Chicanos in a Changing Society

D0167351

Chicanos in a Changing Society

From Mexican Pueblos to American Barrios in Santa Barbara and Southern California, 1848–1930

Albert Camarillo

HARVARD UNIVERSITY PRESS

Cambridge, Massachusetts, and London, England

Copyright © 1979 by Albert Camarillo
All rights reserved
Printed in the United States of America

10   9   8   7   6   5

Library of Congress Cataloging in Publication Data

Camarillo, Albert.
    Chicanos in a changing society.

    Bibliography: p.
    Includes index.
    1. Mexican Americans—California—Santa Barbara—
History.   2. Mexican Americans—California, Southern—
History.   3. Santa Barbara, Calif.—History.
4. California, Southern—History.   I. Title.
F869.S45C25   979.4'9'0046872   79–10687

ISBN 0-674-11396-9 (paper)

ACC LIBRARY SERVICES
AUSTIN, TX

en memoria de mi padre

Benjamín T. Camarillo
1902–1978

y

para mi madre

whose lives are part
of the Chicano historical experience
in twentieth-century southern California

Acknowledgments

During the past six years much of the research for this study has been generously supported: by a Ford Foundation dissertation fellowship for Mexican Americans; by a research grant from the University of California, Los Angeles, Chicano Studies Center and Institute of American Cultures; by an independent study and research fellowship from the National Endowment for the Humanities; and by a seed-money grant from the Center for Research on Women (Stanford University).

Several friends and colleagues have made invaluable comments on all or part of the manuscript. I am especially indebted to Norris Hundley and Juan Gómez-Quiñones for their support before, during, and after my doctoral dissertation. I am grateful to Carlos Cortés for his many critiques of the manuscript at different stages, and for permission to use the unpublished manuscripts and research files of his Inland Empire (San Bernardino Valley) Chicano Cooperative History Project. This book has also benefited from suggestions offered by Tomás Almaguer, Pedro Castillo, Leonard Pitt, and David J. Weber. I am appreciative of the research assistance furnished by Lydia Villarreal and Linda Torres on various parts of the study. In addition, the staffs of the Santa Barbara Public Library, the Santa Barbara Historical Society Library, and the San Diego Historical Society Serra Museum Library made my research tasks easier by providing friendly, professional help.

An earlier version of Chapters 5 and 9 was presented as a

Clark Memorial Library Seminar (UCLA) in the spring of 1977 and will be published separately in the Clark Library Seminar Publications.

I am forever indebted to my wife, Susan, who over the years has spent countless hours as editor and research assistant. Without the time and effort she unselfishly has devoted to my work, while at the same time pursuing her own career, this study would never have been completed. Words can never adequately express my appreciation of her patience, support, and help.

Lastly, special thanks go to the many Chicanos of Santa Barbara who shared their life histories with me and who provided information about the early twentieth-century Chicano community. It is the purpose of this study to document the major life experiences of these people, and the tens of thousands of others like them, who lived in southern California between 1848 and 1930.

Contents

TABLES

ILLUSTRATIONS

Chicanos in a Changing Society

Introduction

The search by Americans for their ethnic, cultural, and family roots has become especially prevalent in recent years. Black Americans, for example, have looked to their African origins and to their long history under the oppressive institution of American slavery in order to understand better a major part of their experience. Anglo-Americans who trace their family backgrounds examine in a comparable way the trans-Atlantic immigrations, the Old World life in Europe, and the initial settlement of their ancestors in the New World. American Indians, on the other hand, turn to their North American tribal origins and to a tragic history of Indian-white relations to comprehend their present subordinate status.

In similar fashion the Chicano people learn a great deal about themselves by exploring their Mexican Indian, Spanish, and *mestizo* origins.* Their position in American society, however,

---

*A confusing number of terms—Mexican American, Latin American, Hispano, Chicano, Spanish speaking, Spanish American, and so on—have been used to refer to people of Mexican descent in the United States. For the sake of simplicity, Mexican (or Mexicano) and Chicano are the two main terms used interchangeably in this study. The names American Indian and Native American are also used as equivalents. The general term Anglo (Anglo-American) is used here to refer to persons of European descent, excluding persons of Hispanic origin. The word Californio, which appears in the first five chapters, refers only to the ranchero or land-grantee group of Mexicans in nineteenth-century California. Another term occasionally used, Barbareños, refers to all Mexicans in Santa Barbara.

Unfamiliar words of Spanish origin (as *mestizo* here) are italicized at first use and defined in the Glossary.

cannot be fully ascertained without a knowledge of the historical contours of Anglo-Chicano relations. The history of the Chicano people as an ethnic minority in the United States was forged primarily from a set of nineteenth-century experiences. This country's war of annexation against Mexico (and the Texas Revolution a decade earlier) led to American acquisition of a vast territory and its Spanish-speaking population. Chicano history is, thus, part of that larger history of westward expansion by the United States and its subsequent domination of societies with different racial, cultural, socioeconomic, and political characteristics.

As the history of the Chicano people is written, an important dimension is added to U.S. history. And as scholars discern the major patterns of the Chicano experience, the history of Mexican people in the United States, which has been beclouded by misinterpretation and neglect, will be more fully understood. It is ironic that so little is known about a people who have historically constituted one of the largest ethnic groups in the western United States—a group that many scholars predict will become the single largest minority population in the country during the next two decades if present birth and immigration rates continue. Although the pioneering studies of such writers as Paul S. Taylor (*Mexican Labor in the United States*, 1928–1932), George I. Sánchez (*The Forgotten People*, 1940), and Carey McWilliams (*North from Mexico*, 1948) remain seminal works, it has been only within recent years that a significant body of literature on Chicano history has emerged.[1] Fortunately, historians and other scholars are now engaged in reconstructing the history of the many generations of Mexican people who have lived in the United States since the Mexican War. This book is a contribution to that effort.

Within a larger national historical perspective, this study may be considered as part of the new social history that has focused on various groups of people heretofore excluded from traditional historical studies. At the regional level, it is part of the new urban history of the American West and of California history. More specifically, this volume is a social history of the Mexican/Chicano people who have resided in the towns and cities of southern California. Although the study encompasses the period from the initial colonization of California by the Spanish, beginning in 1769, through the early twentieth century, the focus is on the Chicanos who lived in four of the main areas of settlement in southern California between the Mexican War and the Great Depression (from 1848 to 1930). Major attention is paid to the development of Chicano society in Santa Barbara—the stronghold of Mexican socioeconomic and political influence in nineteenth-century southern California—with comparative overviews of the Chicano communities in Los Angeles, San Diego, and San Bernardino for the same period. Chapters 1 through 4 deal specifically with nineteenth-century Santa Barbara, while Chapter 5 places in comparative perspective the historical processes that occurred simultaneously elsewhere in southern California. For the early twentieth century, Chapters 6, 7, and 8 discuss the case of Santa Barbara, and Chapter 9 documents the history of Chicanos in the three other major cities. The developments in Santa Barbara provide detail for understanding many of the general historical patterns in the other cities of the region. During the twentieth century these same cities still contained the large majority of Mexican people in the region, and their development provides insight into the Chicano urban experiences during the first three decades of the nineteen hundreds. These cities are also geographically representative of early twentieth-century southern California with its large urban center of Los Angeles, its smaller coastal cities like Santa Barbara and San Diego, and its inland valley cities like San Bernardino. As the fast pace of urbanization increased dramatically in Los Angeles, that booming urban metropolis became much more complex than the smaller cities.

The key to reconstructing the history of Chicano society in southern California is understanding the major developments of the half-century after the Mexican War. During the transitional period between "Mexican" southern California and "American" southern California, approximately 1850 to 1875, and during the following quarter-century, the basic socioeconomic and political relations between the two groups were established. In tracing the history of this period as well as that of the first third of the twentieth century, special attention is placed on the development of Chicano neighborhoods or *barrios*. The external and internal factors—social, economic, political, racial, cultural, and demographic—that have shaped the life experiences of three generations of Mexican people in southern California cities are examined. Another major feature of this study is its examination of the origins and evolution of the Chicano working class during the era of the Mexican pastoral economy, the subsequent incorporation of Mexican workers into the capitalist labor market, and, finally, the occupational status of Mexican workers during the predepression twentieth century. This examination of the Chicano working class in southern California, supported by quantitative analysis of occupational information contained in U.S. census documents (manuscript schedules) from 1860 to 1900 and city directories from 1910 to 1930, is an attempt to understand Chicano society "from the bottom up."

In providing new information as well as synthesizing existing literature, this study necessarily refutes some long-held but untenable views. One of these is the claim that Chicanos have a "lost," or apparently irretrievable, nineteenth-century history. Another is the failure of scholars to recognize the influence of nineteenth-century developments on twentieth-century experiences. This view is perhaps best represented in the claim that only "sentimental" continuities exist in Chicano society from one century to another.[2] This study also challenges those writers who have argued that the tense relations between Mexicans and Anglo-Americans following the Mexican War can be attributed simply to a clash of cultures. There was such a clash, but it can be properly understood only within the context of other important but overlooked considerations. The findings presented here demonstrate that the subordinate socioeconomic and political status of Mexicans emanated from the establishment of the dominant Anglo society in southern California and the corresponding growth of the capitalist economic system during the late nineteenth century.[3] In addition, this study reveals that the incorporation of Mexican workers into the capitalist labor market locked them into the status of a predominantly unskilled/semiskilled working class at the bottom of the occupational structure. The major occupational, residential, political, and social patterns evident in the nineteenth century continued into the new century and through the Great Depression. But with the fundamental continuity there was also significant change; continuity and change were not mutually exclusive.

This examination of Chicanos in southern California during the period 1848 to 1930 will, it is hoped, provide the basis for better understanding a people who have greatly influenced the formation of the region's society for two centuries. While this history may provide insight into the status of contemporary Chicano society, it endeavors—more importantly—to document the historical roots of an ethnic group virtually forgotten in history.

The Mexican Pueblo
of Santa Barbara

1.

The United States annexation of California in 1848 and the subsequent immigration of the first sizable population of Anglo-
Americans into Santa Barbara during the 1850s posed a serious
threat to the foundations of Mexican society. From the beginning, conflict manifested itself between the newly arrived
Anglos and the Mexican residents. Importantly, however, the
racial, cultural, social, and political conflicts overshadowed the
less obvious economic penetration of Mexican society by American capitalism. The long-range economic changes that ensued
would ultimately alter the nature of the Mexican pueblo. But
the Mexicans of Santa Barbara—the socioeconomic and political
stronghold of Mexican southern California—succeeded in keeping their society intact at least through the late 1860s as they
defended against the first significant Anglo intrusion into their
community.

Mexican Society before the War

At the time U.S. military forces arrived in Santa Barbara during
the Mexican War, the pueblo could be described as an amalgam
of Indian, Spanish colonial, and mestizo elements. These factors
had contributed to the making of a Mexican pueblo society that
for many years after its incorporation into the United States was
only nominally American. Although the Chumash Indian population had significantly declined since the beginning of Spanish

colonization, it was still visible in and near the pueblo. The Spanish colonial heritage was also deeply felt in Santa Barbara, even though its dominant institutions—the presidio and mission—had ceased to exist as strong influences. The Catholic church, the Spanish language, and the Hispanic culture, however, remained long after the end of the colonial period in 1821. The most pervasive influence in Santa Barbara pueblo society was the Mexican mestizo. Predominantly from the interior of Mexico, these settlers formed the majority population and were largely responsible for shaping the cultural and pastoral life styles that characterized Mexican Santa Barbara.

The American occupational army that remained in Santa Barbara during 1847 and 1848 was largely ignorant about the complexities of Mexican society. Most of the soldiers were unaware of the historical developments that had affected the pueblo population since the Spanish-speaking settlers had first arrived during the 1780s. The Indians whom the Americans encountered, for example, were only a remnant of the once numerous Chumash tribe. At the start of the mission period in the 1780s, approximately 8,000 Chumash inhabited the coastal regions between present-day Los Angeles and the areas just north of Santa Barbara as well as the small Channel Islands. These hunting-fishing and seed-gathering people lived in well-defined social and residential communities. Over the next five decades the missionization of the Chumash resulted in conversion of about half their population. The three Chumash *rancherías*, or villages, near the Santa Barbara mission, numbering in total 1,000 persons, ceased to function as viable communities by the early 1800s after many Native Americans became neophytes (Indian wards of the mission) under the control of the Franciscan missionaries.

Besides missionization of the indigenous residents, the historical trend that would have the greatest impact upon Indian society was the constant population decline. Throughout the mission period from the 1780s to the mid-1830s, the Chumash population steadily decreased. Diseases, the mission labor system, overcrowded living conditions, violent resistance to mission life—such as the 1824 neophyte revolt, which resulted in many deaths—and other factors help explain the continuous decline of the Indian population. At the time of the secularization of the California missions the total number of local neophytes and nonmission Indians had been reduced to about 2,500. When the United States officially annexed California after the signing of the peace treaty in 1848, the total number of Chumash was estimated at 1,150. During the early American period the Chumash were all but exterminated; by 1880 only a few dozen had survived the devastating effects of missionization, secularization, and treatment by a new people—the Americans—who had historically demonstrated little regard for Indian society.[1]

Although Mexican society did not experience the same traumatic types of change, it did undergo significant social and institutional change, especially during the two decades prior to the arrival of the occupation troops. To the Americans who occupied Santa Barbara in 1847–1848, the decaying presidio and mission buildings must have appeared as relics of a Spanish past that had existed within the Mexican pueblo society. But the influence of these Spanish colonial institutions had only begun to wane during the 1830s. Throughout the colonial period, and for another decade after the beginning of the Mexican national period in 1821, the presidio-mission complex remained the bulwark of the northern Mexican borderlands frontier in California. Both the mission and the presidio were deemphasized in the plans of the new Mexican republic to strengthen its frontier settlements. During the 1820s and 1830s the military presidio in Santa Barbara, for example, rapidly lost its importance to the contiguous pueblo settlement. The Santa Barbara pueblo, much like the other pueblos of southern California, was an outgrowth of the presidio. Ex-soldiers and their families, together with new civilian colonists from Mexico, constructed adobe houses near the old quadrangular presidio and its inner buildings (a chapel, storehouses, and the soldiers' barracks). The pueblo was located picturesquely on the gradually rising plane between the bay, the nearby mission, and the coastal mountains. Here, approximately 200 one-story adobe dwellings with red-tiled roofs were scattered throughout the original area of the presidio. In

1834 the pueblo officially was proclaimed a municipality within the California province. It contained the great majority of the approximately 600 Mexicans and a few resident foreigners; most of the Indians in the immediate area lived as neophytes on the nearby mission grounds. The year that marked the death of the presidio and the birth of the municipality of Santa Barbara also marked the beginning of the end for the other remaining colonial institution—the mission—throughout California. The Santa Barbara mission, economically prosperous over the years through the efforts of the missionaries and the labor of hundreds of neophyte Indians, was rapidly dismantled under the provisions of the 1834 Secularization Proclamation. Mission livestock, lands, and buildings were handed over to secular administrators at the same time as the neophyte Indians were released from mission service.[2]

The secularization of the missions had profound effects on Mexican California society. On the one hand, the economic and political influence of the mission padres was eliminated, even though the religious influence of the Catholic church persisted. On the other hand, mission secularization radically changed the system of land tenure and land disposal in California. In fact, the breakup of the California mission lands was the signal event for the introduction of what has been called the Golden Age of the *ranchos,* the period from 1834 to 1846. The earlier conservative land-grant policy of Spain, which deemphasized the granting of land to individuals, was discarded by Mexico in favor of a policy by which the gargantuan mission holdings were subdivided and parcelled out to *rancheros.* As a result, the Californios, predominantly members of the ranchero class, increasingly concentrated their economic and political power as mission influence waned during the 1830s and 1840s.[3]

At the local level, mission lands that were not directly granted by the provincial administrators to rancheros and military colonists were acquired through extralegal means. According to the secularization proclamation, half of the disposed mission lands were to be divided among the colonists and ex-neophyte Indians; the remaining property stayed in the control of appointed *mayordomos* or executors of the provincial government. However, the ex-neophytes often became the victims of manipulative, unscrupulous mayordomos and aspiring rancheros. Throughout the period the Santa Barbara ranchos increased in number, size, and wealth. Nearly all of the ranchos located in what is now Santa Barbara County were granted between 1834 and 1846. They ranged in size from 3,000 to over 50,000 acres, with the average approximately 25,000 acres. But certain rancheros were able to acquire vast tracts of land through interfamily ownership. Such was the case of Santa Barbara's largest landowner, José de la Guerra y Noriega, who in 1846 reportedly possessed a rancho domain of over one-quarter million acres stocked with 58,000 head of cattle and an equal number of horses and sheep.[4]

Social Class Structure and Community Cohesiveness

The secularization of the mission and the redistribution of land in Santa Barbara shifted the center of production of the pastoral economy from the mission to the ranchos. The transformation of the land tenure system and the demise of the mission labor system affected the community's distribution of wealth, political power, and occupational structure. All of these factors contributed to modification of the socioeconomic class hierarchy in Mexican society.

Socioeconomic stratification characterized by a three-level class structure existed in both the pueblo and the nearby mission prior to secularization. The small number of colonial/ provincial governmental administrators, military officers, and rancheros, along with the mission fathers, formed the elite sector of society. Wealth, family influence, political power, and claim to direct Spanish descendancy separated this group from the majority mestizo population in the pueblo. Soldiers, ex-soldiers, civilian colonists, and their families constituted this mestizo *poblador* sector. Although a few Chumash Indians also lived or worked in the Santa Barbara pueblo, the great majority lived in the nearby mission, where the padres maintained a tight religious and economic hold on the neophyte population. In the overall mission/pueblo society, the colonized mission Indians were clearly at the bottom of the social class hierarchy.[5]

Secularization significantly altered every sector of the social class structure. Although the ecclesiastical officials were, for the most part, eliminated, other elements of the upper class expanded considerably as the ex-mission lands were granted to individuals. The established Californio families, more prosperous after secularization, were now joined by a number of new land grantees. This class of large-scale landowning rancheros together with a small group of high-ranking civil officials (the *alcalde, ayuntamiento* members, and justices of the peace) and a few merchants occupied the top level of pueblo society. Although several of Santa Barbara's leading Californios were in fact Spanish, most members of the ranchero class were mestizo. Within the pueblo the Californios resided in spacious adobes, while their isolated ranchos were administered by mayordomos or relatives. In addition to these upper-class Californios, a few Anglo pioneers, assimilated into Mexican society through intermarriage, attained high economic and social status.[6]

Far below this elite group of wealthy Californios was another group of landowning ranchers and farmers. This second sector in the class structure engaged in small-scale ranching and subsistence farming on tracts of land granted to them or to their relatives by the provincial government. They did not possess the economic, political, or social prestige that was monopolized by the large Californio rancheros. This group of mestizo rancher-farmers, larger in size than the elite Californio class, were the ex-soldiers and civilian colonists whose previous services to the provincial government had been repaid by small land grants. These small-scale rancheros and farmers were much closer in socioeconomic status to the third sector in the social class structure of pueblo society than to the wealthy Californios. The third identifiable sector, which formed the bulk of the majority mestizo population in the pueblo, was composed of artisans, other skilled workers, laborers, and seasonal *matanza* workers all employed in occupations related to the pastoral economy. Most of these working-class families possessed humble one-room or two-room adobes on a single lot within the pueblo. Many within this group engaged in customary subsistence farming and livestock grazing on small parcels of communal pueblo lands surrounding Santa Barbara.[7]

The bottom of the pueblo's social class structure was occupied by a declining ex-neophyte Indian population, which probably numbered between 100 and 150 during the postsecularization period. Although this estimate represents the number of ex-neophytes who chose to relocate in the pueblo, more of them remained near their deteriorating mission dwellings. Within the pueblo occupational structure these people performed menial tasks, especially as servants in the households of the wealthier Californio families. The declining Chumash influence in the Santa Barbara Mexican community was further diminished as some ex-soldiers intermarried with Chumash women and as orphaned Indian children were adopted by Mexican families in the pueblo.[8]

Life on the large isolated ranchos reflected the class divisions of the pueblo. The ranchero and his family were, of course, at the top of the social ladder, while the mestizos made up the small skilled working class. They served as mayordomos, vaqueros, leather craftsmen, and blacksmiths, and they often helped maintain the rancho subsistence agriculture. The Native Americans served as the chief source of manual labor. They were either resident ex-neophytes or they were contracted from neighboring rancherías. Living quarters for the mestizo and Indian workers were often separated from the main rancho structures.[9]

Although there were distinct social classes within Mexican society in Santa Barbara by the time of the Mexican War, certain important qualities imbued that society with a cohesiveness, solidarity, and common tradition. Social class stratification, as a result, softened and became less rigid. One important element of societal cohesiveness was baptism and the accompanying *compadrazgo* system of godparent relationships. Compadrazgo established bonds between families that transcended class and racial lines and went beyond mere religious significance. The rites of baptism established kinship networks be-

tween rich and poor—between Spanish, mestizo, and Indian—
and often carried with them political loyalty and economic-occupational ties. The leading Californio patriarchs in the pueblo
played important roles in the compadrazgo network. They sponsored dozens of children for their workers or poorer relatives.
The kindness of the *padrino* and *madrina* was repaid with respect and support from the pobladores.[10]

Other religious and secular social activities further bound the
Mexican people together. A common culture, religion, nationality, and language, along with familial-economic ties within the
pastoral economy, all figured very prominently in uniting Mexican society. These qualities of cohesiveness played a crucial
role in preservation of the Mexican community after the annexation of California by the United States.

The Mexican War and Its Aftermath

Although no significant military confrontations took place in
Santa Barbara during the Mexican War, the contact between
pobladores and Americans of the occupation army set in motion
a pattern of racial conflict that became ingrained in Santa Barbara society. At first, Santa Barbara Mexicans did not resist the
small detachment of American troops stationed there in 1846 to
prevent the outbreak of hostilities. However, a resistance movement that originated in Los Angeles and successfully ousted the
small U.S. occupation force there soon reached Santa Barbara.
The Mexicans in nearly every pueblo throughout southern California had, at least for a short while, regained control of their
communities. Realizing that southern California pueblos would
have to be forced to capitulate, Col. John C. Fremont mounted
his military drive to pacify the remaining pockets of resistance
in the south. The Mexicans of Santa Barbara, supported by
compatriots from other parts of the region, had prepared a surprise ambush of Fremont's army. But an Anglo pioneer in the
area averted this military battle by forewarning Fremont of the
trap. Their plan having failed, the Mexicans departed from the
area and partially evacuated the pueblo of Santa Barbara as
Fremont's troops peacefully reoccupied it.[11]

Whereas Fremont's temporary stay in Santa Barbara did not incite more resistance from the local Mexicans, the main occupation force (Stevenson's Regiment from New York), which remained in Santa Barbara for the duration of the war, created intense racial antagonisms. The Mexicans resented the American soldiers' disrespectful behavior and their destruction of Mexican private property. In addition, the theft of a United States naval vessel's cannon by suspected Mexicans, and the subsequent American military order to tax every Mexican resident for the lost cannon, inflamed Mexican hatred of the Americans. Racial feelings were further aggravated over this incident when American troops were ordered from Los Angeles to Santa Barbara to ensure collection of the $500 tax exacted for reimbursement of the still unrecovered cannon. Apprehension over a suspected Mexican revolt led the American officer in charge of the Santa Barbara occupation force to request the aid of the California military commander in Monterey. Finally, as the Stevenson Regiment volunteers were mustered out of service in September 1848, many stayed on in Santa Barbara. Although several became leading Anglo citizens in the town, others contributed to the existing racial enmity through their criminal activity.[12]

Early Racial Controversy   The racial conflict that emanated from the Mexican War was intensified during the 1850s as more Anglos entered Mexican Santa Barbara.[13] Anglo-Americans arriving in the early 1850s were highly critical of the dominant Mexican character of the pueblo and of its inhabitants. Unlike the small number of Anglo pioneers who had lived in or near the pueblo before 1846, many of the newcomers had difficulty coping with Mexican society in Santa Barbara. Charles E. Huse, one of the first Anglo lawyers to settle in the town, noted in his diary that one "becomes negligent, rude, disattentive and to a certain degree discourteous" as a concomitant of living in Santa Barbara and being deprived of Anglo cultural-religious institutions. "Here Sunday is for Americans a sad and heavy day," he complained, "I regret exceedingly that there is not a Protestant church in this town. We are barbarians or soon will be from the entire elimination of public cultural exercises."[14] Santa Barbara also disappointed those Anglos interested in developing professional business concerns. Perhaps part of Huse's dissatisfaction stemmed from the slow growth of his own legal practice.

The Anglos in Santa Barbara by 1855 constituted a small but growing minority, probably less than 20 percent of the town's total population.[15] As the Anglo colony expanded, the likelihood of continued Anglo-Mexican hostility also increased. The attitudes of Huse, who arrived in Santa Barbara from the East Coast during the early 1850s, were perhaps typical of those held by many recently arrived Anglos. The entries in his diary illustrate the antipathy that Anglos felt toward Mexican society in Santa Barbara. He wrote, for example, that the "dregs of society are collected in this town . . . The greatest part of the population is lazy, does not work, does not pay its debts, does not keep its word, is full of envy, of ill will, of cunning, craft and fraud, falsehood and ignorance." Most of his diatribes focused on Mexican culture and institutions.[16] Huse's New England Puritanistic mores, Protestant work ethic, and anti-Catholic upbringing ensured his enmity for the Spanish-speaking population. He was at first satisfied to limit criticism of Mexican society to his private diary, but later he began to make public his feelings through the avenue of Santa Barbara's first newspaper.

The *Santa Barbara Gazette*, a four-page weekly newspaper circulated throughout the county, was established by a New Englander who later acquired two coeditors. Huse immediately established close ties with the editorial staff. After one of the coeditors resigned, he was replaced by Huse as "editor pro tem." With the two other editors he molded the *Gazette* into a publishing forum for Anglo viewpoints, and it later became a vehicle from which to launch journalistic attacks against Mexican society. In 1855 the *Gazette* began to publish editorials calling for increased Anglo immigration into the area so as to promote expansion of agricultural pursuits. The editors also patronizingly called upon the rancheros "to turn their own attention to some other track or branch of business," preferably farming, rather than to devote all their energies to stock raising. Other editorials stressed the need for civic improvements and advocated further Anglo "progress"—progress being equated with the Americanization of Santa Barbara.[17]

The editors added a Spanish-language page; but since it was primarily a chapter-by-chapter history of Lower California, this addition to the newspaper failed to attract a Mexican audience. Occasionally, editorials in Spanish would lecture the populace on the "American" system of constitutional government. The editors also translated legal notices, especially those that reinforced the fact that Santa Barbara Mexicans were subject to all state laws. For example, the *Gazette* printed the so-called Sunday Law, a state statute enacted in 1855 prohibiting bear-, bull-, and cockfights and other traditional Sabbath entertainment—a direct affront to the cultural-recreational life styles of Mexicans.[18] The *Gazette*'s Spanish-language page was short-lived. Reflecting upon the failure of the paper to attract support from the Spanish-speaking population during its first year in operation, the editors finally realized the reasons for their apparent ill success:

At first this lack of support seemed to us somewhat strange, since three-fourths of the population of this and the adjoining county of San Luis Obispo are native Californians . . . We ceased, however, to entertain any surprise when we came to discover that they are habitually and universally opposed to all progress whatsoever, and that they look with decided disfavor upon every innovation which tends in the slightest degree to alter the old hereditary regime and policy which existed under the Mexican government, and which indeed have not been very essentially modified by the change of sovereignty. The change of flags has wrought little change in their habits, customs, tastes, or sympathies.[19]

The inability of the *Gazette*'s editorial staff to attract support from the Mexican population motivated the newspaper to intensify its editorial crusade. The editors considered Mexican society an impediment to the development of the city as a desirable home for Anglos. At precisely the time the Spanish-language page was discontinued, the *Gazette* aligned itself with the Know-Nothing party nativism being promoted by Anglos elsewhere in the state. The first in a series of local racial controversies generated by the *Gazette* concerned bilingual public school instruction in the town of Santa Barbara. Before 1855 public education had occasionally been available, but instruction had been given in Spanish only.[20] In 1855 the California State Bureau of Instruction proclaimed that henceforth all instruction must be in English. During the previous year the city's Common Council appointed for the first time three school commissioners, two Anglos and one Mexican, in order to establish plans for a new school. The Anglo school commissioners soon joined with the *Gazette* editors in calling for English-language instruction in Santa Barbara's schools. As the editors noted during the height of the controversy:

It is not easy to account for the manifest opposition which has before prevailed to all instruction in the English idiom. It may be that this undisguised aversion has been the legitimate offspring of native prejudice against the dialect of a people who wrested this soil from the domain of a weak and effete government; or that it has had its origins in vague and undefined fears lest the influence of their religious faith might be weakened in proportion as their progeny became versed in English.[21]

The controversy was temporarily settled after the forces backing English-language instruction won a partial victory with the establishment of a separate school conducted in English for Anglos. Because of financial burdens on the municipal treasury, however, the separate Spanish-language and English-language classes were combined into one that was supposedly conducted bilingually. Consequently, Anglo parents withdrew their children from school because they were outnumbered two to one by Mexican children. The failure of the bilingual classroom, the *Gazette* stated, "has been sufficiently demonstrated in this city, and the parents of American children unwilling that they should learn a confused jargon and gibberish, prefer to keep them at home."[22] Anglo students in 1858 were, however, able to receive English-language instruction, after it was again decided that instruction in English should be offered in Santa Barbara. Although Mexicans continued to oppose English-language instruction in the public school, they were less concerned after 1857 when a parochial day school, which attracted many Spanish-speaking students, was established.[23]

At the time the controversy over the school issue occurred, the editors of the *Gazette* began criticizing the most sacred institution in the lives of many Mexicans—the Catholic church. Reacting to the announcement that a new cathedral was to be erected in Santa Barbara, the editors asked, "Is this an indication of the progress of civilization or does it indicate a retrogression toward the medieval age?"[24] This editorial jibe moved an outraged Mexican citizen to accuse the *Gazette* staff, in a letter to the editors, of "unmitigated bigotry towards the religion of the majority of the inhabitants of the South . . . I am sick," the author concluded, "of an exhibition of sneering ignorance, bigotry, and intolerance."[25]

Racial Violence of the 1850s   As the *Gazette* contributed to the growing discord between Anglos and Mexicans through editorial attacks, others resorted to physical violence. Like its sister city to the south, Los Angeles, Santa Barbara during the mid-1850s experienced a series of race-related crimes. Much of this criminal activity manifested itself in the form of Mexican banditry, murders of Mexicans and Anglos, and vigilantism. Some individuals like William Streeter, an early Anglo pioneer to Santa Barbara, attributed the emergence of racial violence to the post–gold rush "influx of rough characters." These adventurers

exposed the simple Californians to many dangers, not to speak of the ill treatment and the advantage taken of their simplicity . . . The majority of these rough, reckless men had little respect for the persons or property of the Californians. The generous hospitality of the latter was often repaid with insult . . . This treatment embittered them towards the Americans and together with other causes prevented their reconciliation to the American occupation.[26]

Others have pointed to the influence of liquor, gambling, and an unfamiliar system of U.S. jurisprudence as possible reasons for the proliferation of crime in Santa Barbara. Whatever the immediate factors, racial antagonism underlay much of the violence.

"It is easy to see the hatred which exists in this town," Charles E. Huse confided in his diary, "between the two classes, American and Californian . . . I pray God," he concluded, "that this repugnance will not be manifested by serious acts, but I am ever fearful."[27] Huse had good cause for alarm. By 1856 Santa Barbara was experiencing a "racial crime wave" similar to that of Los Angeles. Once again the *Gazette* was indirectly responsible for inciting the dissension that contributed to increased lawlessness. The newspaper highlighted local and statewide crimes of violence, particularly those reportedly involving Mexicans. The *Gazette* editors also called for strict enforcement of California's newly enacted antivagrancy law, popularly known as the Greaser Law, which was directed specifically against the Mexican population. The nonenforcement of this and other anti-Mexican state laws by the Mexican city marshal infuriated the editors as well as some *Gazette* readers.[28]

By 1856 the situation had reached the point where the editors of the *Gazette* and Anglo citizens were calling for vigilantism; they were evidently encouraged by the successful efforts of vigilante groups elsewhere in the state. Unable to acquire enough horses to outfit a posse and generally unfamiliar with the local terrain, the Anglo vigilante movement sought the aid of the powerful rancheros. Prior to the vigilante movement, however, the editors of the *Gazette* had succeeded in alienating the rancheros, especially the important De la Guerra family, by their attacks on the Californio style of politics and on their nonagricultural-oriented economic pursuits. Charles Huse was particularly despised by certain members of the De la Guerra family. In addition, the *Gazette* reinforced ranchero noncooperation with Anglo vigilantism after the editors presented a case to the Santa Barbara grand jury against the members of the Californio-dominated County Board of Supervisors. Supervisor Antonio María de la Guerra, one of the most powerful men in the region, was charged with misconduct and negligence. Realizing that ranchero support was not forthcoming, the editors began accusing a number of well-known Californios of harboring criminals.[29]

In order to diffuse any possible Anglo vigilante threat in the town of Santa Barbara the recently elected mayor, Antonio María de la Guerra, soon took decisive action. The only Anglos to pose a real threat as vigilantes were the quasi-military members of a group known as the Santa Barbara Mounted Riflemen. Composed primarily of former U.S. military personnel and the more militant citizens of the Anglo community, this force was soon neutralized by Mayor De la Guerra when he ordered the confiscation of the riflemen's arsenal.[30]

Unlike other pueblos of the mid-1850s (such as Los Angeles), the Santa Barbara Mexican community was able to forestall Anglo vigilante activity. "Whereas the forces of order had prevailed on [Los Angeles'] Fort Hill with the cooperation of the ricos," a historian noted, "Santa Barbara's vigilantes . . . had to reckon without substantial aid from ricos and with considerable opposition from the lower classes," who supported the Californios.[31] During the 1850s when the Santa Barbara Mexican society was threatened by a militant Anglo minority, the community, through the leadership of the *políticos*, responded in kind. Some members within the Mexican community attempted to eradicate the Anglo influence. Whereas Mexicans did not tolerate Anglo groups outside the law, they tacitly supported the activities of one of their outlaw compatriots: Santa Barbara's *bandido* leader, Solomón Pico.

As with the more notorious California bandit, Joaquín Murieta, little is known about Pico. Solomón was the son of José Dolores Pico, a relative of the influential former provincial governor from Los Angeles, Pio Pico. In 1844 he received claim to a rancho in the Los Alamos area in northern Santa Barbara County. During the late 1840s and 1850s Pico and his gang of approximately forty *compañeros* preyed on Anglo cattle drivers and gold-rush travelers. The Pico bandidos were most active during the early 1850s, but Solomón may have remained in the area as late as the early 1860s. William Streeter, in recalling the activities of Pico, claimed that "it was commonly reported especially by his countrymen, in hope perhaps of justifying his crimes, that he had been cheated out of his property by Americans and in consequence had vowed that he would kill every American falling into his hands . . . Be that as it may he certainly spared no American."[32] Because of the ethnic loyalties of the Mexican populace and a policy of noninterference on the part of the Californios, the activities of Pico were seldom discovered or brought before the law. By the mid-1850s Solomón had refrained from further acts of banditry, although some of his followers supposedly joined the gang headed by a former Stevenson's Regiment soldier, Jack Powers. It was rumored that Solomón had been killed in San Diego in about 1862, or that he left for Baja California.[33] The stories about Solomón Pico became a source of local Mexican folklore for many generations in Santa Barbara.

After the first attempts to create an Anglo vigilante group had been thwarted in 1856 and the activities of Solomón Pico had ceased by 1857, relative normalcy returned to the Santa Barbara community. The apparent calm was shattered, however, by renewed violence in 1859. A racial war between Mexicans and Anglos in Santa Barbara appeared likely after a dramatic incident at nearby Carpinteria. An elderly man named Francisco Baldillo, a suspected horse thief, and his son were summarily hanged without trial by a group of local Anglos. When word reached Santa Barbara, the outraged Mexican community sent a group of men to investigate. The son of a local Anglo settler was identified by a witness as the murderer, and he was nearly killed by members of the Mexican posse before being taken into custody and returned to Santa Barbara to stand trial along with his brothers (his accomplices). But the suspect was able to prove his innocence, whereupon those Mexicans who had attacked him prior to his arrest were in turn arrested. A grand jury was summoned to try the arrested Mexicans and the brothers of the suspected culprit. The grand jury, eight Anglos and eight Mexicans, could not reach a verdict on either group of defendants because it was split along racial lines. A compromise was finally agreed upon by the jurors, which called for the release of all prisoners. Unsatisfied with the decision, a newly formed Anglo vigilante group issued an ultimatum to the released Mexican suspects to leave town or risk physical harm. On the advice of the mayor, Pablo de la Guerra, they left.[34] However, feelings remained so intense that U.S. army troops sent from Fort Tejon occupied Santa Barbara to prevent bloodshed. One of the military officers, in a report to his commanding officer, evaluated the situation:

The Americans here will not brook restraint on the part of the Californians, and are exceedingly intolerant of the political as well as official control of any of that people. This sentiment on the part of the Americans seems to have become so intense as now to be almost a monomania . . . They do not seem disposed to concede to Californians the same civil rights which they claim for themselves.[35]

The Baldillo affair and its aftermath, as one historian of Santa Barbara concluded, "marked the climax of racial prejudice between the 'native' group [Mexicans] and the 'American party' [Anglos]"; antagonisms generated during this episode "remained keen even into the seventies."[36]

Mexican Control of Politics

Anglo-Mexican conflict was not limited to individuals or groups of individuals; it also permeated the institutional levels of Santa Barbara society. Within the political and judicial system the dominant power of the Californio políticos, who were supported by their mestizo constituents, caused frustration and disappointment for Anglos desirous of changing the status quo. But the transition from the Mexican Republic's form of ayuntamiento local government was only a token change. The 1850 legislative act, which specified that California cities would be governed by a mayor, recorder, and common council, had little effect in Santa Barbara where the informality of the preconquest Mexican municipal government carried over into the early American period. The practice of recording common council minutes in Spanish, for example, remained in effect until 1870.[37]

Prior to 1850 Californio políticos controlled local political office holding; and they continued to do so for the next two decades. As more Anglos settled in the area during the 1850s, the Californios prevented them from acquiring the more important political posts. The powerful ranchero families (such as the De la Guerras, Carrillos, Oreñas, and Covarrubias) dominated the political arena. From the perspective of both groups, control of the political apparatus was essential. The Mexican políticos realized very soon after annexation that the preservation of Mexican society in Santa Barbara was dependent upon their controlling the new system of American politics. Political control by the Californios, with the support of their fellow Mexicans, also ensured the continuation of their ascendant socioeconomic class position in society. Anglos, on the other hand, vied for political power knowing that without it they were in a disadvantageous position to establish a solid socioeconomic foundation in Santa Barbara. These circumstances laid the basis for the political confrontation between the two groups that continued for three decades. [38]

By 1855 Anglos began to contest the political power arrangements of Mexican Santa Barbara. Through the columns of the *Gazette* the editors and other Anglos directed attacks against "bad city politics" and the Mexican practice of bloc voting. Nevertheless, local elections usually resulted in the Mexican voters' electing their own people to office. The 1855 city, county, and state elections are good examples of Mexican election control. In other southern California communities Know-Nothing party candidates were elected to office, but they were all defeated in Santa Barbara. Lamented Charles Huse:

The Americans have very little influence in the elections, but in a few years they will have all the power and they won't consult the Californians about anything . . . The Californians have a majority of the votes. When they are united [which was usually the case when an Anglo and Mexican candidate vied fro the same position] they can elect whomever they wish. [39]

Although Anglos were able to elect representatives to the Common Council in 1857, they remained a subordinate political force in the city and county throughout the 1850s and early 1860s. [40]

As with other elected political offices, the judicial system remained in the hands of políticos and Mexican jurors. But most Spanish-speaking people did not understand the U.S. criminal justice system and the function of juries, lawyers, and courtroom procedures. Thus, most Mexican jurors seldom convicted Mexican defendants, regardless of the offense. Anglo attorneys like Huse realized the futility of their occupations when juries were predominantly filled by Mexican citizens. Huse came to the conclusion that "it would be better to close the doors of the Courthouse . . . It makes no difference what the testimony is, if the criminal is Spanish or Californian, he is always set free by a jury of 'native sons'."[41] In retaliation, a jury having an Anglo majority would never convict a fellow Yankee. However, at least on one occasion when an Anglo jury convicted a Mexican defendant, compañeros helped effect his escape from jail. Or, as in a case involving Antonio María de la Guerra, public officials sheltered and protected alleged Mexican criminals when they faced possible seizure by Anglo vigilantes. Perhaps the best example of Anglo frustration over the Mexican domination of the legal system occurred in connection with the 1859 grand jury report on the Baldillo case. The Anglo faction on the jury reported to the Court of Sessions of Santa Barbara County that the courts in the city and county, because of juries composed of Mexican majorities, "are entirely powerless in punishing crime." They concluded that "thieves and villains of every grade have been from time to time upheld, respected, fostered, and pampered by our most influential citizens and if need be, aided and assisted in escaping from merited punishment due to their crimes."[42] Mexican jurors continued to absolve compatriots in courtroom deliberations, particularly in cases involving Anglos against Mexicans.

Significant Anglo influence in the judicial system as well as in politics never materialized during the 1850s. In fact, the only stronghold of Anglo public influence and opinion, the *Gazette,* was eliminated in 1858. As a result of the Mexican boycott, the newspaper was forced to rely on its small Anglo clientele and the revenues it collected from the publishing of county legal notices as required by state law. However, because of the powerful political influence of the De la Guerra and Carrillo families in the state capitol, the California legislature passed an act in 1858 permitting county officials to post legal notices on billboards instead of in the local newspapers. The *Gazette* folded that same year. The newspaper was subsequently purchased by two Spanish-surnamed individuals, who renamed the new Spanish-language newspaper *La Gaceta de Santa Bárbara.* In 1859 *La Gaceta* moved to San Francisco, where it was printed and edited; but it continued to be published and distributed by mail in Santa Barbara as late as 1881.[43] The demise of the *Gazette* and its later reorganization as a Spanish-language newspaper was symbolic of Anglo-Mexican affairs in Santa Barbara during the early American period.

Changes in the Mexican Community

The dominant Mexican society manifested few outward changes as a result of the clash between the two groups throughout the 1850s. However, there were alterations in the internal social makeup of the Spanish-speaking community. While the Californio upper class remained stable, demographically speaking, the other sectors of society did not. The Indian population situated in town and near the old mission buildings during the early 1850s probably numbered about 400; by 1860 only a vestige remained. Many of those who stayed in town constituted a servant class in the homes of elite Californios. A United States military report in 1859 concerning the status of the Indian population in Santa Barbara concluded that there was no Indian community "in the vicinity save a remnant of some nearly extinct tribe . . . a lot of squalid, miserable beings."[44] Although there was no demographic or causal relation between the two, the declining Native American population was replaced during the 1850s by an increasing number of Mexicans, most of whom were from Sonora, Mexico.

During the first half of the nineteenth century Mexicans had continuously traveled north to the pueblos of California. This migration pattern was greatly intensified in the initial years of the gold rush as thousands of Mexicans, principally Sonorans, ventured to the California gold fields. A campaign against foreign miners, however, drove most Sonorans and other non-whites from the mining areas. Many displaced Mexican forty-niners relocated in the pueblos of southern California. By 1860 recent immigrants from Mexico in Santa Barbara constituted 40 percent of the Spanish-surname households. These more recent additions to the Santa Barbara community lived close together within the pueblo and were evidently well integrated into the existing Mexican society. For example, very few of these Mexicanos were married or had brought wives on their journey north. Intermarriage with California-born Mexican women was almost universal.[45]

In many ways, the Mexicans who immigrated to Santa Barbara had a significant impact on the existing community. By increasing the size of the Spanish-speaking community, they helped reinforce Mexican culture in the pueblo. Mexicanos also contributed to the growth of the local pastoral economy through their special skills and labor.[46]

Anglo Economic Penetration   A less obvious but more significant change occurred at this same time within the economic structure of Santa Barbara. Whereas incoming Anglos had failed during the 1850s to gain a foothold in the political and judicial power structures, they were more successful in penetrating the economic structure. The Californio rancheros were the first to feel the impact of the Anglo presence. In the early part of the decade rancheros in the Santa Barbara County area were able to realize enormous profits from the trade in cattle that had been stimulated by the gold rush. Thus, like many other Californios in southern California, they were able to afford the litigation fees involved in substantiating their land claims before the Board of Land Commissioners.[47]

The first Santa Barbara County tax assessment in 1850 reflected the ranchero at his economic best. Of the 45 individuals in the county who owned property assessed at more than $5,000, some 33 were Spanish-surnamed Californios. The 1853 county tax assessment indicated that little had changed (see Table 1). Spanish-surnamed individuals continued to dominate the area's property structure. The majority (51.6 percent) of the Spanish-surnamed property holders living in the town of Santa Barbara owned less than $1,000 of total assessed property, which usually consisted of a town lot, a single dwelling, and personal property. An intermediate group of Spanish-surnamed property owners (31.9 percent) possessed between $1,000 and $10,000 in property value. A smaller group of wealthy Californios (16.5 percent of the property-owning population) had property valued in excess of $10,000. This group of rancheros, together with several landowners from the intermediate group, owned city property as well as rancho lands throughout the county. Table 1 illustrates, in addition, that few Anglos in 1853 (with the exception of some pioneers who had married into Californio families) had been able to accumulate large amounts of property. But as the decade progressed, the "gringo" influence became more pronounced.[48]

Table 1   Relative worth of the total Spanish-surnamed and non-Spanish-surnamed property-owning populations, Santa Barbara, 1853.

Total assessed value of real and personal property	Spanish surname		Non-Spanish surname	
	Number	Percent	Number	Percent
$0–499	33	36.2	12	38.7
$500–999	14	15.4	4	12.9
$1,000–3,999	16	17.6	6	19.4
$4,000–9,999	13	14.3	4	12.9
$10,000 and over	15	16.5	5	16.1
Number in population	91		31	

SOURCE: Santa Barbara County assessment roll for 1853.

By 1855 profits in the cattle trade had plummeted and the once wealthy rancheros gradually began to lose their means of livelihood. Recoiling from economic stagnation in the northern cattle trade, many rancheros were faced with rising expenditures and dwindling income, legal fees, and the increasing number of Anglo squatters on rancho land. Delinquent taxes also took a heavy toll. One of the daughters of José de la Guerra y Noriega recalled that by 1858 "the lawyers and the squatters had seized the greater part" of her father's immense land holdings.[49] Although most ranchers were deeply in debt, many were still able to retain the best part of their grants throughout the 1850s; the wholesale breakup of their ranchos did not occur until after 1863.

As the Mexican pastoral economy slowly declined, Anglo influence in the economic-occupational structure of Santa Barbara became more important. Throughout the 1850s Anglos increasingly entrenched themselves in the commercial sector of the town. They began to make considerable inroads into the Spanish-surname property structure by purchasing land formerly owned by Mexicans. The declining prosperity of the region affected Anglo merchants as well as ranchers. However, since many Anglo ranchers held other commerical interests in town, they were in a far better position than the indebted Mexican rancheros, whose assets were almost solely in the form of land and cattle. By 1860 the non-Spanish-surname population in the town of Santa Barbara had become a significant economic sector in the community (Table 2).* Non-Spanish-surnamed in-

Table 2 Occupational structure for the total non-Spanish-surnamed (NSS) male head-of-household population, Santa Barbara, 1860.

Occupation	Percent of NSS work force	Percent who own property	Average recorded value of real and personal property
Pastoral/agricultural			
Rancher	5.6	100	$68,661
Farmer	13.6	95	3,349
Professional	12.4	100	14,875
Proprietorial	16.8	100	10,777
White-collar	2.5	75	1,187
Skilled	16.8	92	1,483
Semiskilled	5.6	90	1,305
Unskilled			
Laborer	14.9	41	620
Other	5.6	44	908
Unknown or unlisted	6.2		
Number in population	161		

SOURCE: 1860 federal manuscript census schedules.

* Unless otherwise indicated, the occupational analyses of non-Spanish-surnamed (excluding nonwhites) and Spanish-surnamed persons in Table 2 and subsequent tables include 100 percent of the male head-of-household popula-

dividuals nearly monopolized the proprietorial and merchant trade of the town; the foreign born, especially the Italians, predominated in this occupational category. Anglos also predominated within the professional sector of the occupational structure and began to comprise a sizable percentage of the skilled artisans in town. Likewise, the emergence of a number of Anglo farmers was evident by 1860. The number of unskilled non-Spanish-surnamed laborers (native and foreign-born) was low compared to the distribution of the work force in the higher occupational categories. Perhaps the most important feature of the Anglo economic structure was the accumulation of real and personal property. The growing number of Anglos in the higher occupational categories and the steady accumulation of property in Santa Barbara were trends that manifested themselves by 1860 and were more pronounced in the future.

Mexican Occupational Structure   Although the non-Spanish-surname element in local society had made important gains during the 1850s, the Spanish-surname population in 1860 still maintained numerical and economic dominance in Santa Barbara (see Table 3). The Californio rancheros and the small number of professionals, most of whom were governmental officials and members of the Californio families, possessed the wealth of the community. The sizable group of Mexican farmers was composed of land-grantee pobladores who owned modest tracts of land adjacent to the town. Here they maintained small numbers of cattle, sheep, or milk cows and engaged in subsistence farming. Those individuals listed as "farmers" in the census schedules represented a middle occupational and propertied group relative to the rancheros and those occupying the lower levels of the economic structure.[50] Others who occupied the middle range of the Spanish-surname occupational structure, but who had substantially less property, were the few Mexican proprietors or merchants; this occupational area was conceded early to incoming Anglo capitalists. In the bottom half

tion. Appendix 1 discusses procedures and methods employed in the analyses, including the method of selection for each group, and Appendix 2 provides a list of specific occupations associated with each classification.

of the structure the skilled artisans, semiskilled workers, and unskilled laborers constituted the lower economic-occupational sectors of the pastoral economy. The distinction between the two groups was that many of the laborers—not all of whom were unskilled—were engaged in several occupations throughout the year (for instance, working as supplemental vaqueros during the

Table 3 Occupational structure for the total Spanish-surnamed (SS) male head-of-household population, Santa Barbara, 1860.

Occupation	Percent of SS work force	Percent who own property	Average recorded value of real and personal property
Pastoral/agricultural			
Rancher	9.2	100	$35,721
Farmer	15.1	95	3,945
Professional	3.1	78	6,178
Proprietorial	1.4	100	775
White-collar	0.7	50	225
Skilled	9.9	72	562
Semiskilled	1.4	100	600
Unskilled			
Laborer	47.9	73	456
Other	5.5	0	0
Unknown or unlisted	5.8		
Number in population	292		

SOURCE: 1860 federal manuscript census schedules.

matanzas or as *trasquiladores* during the sheepshearing season). The skilled workers were involved in such tasks as saddle and harness making, but some were also working as full-time vaqueros, silversmiths, shoemakers, and blacksmiths.

Nativity and length of residence in the community played an important part in determining one's placement in the Spanish-surname occupational hierarchy. For example, the small number of Spanish-born heads of household were scattered throughout the higher occupational categories. Those born in

Spain also generally possessed more property than the majority of the Spanish-surname population. But the bulk of the work force was made up of the California-born and those residents born elsewhere in Mexico (54.4 percent and 40.0 percent, respectively). Although the California-born contributed the largest number of rancheros and farmers to the overall Spanish-surname occupational structure, few of them occupied the skilled and proprietorial sectors. The Spanish-born and California-born together contributed the great majority of people to the upper occupational levels, whereas the non-California born Mexicans were most heavily located in the lower levels. Significantly, Mexicans born outside California, mostly from Sonora, comprised the majority of skilled artisans in Santa Barbara, but in the ranchero, farmer, and professional occupations they were few in number and only moderate in wealth.[51]

Nearly all of the jobs held by Mexicans in 1860 were still directly tied to the pastoral economy, which intimately linked employer and employee in other than just occupational relations. The continuing decline of the cattle industry would, however, begin to change these existing relationships. Anglo capitalist interests during the 1850s and early 1860s, which slowly began to penetrate the economic structure of Santa Barbara by establishing mercantile interests, also began to capitalize on the weakening economic position of Mexican pastoralists. This first economic penetration by Anglos was part of the larger movement of capital investment reaching southern California from northern California and other parts of the United States.

Summary and Conclusion

Notwithstanding the subtle changes that Anglo economic interests were beginning to make in Santa Barbara, the dominant Mexican community showed few signs of alteration over a decade after the Mexican War. In 1860, Spanish-surnamed persons, numbering over 1,500, still comprised 70 percent of the total population of the town; the town contained over 60 percent of the total county population.[52] In fact, the town of Santa Barbara remained the Mexican stronghold of southern California until the late 1860s. The early attempts by a growing number of Anglo-Americans to penetrate the social and political institutions of Mexican Santa Barbara had ended in frustration. This first significant period of contact between Mexicans and Anglo newcomers produced a legacy of mutual racial antagonisms that were to characterize future relations between the two peoples. The growing Anglo presence, however, portended change for Mexican Santa Barbara.

From "Mexican" to "American" Santa Barbara

2.

Over the decade from 1863 to 1873 developments in Santa Barbara began to alter substantially the nature of Mexican society. The socioeconomic, cultural, institutional, and political systems that Anglos brought with them to southern California and the Southwest, which had begun to be imposed during the previous decade, now began to gain ascendancy. The increased pace of Americanization in Santa Barbara during the 1860s was given added momentum by unfortunate natural disasters, which destroyed the already declining pastoral economy. The demise of the cattle industry hastened the dispossession of Mexican landowners and resulted in the dominance of the new Anglo capitalist economic order. During this period of transition, when the Anglo population steadily increased, the racial conflict in Santa Barbara that had been characteristic of the 1850s was renewed. By 1870, however, racial dissension focused primarily on the control of political power. But unlike the 1850s, the Mexican community was now reduced to minority numerical status and in a much weakened economic position. Mexicans could no longer thwart the Anglo social, economic, and political takeover. By the end of the transition decade between 1863 and 1873, Santa Barbara was undeniably more "American" than "Mexican."

Destruction of the Pastoral Economy and Land Loss

Although the changes that radically transformed Santa Barbara began in the early 1860s, the outward appearance of the Mexican community, prior to the arrival of larger numbers of Anglos beginning in 1869, remained much the same. Up to 1868 Anglo observers characterized Santa Barbara as a small Mexican village that had existed basically unchanged for generations. The "business block" of the community was still located in the heart of the pueblo, and adobe houses remained the predominant form of domestic architecture. The adobe homes—irregularly located on footpaths and small dirt streets and constructed for maximization of sunlight, drainage, and adaptability to other ecological factors—often drew the ire of Americans. The strong adobe influence led one traveler in 1867, for example, to conclude that "Santa Barbara disappointed me—not in what Nature had done, but in what man [the Anglo] has not done . . . Fully eight out of every ten of the houses are one story adobe structures."[1]

According to many Anglos, Santa Barbara before 1868 still was decisively more Mexican than American. Yet Anglo observations during the 1860s did not really reflect the changes taking place in the pueblo or in the countryside. The multiple effects of a slumping cattle industry and a cycle of flood and drought led to the economic demise of Mexican ranchers and farmers throughout southern California. The pueblos were also affected, since they were the social and trade centers of the pastoral economy.

Since the late 1850s the pastoral economy had been in a state of depression. The demand for California range beef had greatly decreased as a result of the importation of a superior breed of Texas cattle. Consequently, the open-range California herds proliferated in numbers that could not be effectively reduced by the annual matanzas. "Everybody in this town is broke," a local ranchero stated, and "cattle can be bought at any price."[2] The situation for rancheros and farmers further deteriorated, especially after the winter of 1862 when heavy rains resulted in extensive flooding. Homes and property were destroyed and cattle drowned. The floods were followed by a prolonged drought, which had calamitous effects on the countryside. Prior to the floods and drought Santa Barbara County herds contained more than 300,000 head of cattle. By the fall of 1865 only less than 7,000 remained. Although the effects on the sheep industry were less severe (primarily because sheep withstand drought conditions better than cattle), only one-third of the sheep survived in 1865. Horse herds were similarly decimated. The Santa Barbara hinterlands became wastelands comparable to an immense cemetery "strewn with the fallen creatures and their bleaching bones."[3] Not until the fall of 1865 did normal weather conditions return.

In the pueblo too the situation became grave. A local ranchero writing to relatives in San Diego during the fall of 1864 stated that "half of the people in this town would have died of starvation if provisions had not been sent from San Francisco, and if winter is severe many may yet perish."[4] During the drought a relief committee formed and distributed the donated food and supplies to nearly 400 people in the county. However, at least one Anglo, who considered himself representing "the opinion of the mass of the foreign [American] population, who are the producing class, and bone and sinew of the country," criticized the welfare requests of the relief committee. Asking for outside relief, he complained, placed Anglos "in a humiliating position." He purported that Anglos were not destitute "owing to their frugal and industrious habits, which cannot be said of the native Californian population."[5] Times of crisis failed to ameliorate racial antagonisms.

Prior to 1862 the Californio rancheros had managed to cope with legal fees, taxes, and other debts without relinquishing ownership of most of their land, but now they had dim hopes of recovery. Some Californios abandoned their ranchos altogether. Others faced the grim reality of slowly watching their rancho lands slip from their control. During the first years of the economic downturn, when cash was in short supply, many landowners began mortgaging portions of their lands in order to pay debts and buy supplies. The floods and drought caused this practice to increase. "Merchants took over large properties,"

one ranchero recalled, "in exchange for anough [sic] to keep
families alive . . . This was the beginning of poverty for many
old California families."[6] Sixty years later an old Barbareña
vividly recalled:

The Spanish people had to live and as the dwindling herds would not
pay their bills, they mortgaged their land to the Americanos. A store
stood where now the Lobero Theater stands, and it was run by two tall
dark, gloomy men who dressed in black. The Spanish people called
them "Los Evangelistas" because they looked like the evangelists who
preached the sorrowful Yankee religion in those days. They got much
of our lands.[7]

The foreclosure of mortgaged lands accounted for much of the
Mexican land loss in Santa Barbara. Exorbitant interest rates on
loans further buried the unwary ranchero. An unpaid loan of
$1,000, based on lands valued from $.10 to $.25 per acre, at
5 percent interest compounded monthly could cause the foreclosure of an immense rancho in a relatively short time. Many
of Santa Barbara County's finest ranchos changed ownership in
this manner. Dishonest lawyers also manipulated ancestral land
grants away from Mexican farmers and rancheros. For example,
one present-day descendant of a nineteenth-century Santa Barbara ranchero family claimed that his great-grandfather lost his
entire rancho—about 75,000 acres of Montecito land—because
he gave an Anglo lawyer power of attorney to handle his affairs.
Oftentimes speculators and lawyers would conjure up more
elaborate schemes to defraud the owners of ranchos. Charles E.
Huse, of *Gazette* fame, participated in several unscrupulous
land deals that were not always successful. In one case Huse,
acting as the lawyer for an Anglo who had received title to
rancho lands in an isolated valley behind Santa Barbara's coastal
mountains, illegally attempted to extend the real boundaries to
include the rich coastal foothills that belonged to a Mexican land
grantee. When this particular scheme was uncovered, a mob of
angry citizens surrounded Huse's home, threatening to hang
the attorney. In one way or another, however, most Mexican
landowners lost their ranchos and farms.[8]

By 1870 many once wealthy rancheros had been reduced to

subsistence farming on rented lands. Others who retained parts of their rancho lands also turned to cultivation of the soil as a means of living. Some, a group of dispossessed Californios, relocated permanently in the pueblo of Santa Barbara. In contrast, although several Anglo ranchers and farmers experienced financial setbacks during the period, many profited from the Mexican land loss by acquiring new tracts of land. This was especially true of Anglos who also held commercial interests in town. A historian of the period, James M. Guinn, summed up the tragic situation of the dispossessed Californios by stating, "There are few more pathetic stories in the annals of our local history than the story of the decline and fall of the cattle barons of California."[9]

The dismemberment of the once sprawling ranchos continued throughout the 1860s and into the next decade. (Table 5 will demonstrate the occupational and economic decline of rancheros and farmers between 1860 and 1870.) Sale of the subdivided rancho and communal pueblo lands increased dramatically by the late 1860s. Speculators accounted for much of the transfer of land, advertising small farm parcels from $1 to $12 per acre depending on location. The breakup of the ranchos increased as the pace of Anglo immigration accelerated.[10]

The Boom of the 1870s

The post–Civil War Anglo migration to Santa Barbara was evident by 1869. The construction of new buildings introduced a strange architectural composition of Victorian New England homes, with turrets and other embellishments, often located beside the older adobe structures. The commercial area also began to change by the late 1860s. Anglo merchants and other entrepreneurs built a new business block, thereby, as one Anglo noted, "leaving the Mexicans (who will not sell) to themselves."[11]

Perhaps the most obvious symbol of the new Yankee influence was the establishment of Santa Barbara's second English-language newspaper. The *Post* was started in 1868 after the absence of a newspaper for over eleven years. But like the unsuccessful editors of the *Gazette*, the new editor, as one Santa Barbara historian has correctly observed, "bruised the feelings of Spanish-speaking Barbareños with his editorial jibes that Californians were discouraging American immigration and impeding development in Santa Barbara county." The *Post* lasted "one abrasive year" before being sold and renamed the *Press*. [12]

The new editor, Joseph A. Johnson, had migrated to southern California from Illinois for health reasons. Johnson spent his first years in the region as the minister of the Congregational Church in San Bernardino before moving to Santa Barbara. There were several reasons why the Reverend Mr. Johnson was a successful editor and why the *Press* became a successful newspaper. Unlike his predecessor, at least in the beginning, Johnson behaved diplomatically toward the local Mexicans. He was able to gain the monetary backing and influence of Santa Barbara's leading Anglo capitalists, who were eager to support a newspaper that would contribute to the growth of the community. He was, moreover, keenly perceptive as a political opportunist and was an effective muckraker. The *Press* was in a good position to succeed, since it was the only English-language newspaper for the growing population of Anglos in Santa Barbara. Any possible opposition that may have come from Californios, who had previously contested the publishing of an English-language newspaper, was minimized at this time, since most were struggling to survive the effects of the declining pastoral economy. Most importantly, Johnson was an avid "town builder," with an outstanding ability to advertise Santa Barbara to the outside world. It was Johnson who was primarily responsible for attracting large-scale Anglo immigration to Santa Barbara and for stimulating the first real estate boom. [13]

Shortly after Johnson assumed his editorial responsibilities, he set in motion his three-pronged plan to develop Santa Barbara through: (1) agrarian development of the remaining rancho system; (2) advertising of Santa Barbara as a tourist/health resort; and (3) pursuit of his personal capitalistic ventures. At first Johnson had to struggle against the effects of a stagnant economy and a public hesitant to embrace his ideas. But by 1871 his efforts began to pay off. A historian writing about the first full-scale tourist boom in southern California has noted:

Santa Barbara was the perfect example of successful advertising applied to a potential health resort . . . For a time, a veritable human inundation had come upon Santa Barbara, and Johnson was its prime mover.[14]

The following year Santa Barbara became a haven for the invalid and the tourist. "Consumptives in the last stages of the disease thronged to the streets," vying for scarce lodging with the curiosity seekers. As the advertising campaign increased, so did the volume of tourists. In early 1873 Johnson reported that "the town is full of strangers" and that crowds of tourists wishing to come to Santa Barbara and other cities in the South had to be restrained by police on the docks of San Francisco. By spring of the same year Johnson reflected upon the new "urban impulse" of Santa Barbara:

It is no longer "quiet little Santa Barbara," but rushing, pushing, growing, Santa Barbara . . . The sleepy days of Santa Barbara are past. The people are awake, and the spirit of progress and improvement may now be said to have gained ascendancy.[15]

After the winter visitors returned to their respective homes, the real estate speculators—the other protagonists of boom times—remained in Santa Barbara. The initial volume of tourism was equaled by the volume of land speculation and transfer of ownership. Town lots that had sold for $500 in 1870 were bringing $5,000 and $6,000 in 1873.[16]

The incipient tourist/real estate boom of the early 1870s was given an added impetus in 1873 by the activities of two individuals. Charles Nordhoff, a journalist hired by the railroads to promote immigration, published a tourist handbook on the attributes of California. Nordhoff was the first person to nationally advertise "Southern California for invalids" and for permanent settlement. After visiting the area in 1872, he characterized Santa Barbara as an ideal health/tourist resort, claiming that it was "on many accounts the pleasantest of all the places" in southern California. He extolled the salubrious climate and ideal geographic location of the town. Nordhoff's *California for*

Health, Pleasure, and Residence: A Book for Travelers and Settlers attracted the attention of thousands of prospective tourists. Shortly after the publishing of Nordhoff's book, editor Johnson embarked upon a personal campaign throughout the eastern United States. Hailing southern California as the "Italy of America," his campaign provided information about Santa Barbara for eastern travelers who desired vacations out West. To judge from the increased traffic of tourists, the Nordhoff and Johnson promotions were highly successful.[17]

By 1875 the bubble of boom times had burst—a result, no doubt, of the national economic recession following the Panic of 1873. Most of the victims of the boom's collapse drifted back to their respective communities, but some were local residents. These unfortunates of Santa Barbara and other southern California cities, according to a historian of the boom, included a few naive Californios. They had sold their remaining rancho lands and town lots prior to the start of the boom and subsequently rebought the same land at much higher prices, hoping to capitalize on their speculations; they were caught owning expensive land that was worth practically nothing as the boom collapsed.[18]

Boom gave way to economic stagnation, especially after the drought of 1876–1877, but not until it had created irreversible changes in Mexican Santa Barbara. It increased the wealth and power of many Anglos who had invested in preboom Santa Barbara. For example, Col. William H. Hollister, probably the wealthiest rancher in the county, accumulated extensive property holdings within the city by purchasing land early and later selling at the height of the boom for great profit. He also capitalized on the tourist trade by building the two main hostelries in Santa Barbara. The boom attracted, in addition, such Anglo tycoons as Mortimer Cook. The enterprising Cook became one of the town's leading capitalists, building many business structures and later winning election as mayor. These men and others left physical reminders of the boom in the community. A new wharf, telegraph lines, gas street lighting, additional schools, a college, Protestant churches, all obscured the historic features of the Santa Barbara pueblo.[19]

Perhaps nothing symbolized the advance of Anglo society

more than the destruction of the old adobes. Their frequent removal to make way for wood or brick structures bothered Johnson. "We regret the demolition of the tile-roofed adobe dwellings that make our town so quaint and old, in a country so comparatively new to Americans," he complained.[20] In 1873 Nordhoff also lamented, "So extensive and thorough are the improvements since I last saw Santa Barbara [in 1862], that I was relieved to find here and there one of the picturesque old tile-roofed adobes to remind me of what Santa Barbara was."[21]

Practically overnight the tourist/real estate boom of the early 1870s transformed the social milieu of Mexican Santa Barbara and southern California. The Mexican population fell from majority to minority status. As early as 1870 the non-Spanish-surname population constituted over 54 percent of all people in town; the boom increased that percentage. The suddenness with which the social makeup of the community changed must have shocked many Barbareños. One visitor in 1873, for example, observed, "The native population wear a wondering, bewildered look at the sudden change of affairs, yet seem resigned to their unexpected situation, while the conquerors are proud and elated with their conquest."[22]

The apparent resignation of Mexican citizens was the product of their defeat on several fronts. Anglos had not only gained numerical ascendancy by 1870, but had also begun to wrest control of local institutions of power from the Californios and their constituents. As the Anglo population increased during the late 1860s, the political-racial tug of war reminiscent of the 1850s was reenacted. The outcome, however, was different.

The Decline of Mexican Political Power

Throughout the 1860s and early 1870s local politics continued to be divided between the Mexican and Anglo factions. For the Mexican faction control of local politics became increasingly important as the number of Anglo voters expanded. Especially for the Californio políticos who faced severe economic problems, the maintenance of decision-making power, which benefited their own interests as well as the interests of the Mexican com-

munity, became a necessity. To help preserve the dominant political power of the políticos, the Californios and their Mexican
constituents relied heavily upon machine-style politics. That is,
when the need arose, the Californios and their mestizo campaign managers in Santa Barbara and in other pubelos in the
county could muster a solid Mexican voting bloc to defeat Anglo
candidates who split the non-Mexican votes.[23]

The Mexican electorate doubtless supported Californio candidates out of loyalty and respect. But more was involved. For
example, as the Civil War broke out, the Californio políticos
and their Mexican voters manifested Confederate sympathies
partly because of their aversion to the word "Yankee," which revived memories of the invasion of California. William Streeter,
the Anglo pioneer, noted, "The Californians being natural enemies of the Americans were as matter of course in sympathy
with the Confederates, simply because they thought they would
gain their cause."[24] But party loyalty meant little to the Californios. In fact, party affiliation often shifted to accommodate
changing political circumstances. Pablo de la Guerra, for instance, easily led a Mexican voter switch from the Democratic
to the Republican party in order to prevent the hated Charles
E. Huse from being elected district attorney.[25]

Even as late as 1867, county and municipal politics were still
firmly in the hands of the Mexican community. Spanish-surnamed voters comprised 62.7 percent (208) of the electorate in
the town of Santa Barbara. At the county level, they accounted
for 61.7 percent (421) of all registered voters; the Mexican
voters in the city represented nearly 50 percent of all Spanish-
surnamed voters in the county. By 1869, when the Anglo population began to increase dramatically, the Californio políticos
began to concede minor county offices to Anglos, while retain-
ing the most important ones (county assessor, sheriff, district
court judge, representatives on the board of supervisors). The
town of Santa Barbara was still politically dominated by Californios.[26] This arrangement was, however, now being seriously
contested by the growing Anglo electorate.

Johnson of the *Press* was a prime mover in rallying Anglo
voters to action. In 1869 he launched a campaign to help dis-

solve the political control of the Mexicans. In his first editorial of this campaign he called for the "people" to rise up and elect officials who would represent their real interests. Johnson focused first on the so-called assessment question. The common practice of the Californio county tax assessors was to place a low value on vacent lands and a high value on improved property, thus protecting the remaining lands of the rancheros. This favoritism toward rancheros infuriated Johnson, who supported the growing number of Anglo farmers in the county. Other editorials opposed the election of Pablo de la Guerra, the leading politico of the region, as district judge. Johnson and other Anglos contested the election on the grounds that De la Guerra retained "the character of a Mexican citizen" and thus could not be considered a United States citizen. Many Anglos detested De la Guerra's Mexican chauvinism and control of politics.[27]

Neither campaign was immediately successful, but Johnson's expositions and the efforts of other Anglos to acquire political power gradually affected the political environment of Santa Barbara. Yet Anglos seeking political office had to contend with the Mexican voting bloc that remained intact and therefore presented formidable opposition. Johnson summed up the situation in 1870 when he observed:

Now our population is composed of about one-third [this figure is underestimated] native element, 'born to the manor,' and their sympathies are, of course, with any gentleman who is a native [Mexican].[28]

But by the April 1871 municipal elections and the September county elections, the political scene had shifted. The influx of Anglos drawn by the boom now gave them voting parity. Elections became hotly contested between Anglos and Mexicans who actively supported their respective candidates. During the heat of the county election a visitor recalled hearing "political speeches in the Spanish and English languages, [which] attracted a large concourse of both sexes and of each race."[29] The outcome of the election placed one of the most important offices in the hands of Anglos—that of county tax assessor. Shortly after the election, Johnson, a staunch Republican, reported that "probably no election has ever occurred in this county which has approached that of this week in the intensity of feeling manifested . . . For the first time," he proudly claimed, "Republicans began to fill some county offices."[30]

The Californios realized that their political control was being threatened. In a letter to "the Californios of Santa Barbara County," one citizen called for the regrouping of Mexican voters under the banner of the Democratic party.

We are all native Californios, we have all been raised on the same soil, we have lived more or less as brothers. From where, then, and who has come to sow discord among us?

The author claimed that the divisions among the people were created by "our natural enemies"—the anonymous gringos. He asked that the "natives" remain loyal to those who have their best rights and interests at heart, "the learned Californios of the pueblo." "The Democratic Party," he concluded, "has been and will always be the party that offers more guarantees to the native Californians and to our raza [race]: this party is the one that constantly extends its arms to the working class."[31] Several years later the Mexican editor of *La Gaceta de Santa Bárbara* echoed the same political sentiments, claiming that the Democratic party "is the defender of the interests of the pueblo" and "best defends . . . the preservation of your raza, and the future of your families."[32]

By 1873 Mexican voter unity was becoming less meaningful in view of the increase in Anglo voters. Spanish-surnamed voters now accounted for only 34.2 percent (271) of the electorate in the town of Santa Barbara; their proportion in the county was equally small. They were, however, a strong political force as long as the Anglos remained divided along party lines. Prior to the next local election the *Press* reported that in Santa Barbara County "party strength is pretty nearly divided, the Republicans having a small majority, and the natives [Mexicans], who have no very strong political preferences, hold the balance of power."[33] Anglos interested in breaking this balance of power, in efforts to establish their own political dominance, now formed their own coalition party. A political-racial showdown was imminent.

Anglos began to consolidate their voting power by crossing

existing party lines to form a "People's Convention," which reflected the agrarian reform measures of the national Grange movement. Although the "People's Ticket" advocated many of the national reform issues of the day, the primary concern was dislodgement of the remaining California políticos. As the convention commenced, a delegate optimistically stated that "this day inaugurates the dawning of a better era upon the political arena of Santa Barbara." Another delegate recalled, with vengeance, the frustrating days of past political elections for Anglos in Santa Barbara. He remembered, for example, when "Pablo de la Guerra was elected Judge years ago, there was a celebration in Santa Barbara, and the Mexican flag floated proudly, as if a great Mexican victory had been won."[34] In a *Press* editorial shortly after the convention opened, Johnson, perhaps not wishing to alarm the local Mexicans, stated that they deserved representation in proportion to their minority population; but he did "not believe in giving all the valuable offices to them, as has been the custom so long . . . There should be a change in the old order of things."[35] The People's Convention and selection of candidates became for many Anglos a vehicle of political revenge against Californios and their Mexican supporters. The People's ticket largely represented the anti-Catholic, the antiforeign, and the Protestant proagrarian local interests in Santa Barbara.

In response to the People's ticket a group of 150 citizens, the majority of them Spanish speaking, met at the Lobero Theater to organize opposition. The "Citizens' Convention" was also attended by members of the Irish working class and other foreign Catholics opposed to the nativist tendencies of the People's ticket. The delegates at the convention adopted a motion condemning the People's party because it had "totally ignored the rights of all foreign-born citizens, more particularly the native Californians, and the laboring men who compose over six-sevenths of the voters of this county."[36] At a subsequent meeting they nominated a coalition slate of candidates comprised of Californios, Anglos intermarried with Californio families, an Anglo ranchero, and an Irish-American. The designation of Citizens' ticket candidates at the convention proved to be an amusing affair in the opinion of at least one outside observer, who noted: "Think of a political convention having to elect an interpreter, so that delegates who speak and understand nothing but the Mexican patois might know what was going on." He understood, however, the political gravity of the contending forces and predicted that "a strong effort will be made to put Santa Barbara down on the political chart as a portion of the United States, not an appendage of Mexico." Mexicans, he claimed, "are contesting every inch of ground against the influx of the paleface; they sink all party feelings in the resolution to keep their chiefs in the principal offices . . . They are now in their political lava bed; they will make a desperate fight."[37]

As election day drew near, accusations between the opposing forces increased. Backers of the Citizen's ticket denounced the nativist and antiworkingmen characteristics of the People's ticket. Conversely, People's party advocates decried the lawless, backward, and antiagrarian qualities of the opposition. Political concern was also reflected in the Spanish-speaking community of Santa Barbara, where on at least one occasion a group of over 200 Mexicans listened to the issues. Johnson added his personal touch to the campaign, issuing a warning to the Mexicans in the *Press:*

It does not require much good sense to enable the Californians to see that this policy [bloc voting] will soon exclude them from all offices . . . By next election the Americans will elect whom they please, without any reference to the California vote.[38]

Johnson's prophecy became a reality and the 1873 election was the turning point. The county election resulted in the almost complete defeat of the Citizens' candidates. Only one Californio, Nicolás ("Nick") Covarrubias, was elected (as county sheriff); fellow candidates lost the important positions of county assessor, clerk, treasurer, and district attorney. Anglos triumphantly rejoiced in their victory over the Mexican voters.[39] They now controlled city and county political power.

Mexican Economic and Occupational Displacement
The loss of political power coincided with another equally devastating development for the Californios and the larger Mexican

community—an economic and occupational downward spiral. By 1870 Santa Barbara was in a state of rapid economic transition. The impact of the earlier period of flood and drought, economic depression and inflation, and Anglo immigration caused major changes within the demographic and economic makeup of the county and town. An analysis of the 1870 census for the county correctly concluded that the region was experiencing "the collapse of one order and the rise of another."[40] The traditional Mexican pastoral economy was being replaced by Anglo-American capitalism.

The town of Santa Barbara experienced the most rapid changes within the county. Even by 1870 it remained the only community of any consequence in the entire county; more than 50 percent of the county's almost 8,000 residents lived in or near the town. In Santa Barbara proper the non-Spanish-surname population was now in the majority (54.2 percent of the 2,640 residents). Within the town and including areas adjacent to the town, they constituted 64.5 percent of the total population. By 1873, a year that marked the beginning of Mexican political powerlessness and the height of the tourist/real estate boom, the Mexican population was further reduced relative to the non-Spanish-surname population.[41]

With the destruction of the pastoral economy, the steady influx of American capital, and the continued immigration of non-Mexican people, Anglos by 1870 dominated the economic life of Santa Barbara. Since their initial economic penetration indicated in the 1860 census, the number of non-Spanish-surnamed heads of household had nearly tripled. Two major changes within the non-Spanish-surname occupational structure reflected the economic transitions that had occurred by 1870 (Table 4). First, the ranchers as a group had suffered substantial property and monetary decline since the natural disasters of 1862 to 1865. The farmer group, however, had expanded significantly both in number and in wealth. Second, by 1870 the Anglo occupational structure was indicative of the increasing dominance of American capitalism in Santa Barbara. Anglos continued to monopolize the professional and proprietorial sectors of the growing economy. The increase in commercialism in the town and the concomitant need for store clerks, salespeople, delivery personnel, and craftsmen opened up new white-collar, skilled, and semiskilled job opportunities for Anglos. (See Appendix 2 for a listing of occupations.) As a result of Anglos' acquiring these new occupations, the percentage of unskilled Anglo workers began to decline between 1860 and 1870

Table 4 Occupational structure for the total non-Spanish-surnamed (NSS) male head-of-household population, Santa Barbara, 1860 and 1870.

	Percent of NSS work force		Percent who own property		Average recorded value of real and personal property	
Occupation	1860	1870	1860	1870	1860	1870
Pastoral/agricultural						
Rancher	5.6	4.5	100	95	$68,661	$16,978
Farmer	13.6	12.2	95	86	3,349	8,660
Professional	12.4	9.1	100	89	14,875	13,008
Proprietorial	16.8	11.7	100	94	10,777	12,925
White-collar	2.5	5.5	75	74	1,187	3,043
Skilled	16.8	24.6	92	75	1,483	2,813
Semiskilled	5.6	12.4	90	75	1,305	2,185
Unskilled						
Laborer	14.9	11.9 ⎫	42	47	698	775
Other	5.6	3.3 ⎭				
Unknown or unlisted	6.2	4.8				
Number in population	161	419				

SOURCE: Federal manuscript census schedules, 1860 and 1870.

(from 20.5 percent to 15.2 percent). At the same time that Anglos were entrenching themselves in the higher occupational levels of the work force, they were also steadily accumulating more real property in Santa Barbara. By 1870 they dominated the property ownership structure and wealth of the community, as is evident by comparison of the last two columns of Tables 4 and 5.

The economic transition occurring in the town of Santa Barbara was manifested throughout the county. The commercial merchant class was controlled by German, English, and Italian immigrants and by native-born Americans. The growing skilled workmen group was composed largely of northern European immigrants. The Americans, who migrated from all parts of the

Table 5 Occupational structure for the total Spanish-surnamed (SS) male head-of-household population, Santa Barbara, 1860 and 1870.

Occupation	Percent of SS work force		Percent who own property		Average recorded value of real and personal property	
	1860	1870	1860	1870	1860	1870
Pastoral/agricultural						
Rancher	9.2	2.5	100	100	$35,721	$6,110
Farmer	15.1	3.9	95	87	3,945	3,266
Professional	3.1	2.0	78	75	6,178	8,526
Proprietorial	1.4	3.4	100	86	775	3,475
White-collar	0.7	3.0	50	17	225	150
Skilled	9.9	6.4	72	62	562	675
Semiskilled	1.4	5.4	100	37	600	490
Unskilled						
Laborer	47.9	64.0 ⎤	65	50	409	398
Other	5.5	2.0 ⎦				
Unknown or unlisted	5.8	7.4				
Number in population	292	203				

SOURCE: Federal manuscript census schedules, 1860 and 1870.

United States, added to this group as well as to the semiskilled and professional occupations, and constituted the small but growing family farm population. The Irish immigrant could be found at every occupational level.[42] By 1870, therefore, the non-Spanish-surname population had increased in size and economic power not only within the town of Santa Barbara but throughout the county as well.

As Anglos continued to establish themselves in the higher

economic-occupational levels, the Mexican community experienced a corresponding downward occupational shift. The occupational structure for the Spanish-surname head-of-household population between 1860 and 1870 reveals several dramatic changes between the two census periods. The Mexican rancheros and farmers were devastated by the effects of flood, drought, economic depression, taxes, legal fees, and extralegal land dispossession during the 1860s. The 1870 census reflected the erosion of the farming and ranching sectors of the Spanish-surname occupational structure. The professional, proprietorial, and low white-collar occupational categories still had few representatives from the Spanish-surname population. Other important developments altered the composition of the Spanish-surname occupational structure during this decade. A dramatic exodus of non-California-born Mexicans was evident by 1870. Skilled and unskilled Mexican workers, many of whom had settled in Santa Barbara during the 1850s, left the area; the total number of non-California-born Mexican heads of household was reduced almost two-thirds between 1860 and 1870 (from 117 to 44). In addition, the few Mexican-born rancheros who were stock raising in 1860 were no longer present by 1870. Though a large majority of the non-California-born Mexicans migrated from Santa Barbara, those who remained continued to live in the pueblo together with their California-born counterparts. [43]

Unlike many of their compañeros who were born elsewhere in Mexico, the California-born Mexicans chose for the most part to remain in Santa Barbara, particularly those whose roots in the community went back several generations. Like the few non-California-born Mexicans who remained in the pueblo, they too experienced economic deterioration. The California-born rancheros and farmers, who formed the majority of these two occupational groups, suffered the brunt of the Spanish-surname economic collapse. As a group, the California-born witnessed a general downward occupational mobility; many of them joined their compatriots in the lowest levels of the occupational structure. Between 1860 and 1870, for example, the percentage of semiskilled and unskilled Mexican workers, primarily California-born, had risen significantly from 54.8 percent to

71.4 percent. At the same time, fewer and fewer of them were able to find employment in their traditional pastoral-related jobs. [44]

By 1870 Spanish-surnamed persons were becoming displaced workers outside the changing economy of Santa Barbara. They did not share in the increasing prosperity of "Anglo" Santa Barbara. Their representation as professionals, proprietor/ merchants, and skilled workers was insignificant. The majority of the unskilled Mexican laborers also remained outside the economic mainstream of Santa Barbara. Either out of pride, or preference, or job discrimination, most remained tied to the ever diminishing pastoral economy. Occasionally they worked as vaqueros and trasquiladores and in other related jobs throughout the county where some Californios still retained small ranchos. They managed to eke out a living by subsistence gardening and other odd jobs. [45] Significantly, the expansion of agricultural production in and near Santa Barbara began creating demand for a seasonal farm labor force. Likewise, the expanding tourist trade in the city developed a new need for a service-worker labor force and construction laborers. Job openings for domestics, laundry workers, farm laborers, and construction workers were occupied by Chinese, who began to be imported during the early 1870s to fill the menial labor needs of the growing economy of Santa Barbara. Meanwhile, the Mexican community began to experience increasing impoverishment as a result of its occupational and social displacement in Anglo Santa Barbara. By 1873 the town could no longer be correctly referred to as "Mexican" Santa Barbara.

Summary and Conclusion

Within the space of a decade the Barbareños witnessed the transformation of their pueblo from a Mexican to an Anglo community. The natural catastrophes of the 1860s destroyed the already weakened pastoral economy, and it was the Mexicans who suffered the repercussions. As the number of unassimilable Yankees increased by 1870, the fate of the Mexican community was sealed. The economic and political power structures were the first areas of Mexican control that were contested. The influx of an Anglo boom population during the early 1870s caused the demise of the Californio político and his mestizo supporters; political defeat came in 1873. Loss of political power was accompanied by a steady economic slide. Throughout the decade the Mexican community witnessed a decline in its traditional pastoral occupations; by 1870 the Barbareños were at the bottom of the occupational hierarchy in Santa Barbara. As the Anglo population continued to grow during the early 1870s, the influence of the Mexicans was further obscured. In 1873 they constituted a minority ethnic group, increasingly dispossessed of their traditional mode of life by an encroaching foreign element. Yet to the Anglos, the battle had been won over a people who retarded the progress and the development of the community.

Barrioization of the Chicano Community

3.

The loss of land, the decline of the pastoral economy, and the continuation of racial antagonism, together with the onset of political powerlessness, began to create a new reality for Mexican people in Santa Barbara. That new reality was perhaps best reflected in what can be called the *barrioization* of the Mexican population—the formation of residentially and socially segregated Chicano barrios or neighborhoods. Barrioization of mestizo society in Santa Barbara meant more than just segregation from Anglo society; it was also a *process* that involved a great many social, economic, familial, and demographic factors. It was because of the Americanization of Mexican society—and the resultant changes in the class structure—that the process of barrioization in the Santa Barbara pueblo began.

By 1873 the Americanization of Santa Barbara had placed the Anglo community in an ascendant position over the Mexican sector of society. The Americanization process continued steadily during the next decade and was nearly completed by the boom of 1886. Throughout the last quarter of the nineteenth century, at least from the Anglo perspective, the Spanish-speaking community was rapidly disappearing. In actuality, the Mexicans were not leaving Santa Barbara, merely becoming less conspicuous in the American sections of the city. They secluded themselves within the confines of their historic pueblo—the barrio of Pueblo Viejo—where, as before, they could function within a closed Mexican social universe. Faced with their new-found status as a segregated minority and confronted by a hostile outside world, the Mexican community entered a phase of social change and adaptation. Although the internal changes that Chicanos effected within their barrio ensured the continuity of Mexican society in Santa Barbara, the external pressures exerted by Anglo society further eroded the economic, social, and political status of Chicanos.

Anglo Impressions of the Barrio

The barrioization of the Chicano community was well under way prior to the second large wave of Anglo immigration to reach Santa Barbara in 1886. By 1874 the only remnant of old Santa Barbara was the seven-block area in which the Chicanos of Pueblo Viejo were concentrated. This historic location was the original area of Spanish-Mexican settlement in and around the presidio. By middecade most of the adobe structures outside the core area of Pueblo Viejo had been demolished by the Anglos (see map). The boom of the early 1870s accelerated the destruction of the adobes and further obfuscated the dominant Mexican character of the town. "A year ago [1872 or 1873]," a tourist returning to Santa Barbara claimed, "the low, red-tiled adobes, the streets straying round in the most bewildering manner, the rough, wild-looking Mexicans galloping by, the strange sights which met me at every turn, all made me question whether I had not been transferred to Spain or Italy. Santa Barbara," she concluded, "has now emerged from this transitional state; she is no longer a Spanish, but an American town."[1] But within this growing American city Mexican society still existed in the old adobe pueblo.

With each passing year of the 1870s more incoming Anglos were unfamiliar with the existence of the Mexican colony. Curious tourists were still able to catch glimpses of the unobtrusive Spanish-speaking population outside of Pueblo Viejo. During the early morning hours at the State Street stores, observed one such visitor, "Spanish and Mexican people, the greater part of whom are very poor, come to do their day's marketing."[2] Some curiosity seekers actually wandered into the

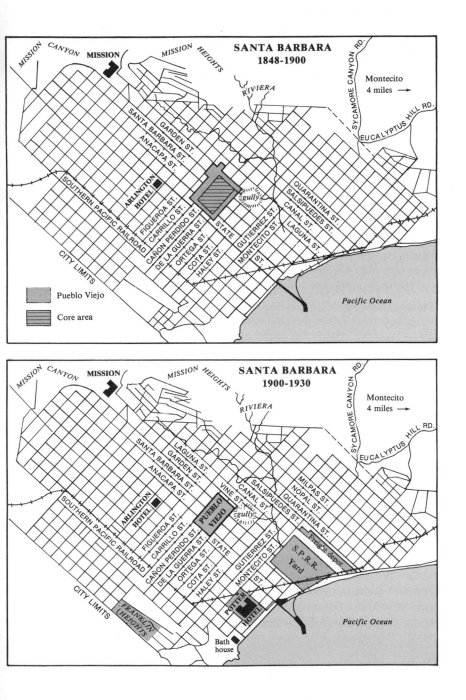

SANTA BARBARA
1848-1900

MISSION CANYON

MISSION

MISSION HEIGHTS

RIVIERA

Montecito
4 miles →

SYCAMORE CANYON RD.

EUCALYPTUS HILL RD.

GARDEN ST.

SANTA BARBARA ST.

ANACAPA ST.

ARLINGTON HOTEL

FIGUEROA ST.

CARRILLO ST.

CAÑON PERDIDO ST.

DE LA GUERRA ST.

ORTEGA ST.

STATE

COTA ST.

HALEY ST.

gully

GUTIERREZ ST.

MONTECITO ST.

QUARANTINA ST.

SALSIPUEDES ST.

CANAL ST.

LAGUNA ST.

SOUTHERN PACIFIC RAILROAD

CITY LIMITS

Pueblo Viejo

Core area

Pacific Ocean

SANTA BARBARA
1900-1930

MISSION CANYON

MISSION

MISSION HEIGHTS

RIVIERA

Montecito
4 miles →

SYCAMORE CANYON RD.

EUCALYPTUS HILL RD.

LAGUNA ST.

GARDEN ST.

SANTA BARBARA ST.

ANACAPA ST.

ARLINGTON HOTEL

FIGUEROA ST.

CARRILLO ST.

CAÑON PERDIDO ST.

DE LA GUERRA ST.

ORTEGA ST.

STATE

COTA ST.

HALEY ST.

VINE ST.

PUEBLO VIEJO

gully

CANAL ST.

SALSIPUEDES ST.

QUARANTINA ST.

MILPAS ST.

NOPAL ST.

GUTIERREZ ST.

MONTECITO ST.

Freight depot

S.P.R.R. Yard

SOUTHERN PACIFIC RAILROAD

CITY LIMITS

FRANKLIN HEIGHTS

POTTER HOTEL

Bath house

Pacific Ocean

"alien" environment of Pueblo Viejo. "It looks as if Time had stood still," remarked a visitor in 1877:

All at once good-bye to modern days . . . Out into the past as through an unseen gateway, you travel into the midst of an array of dull drab-colored adobe houses, broken down and decaying adobe walls, windowless ruins, and dark foreign-looking faces . . . It doesn't seem as if this could be a part of the beautiful city of Santa Barbara.[3]

Other tourists were hesitant to enter the barrio because it had "an exclusive air about it that keeps one at a distance."[4] The more perceptive visitors acknowledged the presence of the Chicanos, but the racial apprehension of Anglos towards the mestizos canceled any desire for greater contact with them. They realized, as one tourist stated, that the "two civilizations do not, so far as we can see, mingle much."[5] William Streeter, who was very familiar with the Mexican population, summarized the status of the Chicanos in Anglo Santa Barbara society in 1878.

The Californian of today is an American citizen in name only. He still maintains his characteristics and his language. His sympathies are as entirely with the Mexicans as they were thirty years ago. He does not assimilate with the Americans. His feeling towards Americans is never less than antipathy, and more generally hatred; latent though it may be.[6]

The social distance characterized by Streeter increased during the following decade.

As the Anglo population again dramatically increased during the second, yet larger, real estate/tourist boom in 1886, Pueblo Viejo was further obscured by the dominant society. As a result, fewer curiosity seekers discovered this hidden quarter of Santa Barbara. However, a resident of the city, a reporter for the *Press* who was intrigued by his recent "stroll through the Spanish settlement," gave a graphic description of the isolated existence of Pueblo Viejo in the late 1880s:

[The area] still retains almost unchanged the features and characteristics of Santa Barbara of forty or fifty years ago. There is to be seen in that quarter a labyrinth of by-ways and alleys, the existence of which most residents of Santa Barbara are unaware. And yet all of these buildings are the homes of the poorer class of Californians, and by strolling through this section many manners and customs peculiar to the early settlement of the place are to be observed.[7]

A group of Santa Barbara Mexican women in about 1880. Reproduced by permission of the Huntington Library, San Marino, California.

As the Anglo population continued to hem in the barrio, their retreat to a familiar environment became ever more important to Chicanos. Here they could, as a writer in the mid-1880s described, "pursue a quiet, uneventful life, in nearly the same manner that they did when Santa Barbara was all their own and was a stranger to all Americans."[8]

By the early 1890s Pueblo Viejo had established an equilibrium within the larger community as the slower population growth of Anglo Santa Barbara corresponded to the small increase in the size of the population in the barrio. Residential segregation, a major part of the new Chicano reality that had evolved during the last quarter of the nineteenth century, was accompanied by increasing economic impoverishment. In addition, the Chicanos now had to manage without the aid of Californio leaders and without political leverage in Anglo society. They were also faced with an enduring heritage of racial conflict. "Considered in light of the existing enmity," Carey McWilliams has perceptively noted, "it is apparent that the framework, within which some measure of acculturation might normally have been expected to take place, simply did not exist."[9] At a time when the existence of Mexican society was in jeopardy because of the many negative forces impinging upon it from the dominant society, the Mexicans of Santa Barbara adopted mechanisms that ensured their continuation as a distinct ethnic and cultural entity.

Residential Concentration and Segregation

The first step in the social adaptation of Chicanos was a response to the demographic changes taking place in the community. As the Anglo population increased, the Spanish-surnamed citizens became more highly concentrated in the area of Pueblo Viejo. Their percentage of the entire population in the city of Santa Barbara was reduced from 46.8 percent in 1870 (approximately 1,200 persons) to 26.8 percent in 1880 (slightly less than 1,000). Between 1880 and 1890 the total population in the city increased by 70 percent; as a result, the Spanish-surname population was reduced to about one-fifth of the total by middecade.

Moreover, since the boom of the early 1870s the Chicano population became less visible every winter as thousands of vacationing tourists entered the city. Chicanos continued to comprise about 20 percent of the city's population throughout the 1890s.[10]

As the city grew, the adobe homes outside the concentrated area of the barrio became victims of "Anglo progress." As the initial wholesale destruction of adobes occurred during the first boom period, Anglo town builders and entrepreneurs began reconstructing Santa Barbara along lines that reflected their midwestern and eastern backgrounds. While some Anglo tourists as well as residents rejoiced in the destruction of the "ugly" adobes, others witnessed the demolition of the "picturesque" old buildings with remorse. To Chicanos the razing of these adobe structures meant dislocation for many families; some sought greater isolation by moving to more remote areas, but most joined their compañeros within the barrio.[11]

The barrioization of Pueblo Viejo continued during the 1880s as destruction of outlying adobes proceeded. The few that remained intact, once the homes of prominent Californios, became by 1890 ruins inhabited by "only those too poor to find lodging elsewhere."[12] The pace quickened as residential and business development closed in around the boundaries of the Spanish-speaking neighborhood. A popular writer of the period captured the mood of at least one Chicano, who agonizingly witnessed the developments affecting his community during the late 1880s:

Sometimes it does not seem Santa Barbara anymore—the new houses and strange people and hotels. Some of us have little to do now, and our own town is no longer beautiful or gay. Even our houses are being pulled down, as you can see, and in a few years, I think, there will be no Spanish town.[13]

By the mid-1890s, Anglos took advantage of cheap land values and built the first public and commercial structures on the outskirts of Pueblo Viejo. The steady encroachment of Anglo society near the barrio increased the density and segregation of the Spanish-surname population. In 1888, 67 percent of all home and property owners in the approximately eleven city blocks of Pueblo Viejo had Spanish surnames (see map). Within the seven-block core area of the barrio, nearly 72 percent of all property owners were Chicano. In addition, many of the non-Spanish-surnamed property owners in Pueblo Viejo were individuals who had married into Spanish-surnamed families. By 1890, Pueblo Viejo contained over 90 percent of the combined property-owning and non-property-owning Chicano population in Santa Barbara.[14]

Social Change and Adaptation

As the Chicanos became increasingly more segregated in Pueblo Viejo, they were no longer able to function socially as before. Sociocultural activities were adapted to conform to the new reality of the Chicano community. The historic community-wide Mexican fiestas or celebrations were replaced by modified, usually exclusive, forms of entertainment. In the years immediately following the gold rush, for example, the Barbareños had been entertained annually by a traveling Sonoran-Mexican circus; this circus was actually a troupe of acrobats and musicians who performed feats of physical ability and other entertainment. In 1874 the Mexican circus discontinued its performances in the community and was replaced shortly thereafter by an American circus from San Francisco. The new circus of clowns and animals could not fulfill the cultural traditions of the old Spanish-speaking community. A few local Chicanos therefore organized an acrobatic troupe purely for the entertainment of Santa Barbara's Chicanos and carried on this modified cultural activity throughout the nineteenth century.[15]

Mexican social and ethnic persistence manifested itself in other forms of cultural recreation. For generations the holiday horse race and bear-bullfight were forms of entertainment enjoyed by elite Californio and mestizo alike. By the mid-1870s Anglos had capitalized on the commercial value of the horse races by introducing new, alien forms of competition (the steeplechase and the Irish hurdles). A formal racetrack was constructed, and an admission charge ended the customary free

Home of a Mexican working-class family (Jesus Valenzuela adobe) before and during its decline, Pueblo Viejo, Santa Barbara, circa 1880s. Courtesy of the Santa Barbara Historical Society Library.

Sunday amusements. Few Chicanos were interested in the new-style horse races, and they began attending separate bearfights and bullfights. By 1880 bearfights and bullfights were outlawed and horse races remained exclusively Anglo events. The Chicanos replaced these forms of entertainment with activities that could be practiced within their own neighborhood such as cockfights, games of horsemanship, and impromptu horse-breaking exhibitions. Wild horse-breaking contests, an occupation-related activity among competitive compañeros, sometimes attracted large Chicano crowds.[16]

While some traditional forms of entertainment were modified by the Chicanos, other activities were initiated in order to bring together the Spanish-speaking community on special occasions. Perhaps as a response to the Yankees' July Fourth celebrations and as an expression of their Mexican nationalism, the local Chicanos began celebrating Mexican Independence Day, the *Dieciséis de Septiembre*. At the first celebration in 1873, planned by a group of locals called La Junta Patriótica Mexicana, there were music, speeches, and plays. "We are Mexicans, almost all of us here present at this reunion or celebration, by our fathers or ancestors," one of the speakers announced in Spanish, "although we are now under a neighboring nation's flag to which we owe respect. Notwithstanding," he concluded, "this respect does not prevent us from remembering our Mexican anniversary."[17] The Dieciséis celebrations throughout the 1870s and 1880s became the only days on which Chicanos could openly demonstrate their pride in being Mexican. The activities were well attended; sometimes 200 to 500 people participated in the traditional community dances. In 1878 William Streeter recalled the distinctiveness of the Mexican national celebration in Santa Barbara:

They join reluctantly in the celebration of our independence, while they all are enthusiastic in the celebration of that of Mexico.[18]

The Mexican Independence Day celebrations were augmented by another patriotic festivity, the *Cinco de Mayo*, beginning in the early 1890s. Thus, in the absence of the former celebrations of the Spanish-speaking community, Chicanos after 1873 supplanted their cultural-ethnic festivities with events that became symbols of patriotism and highlighted the distinctiveness of the Mexican community.[19]

There were religious as well as secular celebrations in which Chicanos participated. The traditional celebration of Corpus Christi Day at the old mission continued throughout the nineteenth century. But by the 1880s there was little other than tradition that attracted the Chicanos to the church. Importantly, after 1883 a Spanish-surnamed priest was seldom resident at either the local parish or the mission.[20] As Leonard Pitt concluded for Chicanos in southern California during this period, the Chicanos of Santa Barbara may have "neither returned to religion as a source of comfort from their new social woes, nor broke away from the Church because of the temptations of the new life. They still adhered to the minimum rites, although without a conviction deep enough to satisfy the clergy."[21]

Occasionally, however, festivities with some traditional religious content were adapted by Chicanos to facilitate collective social celebrations. A church-related activity in the Santa Barbara area which retained the character of a pre-American fiesta throughout the nineteenth century was the birthday celebration of Montecito's patron saint. By the mid-1870s this historic celebration took on a new significance for the Spanish-speaking people in the Santa Barbara–Montecito area and outlying regions. The suburb of Montecito, unlike Santa Barbara proper, never experienced rapid urban expansion. Prior to 1850 the Montecito Valley remained an isolated pocket of settlement. During the early American period it was renowned as a hideaway for bandidos—a place Anglos would not dare enter. By the 1880s and 1890s Montecito had become a suburban appendage of Santa Barbara, inhabited by a few ultrarich Anglos and by the original small colony of Chicanos. The isolation of Montecito provided the Chicano people with an opportunity to enjoy the celebration of Nuestra Señora del Carmen's birthday away from the presence of Anglos in the urban atmosphere of the city of Santa Barbara. The celebration represented the only social activity that rivaled the pre-American fiestas; this annual event, however, was predominantly a working-class, not an elite Californio, celebration.[22]

As other historic forms of amusement were discontinued or modified because of the Anglo influence, the Montecito celebration became more important as an exclusive Chicano affair. The large migration of Barbareños to the Montecito celebration in 1877 prompted the *Press* to report that it "was a great day with the Spanish and Californians, [drawing] one of the largest crowds that has been seen for some time."[23] The celebration lasted two full days and comprised a religious mass followed by horse racing, bullfights and cockfights, feasting, and a nighttime dance. The annual activity was never scheduled on the patron saint's actual birthday, since this would mean that "the laboring classes could not attend in full force"; it was always celebrated on a weekend. By the 1880s the celebration was attracting crowds of over 1,500 Chicanos and even a few Anglos, who "visit the scene out of curiosity to behold an old time Spanish American celebration."[24] The annual Montecito celebration represented the continuation of a historic religious-social event which, after 1873, facilitated greater isolation and temporary escapism from Anglo Santa Barbara society for the local Chicano community.

Besides the changes in the group activities of the Chicanos, there were modifications in the form of individual entertainment. By the late 1870s and 1880s Chicanos seldom socialized outside the immediate area of Pueblo Viejo. For example, the saloons frequented by Mexicans were located on State Street adjacent to the barrio or within the boundaries of the neighborhood. Family functions were also modified during this same period. The traditionally "open-to-all" wedding fiestas, for example, disappeared, but were replaced by single-family and interfamily social gatherings, especially barbecues. These affairs occasionally became large fiestas, but most were nuclear or extended-family backyard functions. The family "barbacoa" became a cultural fixture in the lives of most Chicanos through the first third of the twentieth century—one of the few pastoral pastimes that was perpetuated. The only other individual form of entertainment that continued to take place throughout the nineteenth century was the Sunday night dance at the local Mexican dance house.[25]

The adaptability of the Chicano community enabled it to preserve many distinctive cultural features during a period when social disintegration was likely to occur. The tenacity of the Spanish-language and Mexican culture prompted a local author to write in 1888 that "Spanish traditions are clung to" and "Spanish customs are preserved."[26] What this writer did not realize, however, was the extent to which traditions and customs were necessarily modified in order to survive. Some cultural activities disappeared altogether, while others became intrabarrio events cut off from possible Anglo contact. Social happenings were broadcast by word of mouth or by the Spanish-language press and Anglos usually learned about them only after they had taken place.[27]

Out-Migration and Poverty

Not all Spanish-surnamed people who lived in Santa Barbara responded to the Americanization of the city by insulating themselves in the Mexican social world of Pueblo Viejo. Some continued to leave the area during the 1870s and 1880s either as part of a colonization effort to resettle certain parts of Mexico or as individuals headed for cities elsewhere in California or other southwestern states. Colonization schemes were particularly common during the mid-1870s.[28] The out-migration of foreign-born and native-born Mexicans was sizable throughout the late nineteenth century. (The term *native-born Mexicans* refers to those whose nativity was in the present-day United States, either when it was part of Mexico or after annexation.) By 1880 only five foreign-born family heads of household still resided in the city, and only three native-born sons of Mexican-born fathers remained. Thus, over a twenty-year period from 1860 to 1880 a veritable exodus of Mexicans of the post-1848 migration had occurred. Whereas some 117 Mexican-born family households were enumerated in Santa Barbara in 1860, only 8 were listed in 1880.[29] The California-born wives and native-born children left with the Mexican-born fathers. Some native-born children of native-born parents also left the area, mostly during the 1880s. Included among these out-migrants were such prestigious local Californio names as Oreña, De la Guerra, and Ortega. The *Press* reported the destination of most as either Mexico or one of the southwestern states other than California.[30]

A majority of the Chicanos of Santa Barbara chose to remain in their native community despite their increasing impoverishment. As the local economy stagnated during the postboom periods of the nineteenth century, the plight of the Chicano community worsened. By 1876 the County Board of Supervisors established welfare relief for paupers, the indigent, and the sick. From the beginning many Spanish-surnamed persons, particularly elderly women, appeared on the county indigent lists. Throughout the period from the late 1870s to the 1890s as many as sixty Mexican people were receiving $4 to $10 per month of county aid.[31] In 1891 a local historian noted that the county pensioners on relief were of "mostly Spanish-American blood." By the early 1890s the problem of relief for the poor was partly taken over by a coalition of religious and charitable organizations, but the welfare status of Chicanos remained unchanged.[32]

Most Chicanos struggled to provide their families with a simple living. Even holiday occasions were spent without special amenities. When a recently arrived Chicano merchant-resident learned that many Mexican families could not adequately celebrate Christmas, he posted a notice in the *Press*.

I have been informed at my intelligence office that there are here several families, particularly amongst the old Spanish, who have not even the necessities of life for a Christmas dinner.

His plea for Christmas food and clothing became a yearly request until a charitable organization permanently established a Christmas dinner for the poor in 1897.[33]

The poverty within Pueblo Viejo was also increased by municipal neglect of the barrio. Community health care and city services were totally lacking. Anglos apparently considered the barrio an area unworthy of municipal concern and taxpayer dollars. For example, the Chicano third-ward public school, located in the barrio, was a dilapidated fire hazard in the early 1890s. "This part of town," it was reported in the *Press* in 1898, "has never had adequate fire protection." The absence of fire hydrants in the area of Pueblo Viejo was especially serious because many structures were considered to be "inflammable shanties."[34] Anglos also evidently ignored the conditions in the barrio that bred disease. The local newspaper claimed that in Santa Barbara contagious disease seldom spread beyond a local area in the city and little precaution was taken, therefore, in 1876 when it was reported that diphtheria was widespread among the young people of the Mexican community. The disease reached city-wide epidemic proportions when adequate medical care was not provided for the barrio children. Periodic epidemics contributed to the poor health of the barrio residents throughout the nineteenth and early twentieth centuries.[35]

From Riches to Rags

The poverty that existed in Pueblo Viejo affected most Mexicans regardless of previous economic or family status. But perhaps the most pitiful cases of impoverishment occurred within the class of Spanish-speaking people who had once possessed substantial wealth—the Californio rancheros. At the time of the 1860 census Mariano José María Valenzuela, for example, was a ranchero who possessed a moderate amount of property. By 1870 he no longer had an occupation and had lost all his property. In 1885, at age fifty, he died a propertyless man in Pueblo Viejo after having been an alcoholic for fifteen years.[36] The case of Valenzuela was not unusual. Most rancheros and farmers were unable to withstand the economic crises of the period. As their land passed from their control, they lost the means to be self-supporting. Even many once wealthy rancheros were reduced to humble status by the late 1870s and 1880s. One prestigious local ranchero, Teodoro Arrellanes, whom some considered "the wealthiest man in Southern California, his acres and cattle being numbered by tens of thousands," died in 1877 "comparatively poor" after living on a rancho "through the favor of the owners." Another original presidio soldier, Pacífico Or-

Crumbling ruins of a Santa Barbara Pueblo Viejo adobe, circa 1880s. Reproduced by permission of the Huntington Library, San Marino, California.

tega, a land grantee who was once "considered quite wealthy, . . . died in very moderate circumstances" in 1885, a victim of the changing socioeconomic environment of Santa Barbara.[37] Still more unfortunate were those who lost their wealth and, as a result, lost their sanity. One of the town characters who was out of touch with reality, for example, rode around town on a white horse brandishing an old sword. A local historian recalled the sad case of another former ranchero in Pueblo Viejo:

There was one paisano whose estate had narrowed down to an acre or two, but nevertheless maintaining the tradition of the ranchero, he would have his horse saddled at first thing each morning, and would spend the day on the horse riding around directing the people or person working for him in his little garden patch.[38]

The transition from riches to rags was accompanied by other developments. As the "gente de razon lost their money and holdings," observed Carey McWilliams, "they began to be called Mexican and the old practice of referring to them as Californios or native Californians was abandoned."[39] Not all rancheros, however, became "Mexicans" in Santa Barbara. A small elite core of the once wealthiest and most influential ranchero families was able to maintain its prestige by identifying itself as the "Spanish" element.

By the late 1870s the most important representatives of the prominent ranchero families had died. Yet such family names as De la Guerra, Carrillo, Oreña, and Covarrubias still carried a high social status among the upper-class sector of the Anglo population. Moreover, most of the native women of this elite family group had married wealthy Anglos prior to 1870. But once the boom of the 1870s had brought new Anglo arrivals to Santa Barbara—most of whom were unfamiliar with and insensitive to Californio customs—the remaining Californio families tended to withdraw from contact with them. "I fail to penetrate their life," an Anglo visitor noted, "and learn whether stoical acceptance of fate, repressed resentment, or recognition of the inevitable mastery of the Anglo-Saxon race, is veiled by the soft courtesy and gracious greetings of our southern neighbors."[40]

As the older generation of Californios began to die off, the declining socioeconomic status of the younger generation was further jeopardized by the in-migration of thousands more Anglos during the 1880s and 1890s. Education as a vehicle to ensure high social status was becoming infeasible by the 1880s. Californio families could no longer afford to send their young sons to the Franciscan College at the mission or their daughters to the private Catholic school in the city, as they had done since the 1860s. However, through the skillful use of family names and the earlier ties established through intermarriage of older relatives with prestigious Anglos in the community, a small group of younger-generation Californios retained a measure of high social status. This small elite group ironically became the *Spanish* links to the glorious past Golden Age of the Ranchos. The social climate of Santa Barbara within a few years reversed a trend that had existed for two generations: whereas in "the older days the dominant Mexican culture had transformed some Yankees into 'Mexicanized gringos'," as a noted historian concluded, "now the new culture created a class of 'gringoized Mexicans.'"[41]

As early as the mid-1870s some of the younger relatives of the

Californio families began participating in the all-Anglo Fourth of July celebrations. By the 1880s these people participated annually in the Independence Day parades as "Spaniards in their native costumes." Mimicking Anglo society, the children of a few Californio families organized themselves into cultural and recreational groups to promote "Spanish" culture, thus obscuring further the mestizo influence in Santa Barbara. A Spanish dramatic club, a Spanish orchestra, and a Spanish dancing club catered to an Anglo culture increasingly fascinated by the past romance of "Spanish" traditions.[42] (The Anglo glorification of things Spanish ironically manifested itself at the same time that the Mexican community was virtually cut off from contact with Santa Barbara society outside Pueblo Viejo.) These types of activities earned several Californio descendants a special social status in Anglo Santa Barbara, a status few other Mexicans could claim. Moreover, social acceptance into the elite Anglo circle was facilitated by the continued trend of marriage of Californio daughters to wealthy Anglos. For the sons, marriage with daughters of other well-known native families perpetuated a small class of elite Californio descendants. Unlike the great majority of the Chicanos who remained socially and residentially segregated in Pueblo Viejo, this elite corps of Californios—

Casa Aguirre, once the home of a prominent Californio, which by 1890 had become a ruin inhabited only by those too poor to find lodging elsewhere. Courtesy of the Santa Barbara Historical Society Library.

probably less than 5 percent of the Spanish-speaking population—became assimilated into Anglo society.[43]

Mexican Political Ostracism

As the younger generation of elite Californios defected and as the older Californio políticos died, the Chicanos became a leaderless and defenseless people in a hostile Anglo society. Taking advantage of the changed situation, Anglos moved to ensure the powerlessness of the Mexican electorate in the local and county political arena. In 1873, although Anglos had achieved political ascendancy by this time, the Spanish-surnamed voters in the city still constituted over a third (34.2 percent) of the electorate.[44] However, the following year a movement was spearheaded by a large group of Anglos that nullified the remaining Chicano voting power.

A drive to reincorporate Santa Barbara was launched in early 1874. The city was first incorporated in 1850, but was changed to the status of a county township in 1864. The new incorporation of Santa Barbara as a city coincided with the political dominance of the Anglo population. The most important aspect of the new city charter movement was the creation of a political wardship system that divided the city into five neighborhood wards—one of which was Chicano. Anglos were apparently satisfied by the new arrangement, which allowed Mexicans to elect one city councilman but neutralized their voting power outside the "Mexican ward." Previous to the ward system of voting, the board of trustees (city councilmen) was elected at large; the board members then selected a mayor from among their group. The Chicano voting bloc effectively capitalized on this arrangement by electing as many trustees as possible. The new wardship system brought to an end the influence Chicanos once wielded in local general elections; now they were able to elect only one city councilman, whose voting power was negated by a four-to-one margin. "Most of the Spanish element live in this section," observed a reporter of the *Press* about the gerrymandered Chicano third ward, "and with some exceptions

everything in that quarter, in the shape of improvements, remains in status quo."[45]

The ratification of the new city charter was conveniently ex-
ecuted prior to the municipal elections in April 1874. Even
J. A. Johnson of the *Press* claimed that the incorporation movement was directed toward the removal of the incumbent board
of trustees, which included a Californio mayor/chairman and
two of the five trustees. The city elections sealed the fate of
Chicano political influence. Only one Spanish-surnamed person
was elected to a position of power—the councilman of the third
ward.[46]

Thus, the city elections of 1874 represented a major revolution in local politics. Not only was representation of Chicanos
reduced to the tokenism of one councilman, but more importantly, the Chicano voting bloc began to dissolve. The 1874 city
vote, in addition, resulted in the election of the first Anglo
mayor. Mortimer Cook, the mayor-elect, was one of the leading
capitalists of the city, a symbol of the "new" Santa Barbara.
Never again would a Spanish-surnamed individual fill the highest office of the city. The city council, now Anglo dominated,
lost no time in passing ordinances to restrict the traditional
social customs of the Spanish-speaking. There were prohibitions
against "public performances and balls on the Christian Sabbath," including such "noisy and barbarous amusements" as
cockfights and bear-bullfights. Even Mayor Cook realized the
potential reaction to this ordinance; he refused to ratify it,
claiming "any law that cannot be enforced had better not be or-
dained, as it engenders disrespect for all laws."[47] Since the city
councilmen had the power to create new wards and change the
boundaries of existing ones, the Chicano voters of the third
ward could never again pose a serious threat to Anglos.

At different times throughout the last quarter of the nineteenth century, however, a few young Californios did contest
Anglo political supremacy. All suffered ignominious defeat because of a disorganized Mexican electorate, weak leadership,
and a politically dominant Anglo population. A typical example
occurred in 1878. The third-ward Californio councilman, Caesar
Lataillade, complained about the unnecessarily rough treatment

by the Anglo city marshal of Mexican suspects from the third
ward. As a result, a campaign to elect a young member of the
once powerful Carrillo family as the city marshal began. As the
election drew near, Anglos organized their campaign to counter
the Chicano vote. To discredit the candidate for marshal the
Daily Press shortly before the election printed a letter from a
citizen who claimed that Carrillo would "carry the Californian
and hoodlum vote solid . . . and nearly all the American vote
will be solid against him." The third ward was the only ward
with a majority vote for Carrillo. The *Press's* editor boasted
about the victory of the "better classes" over the "other sort of
voters."[48] Two years later when Carrillo once again ran for city
marshal, the Chicano vote could no longer be rallied. "The
town," claimed *La Gaceta de Santa Bárbara*, "took little interest [in the election] and the vote was small especially the native
vote."[49]

In the same election in which Carrillo was first defeated, incumbent councilman Lataillade was the only Chicano representative in city government. After an earlier unsuccessful attempt
to oust Lataillade on charges of illegal voting in the third ward,
Anglos succeeded in obtaining his forced resignation in a case of
battery against an Anglo. Thus, the last Californio político who
could rally Chicano voters left the third-ward seat vacant. In a
special election an Anglo was elected to fill the vacant post as
the apparently demoralized and now leaderless Chicanos withdrew from further political participation. The Chicano citizens
remained leaderless and unrepresented until 1886, when Lataillade, who returned to Santa Barbara after having lived in
Mexico, was again elected to the council seat of the third
ward.[50]

The defeat of a Carrillo for marshal, of a De la Guerra for justice of the peace, of an Arrellanes for constable, and of a California newcomer for mayor during the period 1878 to 1898 all
graphically illustrate the inability of Spanish-surnamed candidates to obtain political office. The requisites for victory had
been removed. The respected, old Californio políticos were
passing on, and their sons could not wield the same degree of
influence. Even if they had, the establishment of the gerryman-

dered wardship system would have severely limited Chicano voting power. Although the Spanish-surnamed voters in 1890 still constituted 21.5 percent of the electorate in the city of Santa Barbara, their potential for electing representatives other than the third-ward councilman was almost nil.[51] This Chicano powerlessness in city politics, which began in 1873, continued throughout the nineteenth and twentieth centuries.

The eradication of Chicano political influence at the county level, which had been almost accomplished in 1873, required a few years longer. Although Anglos had to employ different tactics from those used in city politics to achieve their goal of political hegemony, they were, nevertheless, equally successful in eliminating Californio county office holders by 1880. By 1874 Sheriff Nicolás Covarrubias was the only Californio of major political significance remaining in the county. He was able to survive as sheriff by siding with any political party or faction that enhanced his chances for reelection. Since the county vote was almost evenly divided between the Republicans and Democrats during most of the 1870s, Covarrubias and his Chicano constituency maintained a crucial balance of power.[52]

By 1877 both Republican and Democratic Anglos, dissatisfied with Covarrubias' partiality and favoritism to friends, joined in an effort to oust the last Californio político. Prior to the September county elections, the *Press* initiated a campaign called "Anything to Beat Nick." The campaign began with a felony charge brought against Covarrubias for an alleged appropriation of part of the county jailer's salary. The custom of the jailer's giving the sheriff a small percentage of his wages, to show gratitude for obtaining the job, had been a Mexican tradition for years. However, a state law enacted a few days after Covarrubias' election in 1872 forbade the practice. The case was sent to the district court. Meanwhile, attempts by the "anti-Nick insurrection" elements within the county Democratic party central committee to thwart his nomination were unsuccessful. A party follower, disappointed over the successful nomination bid of the incumbent, concluded, "Notwithstanding the notorious feeling of revolt which exists against Senor Don Nicholas Covarrubias in the breast of not a few American Democrats, that dashing caballero got away with the unanimous nomination . . . Now comes the tug of war."[53]

The Covarrubias political machine, run by local Chicano as well as Irish supporters in the different towns of the county, functioned perfectly—the incumbent was reelected. "It must be confessed," admitted several "Americans" in a letter to the *Press*, "that as political strategists or diplomats, the hijos del pais [Mexican native sons] are far in advance of the Gringo. You never find the hijos del pais," they noted, "opposing one another for any office; they skirmish around both parties for nominations to the best and fattest places and somehow manage to get them."[54] The Republican editors of the newspaper sadly concluded that the Mexican bloc vote had caused the defeat of their party's ticket. However, what Anglos could not accomplish through the electoral process, they accomplished through their control of the judicial process. The District Court of Santa Barbara County found Covarrubias guilty of the charges against him. The jury agreed to waive the felony conviction penalty if the sheriff would resign; he resigned, but remained in office until his appeal came before the California Supreme Court. Meanwhile, after the local grand jury convicted him of a misdemeanor on the same pending charge, Covarrubias vacated his office. Two years later, when he decided to run for a seat in the California Assembly, the last of the Californio políticos in the county was overhwelmingly defeated.[55]

The final thrust by Anglos to eliminate altogether the influence of the Chicano voters occurred during the early 1880s when Chicano representatives were successfully purged from participation in the Democratic party conventions of the county. The outraged editor of *La Gaceta de Santa Bárbara*, who had been a staunch supporter of Democratic party politics, concluded: "For the Native Californios the result of said convention cannot be of more significance: it excluded them completely, as if they [the Democrats] didn't need them for anything and did not consider them among citizens they represented or worthy of occupying any public post."[56] As a response to the racial segregation practices of the party, a Democrat, concerned over the loss of the Chicano vote, stated that Chicanos should be granted the same right accorded to other Americans who were represented in party deliberations. Even though Chicanos constituted a significant proportion of the county electorate, he observed, "they are not allowed seats as members of the Central Committee, they are not allowed representatives as Delegates to our State Convention, [and] not satisfied with this, resolutions are offered and passed excluding them from our Central Committee."[57] But the Santa Barbara Democratic party central committee, which reportedly "didn't want any d[amne]d Mexicans," was merely a local manifestation of feelings held by Democrats throughout California. At the San Jose state convention Chicanos, according to a local delegate, were treated "with utter contempt" and were "deliberately kicked out of the party."[58] State and county Democrats evidently did not care that Spanish-surnamed voters comprised 16 percent of the electorate in the county in 1890; the 617 Chicano votes thus were meaningless, since the Chicanos lacked leadership and were unable to participate in party politics. At both the county and the municipal levels, Chicanos had been placed outside the political system.[59]

Foreigners in Their Own City

Without political, judicial, or law enforcement representatives the Chicano people were defenseless against Anglo racism. By the mid-1870s juries seldom included Spanish-surnamed jurors and Chicanos therefore faced the extreme penalties of Anglo law. Fully 70 percent of all arrests and convictions reported in the *Press* for the period after 1873 involved Spanish-surnamed individuals. Cases of assault on Chicanos by Anglos, which might have touched off racial confrontations comparable to those of the 1850s, were now ignored by the authorities. When Chicanos were brought to trial, some requested a change of venue because, as one defendant claimed, the "people of the second township were biased and prejudiced."[60]

For Mexicans of the early 1880s the area outside of their Pueblo Viejo was a foreign city. Anglo immigration, the annual tourist trade, and the architectural changes in the city during the 1870s and early 1880s transformed Mexican Santa Barbara.

After the famous tourist hotel known as the Arlington was built in 1875, it attracted residential and business development away from the lower town and closer to Pueblo Viejo uptown; the barrio receded before the encroachment of Anglos. In the character of the Anglo population and in structural appearance the city, according to many observers, was "like that of a New England town, and not at all Californian."[61] During the 1870s Anglos transplanted to Santa Barbara their social world of dramatic, philharmonic, and literary societies, fraternal organizations, temperance movements, and other associations.[62]

The Great Boom of 1886 further eclipsed the Chicano community. It attracted Anglo capitalists, tourists, workers, and farmers who nearly doubled the population of the city between 1880 and 1890. With the increase in population came expanded residential and commercial developments and other improvements. As the principal historian of the period concluded, "The boom greatly affected the caliber of southern California's population . . . The boom was the final step in the process of making California truly American."[63]

As the boom of 1886 played a key role in obscuring the Chicano community even more, negative Anglo attitudes toward mestizos also were important in maintaining the isolation of Chicanos in the barrio. Many Anglos, in describing the Mexicans of Santa Barbara, characterized them as "an idle, indolent, sleepy set"; an "illiterate . . . wasteful people," who were also "shiftless and indigent, little caring for work, and not given to progress."[64] Others categorized them as unsanitary "riffraff" whose life style "keeps every drop of New England blood tingling in the veins of one who looks on."[65] By the 1890s the inhabitants of the barrio were discounted by many Anglos as a group not worthy of acknowledgment. Obviously, many Anglos viewed the Mexicans of Pueblo Viejo as foreigners in what many of them considered to be "the quiet New England community of Santa Barbara."[66]

Summary and Conclusion

During the last quarter of the nineteenth century the processes of barrioization and Americanization created a new reality for

Mexican people in Santa Barbara. As the Anglo capitalist economic order became dominant during the 1870s, Chicano workers tied to the dying pastoral economy experienced increasing privation. This impoverishment was reflected in the general appearance of the residentially segregated and isolated barrio of Pueblo Viejo. Made politically powerless through various methods of disenfranchisement and gerrymandering and without political leaders, the Chicanos were defenseless within a dominant society that regarded them as foreigners. The external forces of barrioization threatened the very existence of the Mexican community during a period when Santa Barbara was rapidly becoming Americanized. Chicanos responded by insulating themselves in the barrio and by modifying and adapting their community to the new circumstances they faced.

Those Mexicans who lived during the period from the 1870s to the 1890s were the first generation to experience the reality of being "Mexican in an Anglo society"—a reality that would shape the major life experiences of future generations of Spanish-speaking people.

Origins of the
Chicano Working Class
in Santa Barbara

4.

The barrioization of the Santa Barbara Mexican community during the last three decades of the nineteenth century coincided with another equally significant development, the incorporation of Chicanos into the Anglo capitalist labor market. The social, racial, and political subordination of Chicanos—a result of the Americanization of their society—was supported by their class subordination as a group of workers at the bottom of the occupational structure. Mexican men, women, and children were initially drawn into the Anglo labor market when traditional pastoral occupations began to disappear during the 1870s. By the 1880s, as other working-class sectors left the community and as the expanding local economy increasingly necessitated a large pool of cheap labor, Chicanos entered the market en masse. Their position was restricted, however, to the most menial, unskilled, and semiskilled occupations. The subordinate working-class status of Chicanos in the growing capitalist economy not only perpetuated their impoverishment, but also altered traditional familial work roles and established new patterns of employment. Most importantly, the developments that affected the Chicano working class in the late nineteenth century established a set of occupational and class relations that would continue to characterize Chicano workers in the twentieth century.

The incorporation of Chicanos into the labor market of Anglo Santa Barbara did not occur until three interrelated conditions existed: (1) the demise of the pastoral economy and related traditional Mexican occupations; (2) the rise of a capitalist economy based on urban development, tourism, and agricultural production in the hinterlands; and (3) a void in the labor market created by the out-migration of the principal menial work force, the Chinese. The future of the Chicano working class was inextricably tied to the urban and agricultural economy of the Santa Barbara region and vice versa.

The Expansion of the New Capitalist Economy

The tourist boom of the 1870s accelerated the displacement of Chicano workers from traditional occupations in the city. By 1875 tourism was the most important source of revenue in Santa Barbara. Visitors represented dollar signs to the leading Anglo business interests. During the peak winter tourist season approximately a thousand visitors spent an estimated $90,000 per month in Santa Barbara. The tourist boom spurred local businessmen to profit from the increased traffic by building more accommodations and expanding existing commercial establishments. The construction of buildings attracted a corps of skilled Anglo workmen experienced in wood frame and brick construction. The local paper advertised for carpenters and masons, badly needed in the growing construction trades, at the high wages of $3.50 to $5.00 per day. By 1880 the expanding pool of Anglo skilled workmen had created the first labor organization in Santa Barbara.[1]

The boom of the early 1870s marked the emergence of Santa Barbara's tourist industry, but the boom of 1886 established the city's fame as the premier tourist/health resort on the coast. The subsequent building far outreached the activity of the first boom. Real estate development companies sprang up, as well as the new business of construction and construction supply. Prior to 1886, for example, 750,000 feet of lumber supplied the city's building needs for six months; by 1888 as much as 15,000,000 board feet were unloaded on the wharf each year. The building boom attracted Anglo workers from every region of the United States to Santa Barbara and southern California.[2]

The rapid growth of the tourist and construction industries in the city was equaled by the less dramatic, steady growth of agricultural production in the hinterlands. The last of the free-roaming range cattle herds were outlawed when the California legislature passed the No Fence Law or Trespass Act in 1873. This law marked the ascendancy of the agricultural interests throughout southern California. In less than sixteen years the number of range cattle had been reduced from 300,000 head in 1862 to a mere 8,000 head in 1878. Where the cattle once roamed, the Anglo farmer began to settle. As early as 1878 there were nearly 59,000 assorted fruit trees and 144,000 almond and walnut trees planted in the farming areas near Santa Barbara; by 1880 the perishable fruit industry was equal in importance to grains.[3]

Throughout the 1880s and 1890s the agricultural industries of Santa Barbara County experienced substantial growth, as enclosure of once Mexican-owned rancho land continued. For example, in 1860 only 3,990 acres of improved farmland was under cultivation in Santa Barbara County; by 1870 and 1880 the farmland acreage had increased to 40,026 and 108,749 respectively. And between 1880 and 1900, agricultural lands nearly doubled in size within the county.[4] The only pastoral livelihood that survived was sheep raising; but it was confined to the isolated valleys of the county and to the Santa Barbara Channel Islands. For many Chicanos sheep raising was the last traditional source of employment. Together, the growth of the agricultural and tourist-related economy constituted, as one historian has perceptively noted, "the final step in the break-up of the ranchos" and "completed the transition from range-land to agricultural economy."[5]

Chinese Labor and the Anti-Chinese Movement

The labor needs of the expanding economy stimulated the immigration of Chinese workers, who soon were employed as the primary menial labor force within the two main sectors of the economy. The formation of a distinct Chinatown in Santa Barbara coincided with the advent of the tourist rush. The Asians were residents within the city as early as 1861, but by 1870 there were still only 82 Chinese. By the time of the first tourist/real estate boom, however, the Chinese population numbered almost 400. Because of a desire to reside together, and because of the prejudices of an Anglo society that fostered the segregation of non-Anglo peoples, the Chinese—like the Chicanos—were confined to a geographically and residentially segregated section of town. Chinatown was established next to Pueblo Viejo (on Canon Perdido Street, between State and Anacapa streets; see map). The Chinese inhabited many of the adobes abandoned by Mexicans, as the former occupants either left the area or moved from the periphery of Pueblo Viejo closer to the core of the barrio.[6] Thus by 1875 the two major ethnic groups in Santa Barbara—the Chinese and the Chicanos—lived in contiguous enclaves isolated from Anglo society.

In both the urban and rural sectors of the economy the Chinese were important sources of labor. In the city the overwhelming percentage of Chinese were employed in three main areas of work. They predominated as workers in the Chinese-operated laundries, worked as servants in Anglo homes, and engaged in small-scale commercial growing and selling of vegetables in the city. In the hinterlands the Chinese became one of the earliest sources of farm labor. They were also the section-gang employees on the railroads that arrived in Santa Barbara during the 1880s.[7]

Though the expanding economy of Santa Barbara was dependent upon a pool of cheap labor furnished by the Chinese community, discrimination soon altered the situation. As early as 1876 the Chinese of Santa Barbara, like the Chinese elsewhere in the state, became the target of abuse that resulted in their departure. Even before the movement against them, the Chinese of Santa Barbara had suffered malicious harassment from various elements of Anglo society, which considered them "a foul blotch on our fair city."[8] Anti-Chinese sentiments reached community-wide proportions in Santa Barbara after a demonstration was held that called for the termination of Chinese immigration and a boycott of businesses that employed Chinese workers. "Chinese labor was denounced at the meeting last night," the *Daily Press* reported following the anti-Chinese rally, "but no substitute proposed for it. Many of the labors of the Chinamen," the article concluded, "the white men won't perform."[9] The washhouses became the first of the Chinese industries to come under attack by authorities; many were forced to relocate on the outskirts of town. The formation of the Order of Caucasians in 1877 continued the pressure to rid the community of Chinese. In 1879 the establishment of a local chapter of Denis Kearney's anti-Chinese Workingmen's Party and subsequent election of many party candidates to local office placed the Chinese in a precarious situation. The local newspaper reported in 1879 that "Chinamen are leaving here nearly everyday" and that "there is not more than half the Chinamen in Santa Barbara that there were a year ago."[10] Further suppression of the Chinese enterprises (laundries, abalone fishing, and small-scale agriculture) and of the cultural life-styles of the people drove more Chinese workers from Santa Barbara. A prestigious local editor recalled the treatment of the Chinese businesses during his youth, claiming that it was his "first introduction to the controversial application of interference with the economic rights of an individual."[11]

The racial and economic drive to remove the "Chinese menace" was partially successful. By 1880 only 227 Chinese remained in the county of Santa Barbara; they numbered probably less than 150 in the city. Anglos resigned themselves to the presence of these few remaining Chinese, but only after many of the Asians had embraced the missionary efforts of various Protestant sects.[12]

Conditions Affecting the Chicano Work Force, 1860–1880

Anglos who used "reason" instead of "passion and prejudice" realized that the growing economy required a source of cheap labor in the city and on the farms; the declining Chinese work force could no longer meet the needs.[13] The gap hastened the incorporation of Chicanos into the labor market. In addition, the deteriorating economic condition of the Chicano community during the late 1870s and early 1880s forced Chicanos, for the first time in large numbers, to seek nontraditional employment from Anglo employers.

Although increased participation of Chicanos in the Anglo labor market began in the late 1870s, developments during the two previous decades foreshadowed their arrival as workers in an Anglo society. As late as 1860 the pastoral economy, although in a depressed state, was still able to maintain traditional employment for Chicanos. The occupational structure in Santa Barbara for the Spanish-surname population in 1860 was essentially the same as that which had existed for over a generation in the area; no major changes had occurred prior to 1860. But throughout the decade of the 1860s the pastoral economy and the corresponding occupational structure were drastically altered (refer to Table 5).[14] The natural disasters of the early 1860s and the subsequent growth of the Anglo capitalist economy ushered in a period of occupational change for Chicanos. The most notable changes affected the farmer, ranchero, and unskilled labor sectors of the Spanish-surname occupational structure. In addition, over two-thirds of the non-California-born Mexican laborers had migrated from Santa Barbara by 1870. This migration was accompanied by a smaller out-migration of former Mexican-born rancheros, farmers, and skilled artisans. The void left by the transient non-California-born Mexican workers was filled by many downwardly mobile California-born. The group of Spanish-surnamed workers who remained in the pueblo between 1860 and 1870 poignantly illustrates the downward occupational trend that occurred (see Table 6). The farmer group was devastated by the economic turn of events. Most who remained in the pueblo were reduced to the status of propertyless, unskilled laborers. To a lesser extent, the California-born rancheros and skilled workers witnessed an occupational decline. The California-born workers at the bottom of the occupational structure had also witnessed the rapid decline of their economic livelihood as traditional sources of employment disappeared. Moreover, economic conditions initiated a trend of high transiency or nonpersistence among the Spanish-surname population, most notably the non-California-

Table 6 Occupational distribution of Spanish-surnamed male heads of household who persisted from 1860 to 1870, Santa Barbara.

Occupation in 1860	Number in population	Pastoral/agricultural		Profes-sional	Proprie-torial	White-collar	Skilled	Semi-skilled	Unskilled laborer	Unknown
		Rancher	Farmer							
Pastoral/agricultural										
Rancher	6	—	2	1	—	—	—	—	1	2
Farmer	17	—	—	1	—	—	1	—	13	2
Professional	0	—	—	—	—	—	—	—	—	—
Proprietorial	1	—	—	—	1	—	—	—	—	—
White-collar	1	—	1	—	—	1	—	—	—	—
Skilled	5	—	—	—	—	—	2	—	2	—
Semiskilled	2	—	—	—	—	—	—	—	1	1
Unskilled laborer	23	—	—	—	—	—	—	—	20	3
	55									

SOURCE: Federal manuscript census schedules, 1860 and 1870.

born.[15] Thus, by 1870 the Spanish-surname work force was steadily becoming a downwardly mobile, unskilled, displaced working class.

The decline in the size of the Chicano work force by 1870 was particularly notable, as Anglos now outnumbered Mexican workers by a two-to-one margin. The non-Spanish-surname occupational structure reflected the growing dominance of the agricultural and urban commercial economy of Anglo Santa Barbara (refer to Table 4). The number of Anglo workers increased considerably in the farmer, professional, proprietorial, skilled, low white-collar, and semiskilled occupations between 1860 and 1870. The percentage of Anglo unskilled workers, however, declined appreciably over this ten-year period. In addition, the accumulation of property as an index of wealth pointed to the economic superiority of Anglos by 1870. As early as 1860, Anglos were successful in accumulating wealth equal to, and in many cases greater than, the Spanish-surname work force. By 1870 Anglos clearly controlled the greater amount of wealth and property in the city of Santa Barbara. Correspondingly, Spanish-surnamed individuals—especially in the higher occupational categories—suffered substantial property loss between 1860 and 1870.

The downward economic spiral of the 1860s for Chicanos continued throughout the 1870s. As the spread of Anglo capitalism in the region gained greater momentum each year, the pastoral occupations that Chicanos depended upon steadily became obsolete in the growing urban environment of Santa Barbara. The process of occupational displacement increased.[16] The worsening occupational situation during the early 1870s was compounded by a postboom economic recession followed by a drought/flood cycle. The real estate/tourist boom was brought to a standstill by the belated effects of the national Panic of 1873. General economic conditions did not become critical, however, until the notorious dry year of 1876–1877. The lack of adequate rainfall dealt a sharp blow to the sheep industry and caused extensive crop failures. The dry year was followed by a severe storm in 1878, which destroyed still more property. Santa Barbara did not recover from these hard times until the beginning of the next boom period in the mid-1880s.[17]

Those most seriously affected by the developments of the late 1870s were the Chicanos. The drought and flood further reduced the number of local jobs they could secure using their pastoral skills. Moreover, their subsistence gardening was diminished as a means of family survival. "We realize the gravity of a dry year to the country," recalled a visiting writer about the impact of the drought upon local Chicanos, "by the reticence of old Californians on this subject . . . Only by much questioning, by chance expressions, by a look of sudden pain upon the bronzed faces of the pioneers," she concluded, "do we conjure up some conception of that hopeless world, California in a dry year."[18] The worsening plight of the Chicano community, however, did not prevent Anglos from using them as scapegoats. For example, the new editor of the *Press*, Harrison Gray Otis, attributed Santa Barbara's economic woes to the Chicanos' reluctance to accept menial jobs.[19]

As local employment became increasingly difficult to obtain, the Chicano work force began a pattern that has characterized various sectors of the Chicano working class to the present day —part-time, seasonal, migratory work. It was reported in the *Weekly Press* that the "dull times have sent them away to seek employment as vaqueros, herders, teamsters, or what not."[20] At least 200 Chicanos left Santa Barbara County annually to seek temporary work elswhere during the late 1870s. Acknowledging the unavailability of pastoral-related employment in the local area, an article in the *Daily Press* suggested that Chicanos seek such menial jobs as cleaning outhouses, collecting garbage, whitewashing fences, pulling weeds, and trimming trees. "The employing classes," observed the article, will hire "if the help can be procured cheap enough to justify it"; Mexicans, it claimed, should "work at anything honorable at any price. That there are a great many people in our midst, particularly among the native Californians, who are very destitute, there is no reason to doubt. Now that the rain has come, there are none who are able and willing who cannot get something to do at some price."[21]

Chicanos during the 1870s, however, apparently refused to perform the menial tasks available to them. Instead, they continued to support their families by finding occasional work, local and migratory, that utilized their traditional skills. Some *caballeros* hired on as drovers to escort horse herds headed as far northeast as Utah and Montana. Others remained within the county to work as vaqueros at the annual roundups on the rancho circuit. A typical rodeo during the late 1870s employed thirty to forty vaqueros, who branded and slaughtered small herds of about 1,500 cattle. There were some who caught wild horses or purchased them for $20; after having been horse-broken, the animals sold for $75. The more reliable type of temporary employment in the county was sheepshearing. But the temporary work of Chicanos in traditional lines of employment was scarcely enough to maintain the subsistence level of the family. By 1880 the Chicanos were a group of workers dispossessed of traditional occupations and increasingly unable to find local employment in the jobs they knew best.[22]

The census of 1880 profiles the Chicano working class as chronically unemployed, impoverished, and unskilled. Although unemployment also affected the Anglo worker, Chicanos were especially hard hit; 74.8 percent of the Chicano workers were unemployed within the year of the census enumeration, compared with 49.5 percent of Anglos.[23] As Table 7 shows, the occupational structure of Chicanos had reached a new low by 1880. The percentage of unskilled workers rose to 79.7 percent—a considerable increase from 66.0 percent in 1870. The farmer class was now nonexistent, and the percentage and number of skilled workmen had also declined. By 1880 the non-California-born Mexican worker had virtually disappeared from Santa Barbara. Only 5 of the 128 male heads of household listed in the manuscript census had been born in Mexico; the sons of these Mexicanos had also departed from the area. Over 95 percent of the Chicano work force had been born in California. The pattern of unemployment and concentration in the unskilled occupational levels also coincided with continued high rates of nonpersistence; only 16.3 percent of the male heads of household present in 1870 still resided in Santa Barbara in 1880. No doubt this high degree of nonpersistence was attributable to the seasonal migration of Mexican workers, as well as to their general underenumeration in the census.[24] For those individuals

Table 7   Occupational structure for the total Spanish-surnamed (SS) and non-Spanish-surnamed (NSS) male head-of-household populations, Santa Barbara, 1880.

	Number of workers		Percent of work force	
Occupation	SS	NSS	SS	NSS
Pastoral/agricultural				
Rancher	6	12	4.7	2.5
Farmer	0	44	0.0	9.2
Professional	2	69	1.6	14.5
Proprietorial	3	78	2.3	16.3
White-collar	4	49	3.1	10.3
Skilled	4	94	3.1	19.7
Semiskilled	3	43	2.3	9.0
Unskilled				
Laborer	102	40	79.7	8.4
Other	0	11	0.0	2.3
Unknown or unlisted	4	37	3.1	7.7
Number in population	128	477		

SOURCE: Federal manuscript census schedules, 1880.

who remained in the community between 1870 and 1880, nearly 80 percent were now occupationally static—no change in occupation—within the lowest unskilled sectors of the labor market.

As the Chicano working class began to stabilize at the bottom of the occupational structure after over a decade of significant downward mobility, the non-Spanish-surname work force, conversely, had stabilized in the middle and upper strata of the occupational structure (see Table 7). Anglos maintained their dominance of the higher occupational levels (professional, proprietorial, farmer, and white-collar) as well as the skilled and semiskilled jobs. Less than 11 percent of the Anglo work force, as compared with nearly 80 percent of the Chicano work force, were employed as unskilled workers. Even European immigrants, particularly the Irish, were able to experience significant upward occupational mobility from unskilled and semiskilled to skilled and proprietorial positions. Comparatively, as a social mobility study of Irish and Chicanos in Santa Barbara indicated, Spanish-surnamed workers remained occupationally static.[25]

Although the Anglo occupational structure remained much the same between 1870 and 1880, the Anglo community was steadily increasing its wealth in the form of property. By 1875 the non-Spanish-surname population already possessed most of the valuable lands within the city of Santa Barbara (see Table 8); Anglo property owners outnumbered Mexican property owners

Table 8   Relative worth of the total Spanish-surnamed (SS) and non-Spanish-surnamed (NSS) owners of property within the city of Santa Barbara, 1874–1875.

Total assessed value of real and personal property	Number		Percent	
	SS	NSS	SS	NSS
$0–999	68	157	60.2	34.2
$1,000–2,499	26	115	23.0	25.0
$2,500–4,999	7	86	6.2	18.7
$5,000–9,999	5	58	4.4	12.6
$10,000 and over	7	43	6.2	9.4
Number in population	113	459		

SOURCE: Santa Barbara County assessment roll, 1874–1875.

four to one. The majority of Chicanos (60.2 percent) continued to own a single town lot and personal property not in excess of $1,000. On the other hand, a minority (34.2 percent) of Anglos owned property valued under $1,000; 43.7 percent possessed property valued between $1,000 and $5,000, while 22 percent owned property worth more than $5,000. In addition, Anglos predominated among those individuals who owned city property as well as valuable property outside the city.[26]

Incorporation of Chicanas and Children into the Capitalist Labor Market

The Chicano family's response to the dire economic situation during the 1880s altered traditional patterns of employment and familial work responsibilities. The most dramatic change was the entrance of the *Chicana* and her children as important wage earners who contributed to the family's economic survival. As male heads of household faced persistent unemployment, their migrations to secure seasonal work in the other areas of the county or region became more frequent. In these instances the Chicana assumed the triple responsibilities of head of household, mother, and wage earner. No longer able to subsist solely on the income of the husband, the Chicana and her children were forced to enter the unskilled labor market of Anglo Santa Barbara. The work they performed involved domestic services and agriculture-related employment.

Prior to the late 1870s most women and children adhered to their traditional roles, which centered mainly in the home. But by 1880 financial circumstances dictated a break from tradition. For over a decade Anglo women had decried the scarcity of domestic help. Beyond the small corps of Chinese servants, no source of labor was available; Chicanas at that time did not consider work outside their own home. By 1880, however, younger Chicanas began entering the domestic labor pool of the Anglo elite. The 1880 census listed twenty Spanish-surnamed women who were heads of household or who were employed, but living outside their nuclear family. Of those Chicanas seventeen were employed as domestics and two as laundresses; only one had a skilled trade (dressmaking). No doubt many other Chicanas engaged in part-time work that was not disclosed in the census. For instance, during the proposed shutdown of several Chinese laundries in 1882, Chicanas solicited work as washers and ironers. The trend of Chicanas working in the domestic-related services continued throughout the nineteenth and twentieth centuries.[27]

Agriculture and related industries were the main employers of Chicanas and children. The ubiquitous lawyer–land speculator–newspaper coeditor Charles E. Huse wrote in 1874:

There is a good deal of labor that might be usefully employed in a mill; boys and girls growing up in idleness and many of them in ignorance. If we do not build mills, by-and-by we will have to build almhouses to keep these people, or jails to incarcerate them for crimes committed, perhaps, under pressure of poverty.[28]

Huse's hopes for the construction of a wool processing plant never materialized, but the growth of agriculture in Santa Barbara attracted Chicano children and women as the chief source of labor. The first fruit cannery established in Santa Barbara County in 1880 was located near Pueblo Viejo. By 1882 the leading businessmen of the city had made the cannery a successful joint-stock operation. During the peak harvest and canning season, from 100 to 150 women and girls—and a few men and boys—were employed in the cannery. In 1883 the *Daily Press* reported that "about 40 Spanish girls are at work preparing the fruit for canning and drying."[29] They also worked as packers and labelers. The cannery remained in operation until 1886, when fruit crop failures in Santa Barbara and in other areas of southern California forced its closure. A cannery was not established again until 1897, when the Johnston Fruit Company opened its fruit packing plant. Significantly, Chicanas and Chicanos returned as the main laborers in the packing house after an absence of over a decade.[30]

Chicanas and their children were also employed as seasonal agricultural workers on the developing fruit and nut ranches of the area. Prior to the 1880s the economic function of children in the family was limited to grubbing for wild acorns and other edibles. From these natural sources mothers would improvise by making coffee and meal substitutes from acorns for family consumption. But by 1880 mother and child entered the seasonal harvests in order to supplement the family income. The first agricultural sector to entice Chicanas and *Chicanitos* to the fields was the almond industry; they were needed to replace the departed Chinese almond pickers and shellers at the nearby Hollister ranch. Colonel Hollister contracted with a city merchant to hire fifty women and children as shellers at $.04 per pound. The almond shelling season was followed by the longer olive harvest season at the Ellwood Cooper ranch during the fall and winter. Chicano children who worked in both harvests were usually absent from school until February. In 1884 the school census taker reported that about fifty children would return to school after the Cooper ranch harvests. "Those dilatory in coming to school," remarked the school official, "are mostly Spanish children, who are now out picking olives."[31] The olive harvests became an annual source of seasonal employment for women, boys, and girls. By the late 1890s the harvesters would pick a quarter million pounds of olives every season.[32]

The time of year when women and children were employed in the fruit cannery and participated in the almond and olive harvests coincided with the seasons when the men were most likely to be engaged in seasonal migratory work. There were seasons, however, especially in the early summer, when the entire family migrated from the city to pick fruit. This type of family seasonal harvest was evident in Santa Barbara by the 1890s. As walnuts replaced almonds and as the fruit industry expanded, Chicano family labor became essential. The Santa Barbara Walnut Growers' Association claimed that it could realize a very large profit, since the cost of labor involved in harvesting and handling was only 1 percent of the sales.[33]

The Chicano family walnut harvests continued through the first three decades of the twentieth century. Families would often leave their homes in Santa Barbara for several weeks, camping out in the fields where they worked. Goleta and other northern Santa Barbara County locales became the destination of large groups of families departing together. The local newspaper reported in 1897 that "a number of Barbareños" were preparing to spend the summer picking fruit. Shortly after this notice a columnist, surprised at the number of people leaving, reported that "the exodus of men, women, and children from the town to the orchards is something unusual."[34]

The process on a typical ranch during harvest season, as described by the *Morning Press*, required about sixty people, who were recruited from neighboring localities; women and girls performed much of the packing-house work after the men and boys picked the fruit.[35] Thus, within the last two decades of the nineteenth century, Chicanos—especially women and children—originated an enduring pattern of employment that characterized future generations of the Chicano working class in Santa Barbara.

Entrance of Chicano Male Heads of Household into the Capitalist Labor Market

The participation of the Chicano male head of household in the seasonal family harvests by 1890 marked his first exposure to nonpastoral employment. But the male's initial response to the deteriorating economic status of the family during the 1880s was to persist in seeking employment that required his traditional pastoral-related skills. A few Chicanos were employed as leather workers in a local mail-order house and other similar tourist shops. The Anglo proprietors of these establishments advertised "Mexican goods made by old Mexicans now living in and around Santa Barbara" from which a "typical tourist delights to secure mementos."[36] Some worked as vaqueros in the decreasing number of rodeos and local cattle drives. Young men, some only fifteen years old, would leave their family homes in Santa Barbara for the opportunity to become resident shepherds on county ranches. Others had to adapt their skills to new working situations. For example, by 1880 a lucrative trade in the capture of Channel Island sea lions for distant museums required the skills of vaqueros. Only "the Mexicans and Californians who are exceedingly expert with the lasso," noted a local newspaper, could accomplish the task without maiming the sea lions.[37] These types of jobs were, however, usually occasional and could not sustain a large work force.

There was only one historic pastoral-related occupation that many Chicanos followed for several decades after 1880— sheepshearing. After the drought of 1876–1877 and the destruction of large flocks, the sheep industry was relocated on the more temperate Channel Islands; there the sheep proliferated and the industry became a profitable venture until it began to decline after World War I. As early as 1881 the wool clip was valued at $250,000. By the late 1890s the Santa Cruz Island Company grazed from 40,000 to 50,000 head of sheep and employed forty resident shepherds supplemented by fifty to sixty trasquiladores during the fall and spring. The other islands contained an additional 30,000 head.[38] The trasquiladores could usually make their sheepshearing rounds on the small flocks throughout the county before leaving for the islands. Significantly, sheepshearing was the only pastoral occupation in which Chicanos could obtain regular seasonal employment; the same group of men, relatives and friends, migrated together each year. "Among the shearers," the daughter of an Anglo Santa Barbara rancher recalled the annual return of the trasquiladores at her family's ranch in the late 1880s, "were many who had come yearly to the ranch with the crew for as long as my family could remember."[39]

Sheepshearing to the Mexican trasquiladores meant more than just a seasonal income; it was their last occupational link to the traditional pastoral society. Following an old custom, many fathers took their young sons along on the migrations to learn the trade. During the year, when off-season unskilled manual labor in the city became scarce, many trasquiladores migrated to distant sheepshearing camps. During the 1890s several Barbareños joined with compañeros from Ventura County and followed a sheepshearing circuit through several western states. Groups as large as 125 men traveled by train to the shearing camps located in Golconda and Elko, Nevada, in Utah, and in Wyoming; some went as far as central Canada.[40] Trasquiladores stuck tenaciously to an occupation that their ancestors had passed down; unfortunately, sheepshearing did not provide employment for more than a few months of the year. Besides seasonal work as sheepshearers, these Chicanos engaged in various types of employment during the off-seasons. For example, some families and individuals prepared and sold homemade Mexican foods. A family in Las Islitas, a portion of Pueblo Viejo surrounded each winter by the rising waters of the *estero*, sold tamales in the barrio. Lino Ortíz and W. B. Gonzáles, the "tamale men," catered to the Anglo population from their stands on State Street near the barrio. Other Chicanos supported themselves by selling *nopales* and *tunas* to other Chicanos and to a growing Chinese clientele. There were part-time occupations, like the bootblack stand operated by Nick Domínguez; Nick Ruiz and others were hack drivers during the height of the tourist season. These types of part-time jobs helped supplement the income earned from other seasonal employment.[41]

By the 1890s the decreasing seasonal employment in pastoral-related jobs and the meager income from miscellaneous employment forced the male head of household into the general labor market of the construction industry. Throughout the 1870s and 1880s the personnel of this industry comprised primarily Anglo skilled workmen and Chinese unskilled laborers. But as the number of imported and resident Chinese laborers declined, Chicanos during the first half of the decade increasingly became the street graders, ditch diggers, and general manual laborers at construction sites. As recurrent high unemployment prevailed in Santa Barbara during the mid-1890s, more and more Chicanos filled the manual laboring positions once occupied by transient non-Chicano workers. From then on, Chicanos supplied the primary source of manual day labor. The mayor reported in 1895:

We have at [the] present time a great many idle men (not tramps) in our City, men who are residents and have families to care for, many of whom have difficulty supplying the actual necessities of life, because of lack of employment.[42]

A program to hire unemployed local residents for street work marked the institutionalization of the Chicano worker as the chief source of manual labor. Prior to the 1890s few Spanish surnames were recorded for the laborers who worked in the local district of Santa Barbara County's road crews; after 1897 the majority of road workers had Spanish surnames.[43] The pattern of Chicanos as manual laborers in construction and related industries became increasingly prevalent throughout the twentieth century.

During the 1890s the Chicano also increased his dependence upon seasonal agricultural employment. Large groups of men, headed by local Chicanos, began to migrate outside Santa Barbara County for harvests. Even as early as 1889 a certain Alex López left with a crew of twenty-four men to harvest corn in Hueneme, Ventura County. As the sugar beet industry grew in Ventura County and in northern Santa Barbara County during the late 1890s, Chicano labor was recruited. The Santa Maria Sugar Beet Company advertised for labor in Santa Barbara city newspapers, calling for 500 men, women, and children for three months of harvesting. The American Beet Sugar Company in Oxnard attracted a work force of Chicanos and Japanese who created a "forty-niner mining camp" atmosphere in the town.[44] Chicanos as individuals and as families became regulars in the agricultural harvests of the area. This trend, too, was expanded after 1900.

The Chicano working class by the late 1890s in Santa Barbara had established a pattern of employment that continued to characterize Spanish-surnamed people throughout the first three decades of the next century and after. Another development of the decade prior to the twentieth century, and one that persisted thereafter, was the renewed in-migration of Mexican workers. The advance guard of the large twentieth-century Mexicano migration to Santa Barbara came into the community as railroad section-gang workers before the turn of the century. When the first Mexican section crew was established in Santa Barbara, the *Morning Press* reported that the "Chinamen section hands on this branch of the Southern Pacific to Ventura have given place to a gang of Mexicans."[45] Their numbers were soon augmented. The *Morning Press* reprinted an article from the *Yuma Times* which claimed:

Two carloads of Cholos [a disdainful name for Mexicans] were attached to Monday's west-bound express, destined for railroad work at Tecachipi [*sic*] and Santa Barbara, Cal. These cattle are worse than any sort of emigrants that come into the country, and some time the people along the S.P. road will rise up and deport every one of them from the country.[46]

More Mexicans were imported during the late 1890s as the coastal railroad connection between San Francisco and Los Angeles necessitated additional labor for its scheduled completion. "Several Mexicans arrived on the noon train yesterday," noted the *Morning Press*, "and were taken out to the railroad camp."[47] The addition of hundreds of Mexican railroad workers significantly expanded the Chicano working class. They also formed the nucleus of the new Mexicano barrio on the lower east side of Santa Barbara, which would continue to grow during the following decades as other Mexican workers arrived.

The Santa Barbara Occupational Structure in 1900

By the turn of the century the Chicano workers in Anglo Santa Barbara society were fixed in occupational levels where they remained for several decades. Table 9 reveals that in 1900 the Chicano or Spanish-surname working class was primarily an unskilled and semiskilled manual laboring group (57.4 and 15.7 percent, respectively). Over 73 percent of the entire work force was in low blue-collar occupations; less than 20 percent of all Chicano workers were represented in the high blue-collar and low and high white-collar occupational levels. The development of tourism on a year-round basis during the 1890s and the sub-

Table 9   Occupational structure for Spanish-surnamed, non-Spanish-surnamed, and European immigrant male heads of household, Santa Barbara, 1900 (in percent). Appendix 1 discusses the occupational classifications.

Occupation	Spanish surname [a]	Non-Spanish surname [b]	All European immigrants [c]
High white-collar			
Professional	3.7	13.2	8.0
Proprietorial	2.3	18.3	18.1
Low white-collar			
Sales/clerical/			
semiprofessional	3.7	15.1	6.7
High blue-collar			
Skilled	10.2	20.3	33.6
Low blue-collar			
Semiskilled	15.7	12.8	12.1
Unskilled	57.4	14.0	13.4
Unknown or unlisted	6.9	6.3	8.0
Number in sample	216	508	149

SOURCE: Federal manuscript census schedules, 1900.

[a] 100 percent of head-of-household population.
[b] 40-percent sample (including European immigrants but excluding nonwhites).
[c] 40-percent sample of all European immigrants.

sequent need for a larger corps of semiskilled and unskilled service workers gave rise to a group of low blue-collar Chicano employees.[48] This group included hack drivers, delivery personnel, teamsters, hostlers, gardeners, porters, cooks, and others. Spanish-surnamed female heads of household and other employed adult Chicanas contributed significantly to this service-worker labor pool. Sixty-six percent of the total Chicana workers (95) listed in the 1900 census held low blue-collar jobs such as domestics, laundresses, cooks, ironers, and seamstresses.[49] In relation to the overall occupational hierarchy of the city Chicanos, Chicanas, and their children remained at the bottom of the occupational structure.

The non-Spanish-surname occupational structure highlights the continuing disparity between the Chicano and Anglo populations (see Table 9). In comparison to the Chicano low blue-collar workers who comprised nearly three-fourths of the work force, Anglo low blue-collar workers constituted slightly more than one-fourth (26.8 percent) of that work force. Conversely, over two-thirds of the Anglo work force were located in high white-collar (31.5 percent), low white-collar (15.1 percent), and high blue-collar (20.3 percent) positions. Even the occupational breakdown for all European immigrants illustrates by comparison the low status of the Chicano working population. European immigrant workers are more evenly distributed throughout the general occupational structure of Santa Barbara as compared with Spanish-surnamed individuals; their percentages as proprietors (18.1 percent) and skilled workers (33.6 percent) far exceed Chicanos in both categories. Thus, when compared with the overall non-Spanish-surname population of Santa Barbara, Chicanos clearly occupied the lowest economic-occupational levels in the community.

Summary and Conclusion

Within one generation, between the 1870s and 1890s, Chicano workers had been incorporated into the labor market of the newly organized capitalist economic system. The patterns of employment that were established by the turn of the century would continue to characterize the Chicano working class at least up to the Great Depression. The making of the Chicano working class involved a process with origins in the American conquest of California. Through various methods of land expropriation, accelerated by the natural disasters of the 1860s, the Mexican pastoral economy steadily declined and with it, the pastoral-related occupations of Mexican workers. By the late 1870s and early 1880s the economic dominance of American capitalism, and the concomitant displacement of Mexican workers from their occupations, set in motion the impoverishment of the Mexican community. Only after other ethnic-group unskilled or semiskilled laborers—the Chinese—were no longer available did Chicanos enter the Anglo labor market. This incorporation of Chicano workers into the capitalist market had a profound effect on traditional familial work roles and family structure. The Chicanos of Santa Barbara, by the beginning of the new century, were clearly locked into an occupational structure that not only restricted their opportunities for advancement but perpetuated their poverty as well. Although they formed the largest single sector of the manual labor market that was indispensable in building the region's economic prosperity, they did not themselves benefit financially.

The economic position of Chicanos in late nineteenth-century Santa Barbara reinforced their social position, which was the result of barrioization. The social and residential segregation of Mexicans in Pueblo Viejo and their subordinate occupational and class status determined the position that the younger generation of native-born and the larger number of incoming foreign-born Mexicans would assume in Santa Barbara society.

Many of the conditions that affected Mexican society in Santa Barbara during the second half of the nineteenth century were affecting all of southern California. As a result, Mexican pueblos elsewhere in the region experienced similar socioeconomic, political, and demographic changes, which transformed the character of their communities as well. The Chicanos of Los Angeles, San Diego, and of the San Bernardino Valley—to be discussed in Chapter 5—witnessed many of the same developments as their compatriots in Santa Barbara.

Mexican Society
in Nineteenth-Century
Southern California

5.

The forces that radically altered the nature of Mexican society in Santa Barbara were not unique to that city. With varying degree and speed the same forces also ultimately changed the Mexican communities of Los Angeles, San Diego, and San Salvador (located in the San Bernardino Valley).[1] The Mexicans in the pueblos throughout southern California, like their counterparts in Santa Barbara, experienced the manifold effects of the Americanization of their society. They too were affected by barrioization, political powerlessness, land loss, and proletarianization as the new capitalist system replaced the declining pastoral economy. Although the particular circumstances in each locality may have differed from one pueblo to another, the larger historical patterns are clearly evident. During the second half of the nineteenth century, Chicanos in the two largest pueblos of Los Angeles and Santa Barbara, as well as in the two smaller pueblos of San Salvador and San Diego, witnessed the undermining of their society and the ushering in of a new socioeconomic, political order—an order in which Mexicans occupied a subordinate racial-class position.

Overview of Mexican Southern California

For over three generations prior to the Mexican War of 1846–1848, Alta California remained an isolated frontier region. From its initial colonization in 1769 until 1821, Alta California was part of the northern borderlands of New Spain; after 1821 it was part of the independent Republic of Mexico. In the characteristic manner of the Spanish-Mexican borderlands, the mission, the presidio, and the pueblo formed the nuclei of California society. The influence of each of these colonizing institutions varied from one locale to another, and by the time of the Mexican War two of them—the mission and the presidio—had lost much of their importance. After secularization of the California missions during the 1830s and early 1840s and the demise of the economic and political influence of the church, the wealth of the mission system passed into the hands of ranchers. The ranchos then became the centers of economic production (with their hide and tallow trade) and perpetuated the pastoral traditions of the society. The pueblos, however, became the centers of population, social life, and mercantile activity. At the time of U.S. military occupation, Mexican southern California society reflected both its frontier-pastoral past and more recent socioeconomic and political change.

Throughout the Spanish colonial and Mexican national periods the class structure of southern California was largely determined by factors of wealth, land tenure, ethnicity, and family ties. Before secularization the ecclesiastical officials in charge of vast mission domains held much of the political and economic power. Their dominant position was shared by a small group of colonial and/or provincial administrators and by a handful of wealthy ranchers. Secularization of the mission system, however, significantly changed the status of the clergy as well as the other sectors in the population. It was the rancheros who benefited most from secularization. The transfer of land and cattle from religious to secular control resulted also in a transfer of political and economic power to a relatively small group of ranchers and other prominent individuals. Also benefiting from the redistribution of church real estate was a small number of ex-soldiers and minor political functionaries who had served the provincial government. They too received land grants, most of them of modest size, for farming and ranching. Theoretically, secularization should have benefited the former mission Indians who, according to law, were to receive land, cattle, and other resources in order to embark upon a life of independent subsistence. In fact, however, once released from the control of the missions, the Indians were systematically deprived of their property; many were recruited as workers in the rancho cattle industry and in the pueblos. Despite secularization, their social position remained relatively unchanged—they were still at the bottom of society.[2]

Thus, when American troops entered southern California, the class structure in the pueblos included three main sectors, all of which had undergone recent change. The wealthy ranchers and provincial administrators (who were usually members of the rancher families) constituted the upper stratum. They controlled the wealth and political power of the province; they were the benevolent, paternalistic *patrones* of the pueblos. Although most of the elite rancheros were of mestizo origin, many of the Californio families claimed they were of pure Spanish descent and emphasized this as an additional characteristic to set them apart from most other Mexicans. This group in southern California seldom constituted more than 20 percent of the non-Indian population and usually accounted for 10 to 20 percent of the pueblo residents.[3] The middle sector, far below the Californios in socioeconomic status and far larger in numbers, was composed of the mestizo population. Descendants of the original settlers as well as of colonists who migrated later from Mexico, they constituted 60 to 80 percent of the pueblo population. At one end of this intermediate class were the small-scale ranchers and farmers who owned modest tracts of land, and the skilled artisans of the pueblos associated with the pastoral economy; at the other end were the full-time and part-time workers (vaqueros, branders, tanners, laborers) employed in the seasonal cattle roundups. Many also engaged in subsistence farming and ranching on nearby pueblo communal lands. These pobladores were typical of the mestizo-mulatto-Indio people who settled other regions of the northern Mexican borderlands. Below this group in the social class structure were the ex-neophyte and nonmission Indians. Throughout the mission period the neophyte population had steadily declined, and it continued to decline during the Mexican and early American periods as economic exploitation and a legacy of colonial dependency took its toll. Intermarriage between mestizos and Indians and the assimilation of others into Mexican society in some pueblos further reduced the identifiable Indian population.[4]

Although the Mexican pueblos of southern California were stratified, there were elements of cohesiveness and tradition that allowed pobladores to interact positively with others outside their own social class. The community cohesiveness characteristic of Santa Barbara was also common in Los Angeles, San Diego, and San Salvador. Religious, cultural, economic-occupational traditions as well as other practices carried on by Mexicans helped build a unity—a unity that became increasingly important in Mexican society as the influx of Anglos proceeded.[5]

Southern California Mexican Communities

The several pueblos of southern California certainly possessed more common features than differences. There were, however, some variations in the historical and social makeup of the Los Angeles, Santa Barbara, San Diego, and San Salvador Mexican communities. The destiny of each of the pueblos during the second half of the nineteenth century was shaped not only by the larger societal developments that affected all Chicanos, but also by the particular developments within each pueblo.

The two largest Mexican communities in southern California during the nineteenth century, Los Angeles and Santa Barbara, closely paralleled each other in socioeconomic and political background. Los Angeles originated as a pueblo in 1781 and was settled by a group of mestizo, Spanish, Indian, and black pioneers. Its population increased steadily each decade through natural growth and immigration from Mexico. It remained the largest of southern California's pueblos during the nineteenth century. Both Los Angeles and Santa Barbara witnessed the same general effects of secularization (a change in the land tenure system, a concentration of wealth in the hands of a few rancheros, and changes in the socioeconomic class structure). The pueblos had similar social, cultural, religious, and economic

The Los Angeles barrio, or Sonoratown, in 1869. Our Lady of the Angels Church is at the left and the plaza is in the foreground. Courtesy of Historical Collections, Security Pacific National Bank.

characteristics, which helped lessen rigid social class stratification among the Mexican people and which provided that important quality of community.[6]

The smaller of the four pueblos, San Diego and San Salvador, developed somewhat differently from the larger two. San Diego had the distinction of being the first of the Spanish colonial settlements in California; it also became one of the first centers of trade when the mission padres and a few local rancheros profited from the hide and tallow trade with American vessels during the 1820s and 1830s. The pueblo, located several miles from the mission, was colonized by soldiers and ex-soldiers who located their families near the presidio. However, secularization of the once prosperous mission holdings initiated a period of hostilities between the discontented ex-neophyte Indians and the Mexicans. It also created a period of general economic and population decline in the pueblo and on nearby ranchos. As a result of these developments, San Diego grew more slowly than the other southern California pueblos. The small pueblo, nevertheless, remained the center of Mexican population throughout the southernmost region of California for two decades after the war. Within the pueblo itself the main plaza, functioning similarly to plazas in most other pueblos, served as the focal point for such sociocultural activities as bullfights and bearfights, dances, fiestas, cockfights, and other traditional Mexican forms of pastoral recreation. In addition, the nearby pueblo communal lands supported subsistence farming carried on by many pobladores.[7] With one exception, San Diego society mirrored the prevailing class stratification characteristic of the other southern California pueblos. Evidently a larger percentage of the relatively small non-Indian population were rancheros; consequently, there were fewer members of the mestizo working class. The majority of the sizable Indian population lived on rancherías or Indian villages near the pueblo; they occupied the same socioeconomic position as did members of their race in other southern California pueblos.[8]

While comparable in size to the San Diego pueblo, the Mexican community of San Salvador (comprised of the two adjoining pueblos of Agua Mansa and La Placita) in the San Bernardino Valley sprang from very different origins.[9] Unlike the coastal areas of California the inland San Bernardino Valley did not attract much Franciscan missionary activity; the few attempts that were made were abortive because of persistent resistance and attack from nomadic Native American tribes. By the early 1840s only two ranchos of any consequence had been established in the valley, and they too were the repeated targets of Indian raids. The San Salvador community was established to help defend the two local ranchos. Antonio María Lugo, owner of Rancho San Bernardino, induced a number of New Mexican members of the Santa Fe–Los Angeles trade caravans to stay on his rancho and accept free plots of land in return for providing defense against Indian attacks. The New Mexicans, reputedly brave settlers experienced in Indian fighting, accepted Lugo's offer. However, they became dissatisfied with their treatment by the Lugo family and after two years they moved to the nearby Jurupa rancho (owned by Juan Bandini of San Diego), where they accepted similar offers of land in exchange for their services. Here the roots of the San Salvador pueblo took firm hold as more Nuevo Mexicanos as well as California-born and other Mexican-born persons joined the colony during the 1840s and 1850s.[10]

The San Salvador community was located in a beautiful section of the Santa Ana river valley, where fertile farm and grazing lands were irrigated by the river waters. The Salvadoreños owned small private farms that lined the valley, and they grazed their livestock on communal pastures nearby. "Here during many years," District Judge Benjamin Hayes reminisced in 1862, "a simple, frugal, and industrious population had lived, with a considerable measure of prosperity, to me always appearing a happy race, certainly hospitable, kind, and joyous when I met them, whether at the iglesia [church], the baile [dance], or the social hearth."[11] The socioeconomic makeup of San Salvador, because of its different historical background, deviated from that of the other southern California pueblos. Through the 1850s the population comprised primarily Mexican-Indian settlers of New Mexican stock; the Pueblo Indian heritage was particularly strong within this group. There were also many other Mexican-born persons (mostly from the state of Sonora) and a few California-born families. Class stratification was evidently very weak: this rather homogeneous community contained neither large landowning ranchero families nor poor Indians. The majority of families of New Mexican origin engaged in subsistence farming and livestock raising. Perhaps the only consideration that differentiated one group of San Salvador residents from another was the ownership of land. But land ownership was not determined by nativity, for the percentages of New Mexican–born farmers and other Mexican–born farmers and laborers were nearly equivalent. Except for the few Anglo-Americans in the community, the social atmosphere was thoroughly Mexican.[12]

Forging a Legacy of Racism

The few Anglos among the Mexicans of San Salvador were representative of a small group of early Anglo-American pioneers who had come to California, intermarried, and been assimilated into Mexican society. However, by the time of the Mexican War the so-called Mexicanized gringos were becoming anomalies within an increasing population of Anglos with racially antagonistic attitudes toward Mexicans. Especially during the period from the late 1840s to the 1880s, Anglo racism was an oppressive social force.[13]

The military conquest of Mexican California set in motion the racial conflicts. Although a few Mexicans—particularly wealthy rancheros who believed that they would retain their economic and political influence—welcomed American takeover of California, many others resisted the conquest. Outraged by reports of the Americans' atrocities against their countrymen (John C. Fremont's Bear Flag Revolt) in the north and by military occupation of their pueblos, Mexicans formed guerrilla groups that successfully ousted or harassed American troops in every pueblo. They were able, at least for a short while, to postpone the inevitable military capitulation of Mexican California.[14]

Racial conflict during the following decade shook the foundations of pueblo society, especially in the two largest centers of population, Los Angeles and Santa Barbara. Contact between Mexicans and Anglos often manifested itself in mutual acts of violence, which in turn produced more racial tension and new acts of retribution. In Los Angeles race-related lynchings, murders, social banditry, and dramatic court trials approximated a race war. By the mid-1850s Los Angeles had gained a reputation as one of the most unlawful and violent towns in California. With even greater intensity than in Santa Barbara, race relations in Los Angeles during the 1850s erupted into vigilante activity. Racial conflict, both collective and individual, between the newly arrived Americans and the Mexican population shaped the tenor of the times.[15]

Racial conflict and racism in southern California also manifested itself in political tugs of war, discriminatory law-enforcement practices, and judicial proceedings. Whenever and wherever Mexicans lost control of political and judicial influence, Mexican residents were subjected to Anglo law-enforcement agencies, juries, and judges who often meted out excessive penalties. State laws were created especially to restrain Mexican social activity, such as the Sunday Law, which prohibited "barbarous" traditional Mexican pastimes on Sunday, and the anti-vagrancy Greaser Law.[16] Such laws added to the existing enmity. Others affected the economic pursuits of Mexicans. For example, the 1872 No-Fence Law restricted the customary free grazing of livestock by Mexican pastoralists. A justice of the peace in Riverside, near San Salvador, claimed "that he had in

The Los Angeles plaza (*center*), the plaza church (*foreground*), and part of the Sonoratown barrio (*left center*), circa 1875. Courtesy of the Bancroft Library, University of California, Berkeley.

1874 about half of the Mexican population under bonds to keep the peace" after repeated resistance to the strict enforcement of the No-Fence Law.[17] Together with other forms of discrimination, these laws created their own legacy of antagonism and racism.

Patterns of Political Powerlessness

Racial discrimination against Mexicans began in some communities of southern California as early as the 1850s. However, the establishment of Anglo hegemony in the growing towns and cities was also dependent upon American attainment of political domination. During the period between the Mexican War and the 1880s several different patterns emerged in the political interaction between the two groups, which resulted in the complete loss of Mexican political power throughout southern California. These patterns were reflected in (1) racial partisan politics; (2) political accommodation by the elite ranchero class; (3) political harassment and ostracism by neighboring Anglo communities; and (4) adoption of methods to ensure Mexican voter powerlessness—gerrymandering, racial exclusion from political parties, and elimination of Mexican political representatives. Each of the Mexican communities in southern California experienced one or more of these political developments.

Santa Barbara provides perhaps the best illustration of the changes in the political system that affected Mexicans during the third quarter of the nineteenth century. During the early American period Santa Barbara remained the stronghold of Mexican political power in southern California because of an ethnically conscious Californio leadership and a cohesive Mexican constituency. However, by the late 1860s and early 1870s the Spanish-speaking electorate experienced a steady decline in political influence. After successive racial political conflicts, which ultimately ended in their defeat, Mexicans by 1880 were rendered politically powerless.

The political situation for Mexicans in Los Angeles during the three decades after the Mexican War manifested some of the same patterns exhibited in Santa Barbara. During the 1850s a well-entrenched Anglo political faction attracted Californio leaders and Mexican voters to the Democratic party. Unlike the situation in Santa Barbara, however, local politics were never as sharply drawn along racial lines. Still, in 1856 racial issues militated against the possible formation of a strong Mexican political front, as Californio leaders and their followers were divided over which presidential candidate to support (both candidates were regarded as anti-Mexican). This division within the ranks of the Mexicans also caused the Democratic party to distrust Californio políticos, for many had bolted the party over the presidential issue. Through the 1860s the number of Californio officeholders steadily declined and Mexican voter influence became less important. The decline in the number of Mexican voters, and an unstable Mexican electorate because of high rates of transiency, contributed to the loss of political influence. Although several Spanish-surnamed politicians served in elected positions between 1860 and 1880, they did not provide representation for the mass of Mexican people in Los Angeles. The Californio politicians who served in office were elected only after accommodating or assimilating into Anglo society. Even if Californio leaders had sincerely represented the interests of the Mexican population (37 percent of the total population in 1870), Mexican voter influence was negated by gerrymandered political wards and residential segregation. "As a group," a historian of Los Angeles Chicano history has noted, "these men [Californio elected officials] were far removed from the mass of Spanish speaking . . . Not surprisingly, there is no evidence of any effort on their part to ameliorate the pressing social and economic ills that plagued the barrio." In assessing the political situation for Mexicans in Los Angeles between 1860 and 1880, he concluded: "Although superficially the Spanish speaking did not appear to lack political representation, in fact they did and for all practical purposes the masses of laborers in the barrio remained politically inarticulate."[18]

Like Santa Barbara and Los Angeles, San Salvador also experienced racial political conflict. During the first elections in the early 1850s, the inexperienced Salvadoreños were persuaded by Anglos to vote for anti-Mexican candidates who were deceptively presented to them as pro-Mexican. But in subsequent elections they became knowledgeable voters. San Salvador voting precinct in San Bernardino County essentially constituted the Mexican community. As a result of political-geographic division the Mexicans were able to elect their own justice of the peace and establish their own district school with public funds. Politics in the San Salvador district remained firmly in the hands of the overwhelming Mexican majority. The small percentage of Anglo voters in the district did not pose a threat to the Salvadoreños either through gerrymandering or through other tactics used elsewhere to dilute the Mexican voter influence.[19] Mexican political powerlessness was a product of factors external to the community of San Salvador.

The major pattern of political struggle for the Salvadoreños resulted from the establishment of neighboring Anglo communities, Riverside in particular. When the Riverside colony was established within the San Salvador township, the San Bernardino County supervisors appointed an Anglo justice of the peace. His actions soon made him an enemy of the Mexican people, and in the subsequent election he was voted out of office and replaced by a leading citizen of San Salvador. (Spanish-surnamed voters accounted for 75 and 62 percent of all voters in the district in 1868 and in 1873, respectively.) Responding to the requests of the Anglo residents of Riverside, however, the county supervisors divided the district, making Riverside a separate township and reappointing the former justice of the peace. From the 1870s on, political harassment of Salvadoreños—such as confiscation of real and personal property, unjust law-enforcement practices, and contesting of land-grant claims—by Riverside authorities intensified.[20] The Anglos of Riverside widened the political and social gap between the two communities when in 1883 they drew their city boundaries so as to exclude San Salvador; ten years later, when Riverside County was created, San Salvador was left in San Bernardino County. Concluded Donald S. Miller, historian of Chicano history in nineteenth-century San Bernardino Valley:

Systematic separation of the Mexican and Anglo populations became an institution in early Riverside history. By 1880 La Placita [San Salvador] and Riverside had become artificially but completely separated in civic and social affairs . . . The effect of the separation was dramatic. With greater economic resources, Riverside forged ahead with extensive community projects and public works, while La Placita continually declined.[21]

Quite different from the situation in San Salvador were the developments in San Diego. There political powerlessness occurred very early. In fact, the leading Californios of San Diego never contested the Anglo domination of local politics. Many of them had sided with Anglos before and after the war in an effort to protect their own economic interests and social prestige.

Los Angeles Chicanos in front of an old adobe grocery store in Sonoratown, circa 1880. Reproduced by permission of the Huntington Library, San Marino, California.

Eventually, however, these political accommodationists experienced the socioeconomic decline that affected most Mexicans in San Diego. The lack of Californio political leadership no doubt accounted for the minimal interest of Mexican residents in elections. Although they formed a large part of the total population during the 1850s and 1860s, they represented only a small percentage of registered city voters throughout the period (16 percent in 1867 and 4 percent in 1872 and 1879, for example).[22]

Land Loss and Economic Displacement

The loss of political influence by the Mexican population throughout southern California resulted in Anglo control of the judicial system, law-enforcement agencies, elected political positions, and decision-making bodies. This domination of the state apparatus was accompanied by American attempts to divest the "backward" Mexicans of their lands. Loss of Mexican-owned ranchos and pueblo communal lands altered the nature of the economy, radically changed the land tenure system, and resulted in economic exploitation of the Mexican people. Once the subdivision of rancho and pueblo lands had begun, the dominance of U.S. capitalism in the once Mexican province was a foregone conclusion.

The dispossession of Mexican land in California has been sufficiently documented by scholars who have identified the major characteristics of the land loss. They include: (1) prolonged legal struggles to validate Mexican land-grant claims before a board of land commissioners—a body established by Congress, at the urging of Anglo political-economic interests in California, as part of the Land Law of 1851—and other financially costly court proceedings; (2) usurious interest rates on loans, charged by land speculators and others; (3) exploitation by unscrupulous lawyers of the opportunity to acquire land; (4) exorbitant taxes on "unimproved" land, and public sale of lands for delinquent tax payments; (5) Mexican ignorance of the English language and of the American judicial system; (6) spendthrift practices of wealthy Californios; (7) sale of traditional pueblo communal lands by local city governments; (8) passage by proagrarian and commercial interests of legislation against pastoral interests; and (9) confiscation of land by squatters. These factors, together with the decline of the once lucrative beef cattle market during the late 1850s, and a series of devastating natural disasters in the early 1860s, caused the transfer of millions of acres of land previously held by Mexican owners. The process of land loss in northern California, which resulted largely from the Gold Rush and the concomitant demographic and socioeconomic changes, was quite swift during the 1850s. Southern California experienced the same phenomena, but somewhat later and over a longer period of time.[23]

In every Mexican locality in southern California between the 1850s and the 1880s, some or all of the factors described above were operative. In San Diego, for example, the few wealthy rancheros were crippled by litigation fees; by unfair tax assessments levied at the local, county, and state levels; by exorbitant interest rates on loans; by the public auction of their lands for defaulted taxes; by the uncertainty of contested ownership of land grants; and by their own inability to manage financial affairs during "bad times." Essentially the same forces that operated in San Diego, coupled with fraudulent Anglo land schemes, ruined the rancheros of Santa Barbara and Los Angeles. By 1870 Mexican real estate holdings had declined spectacularly and continued to decline thereafter. The transfer of land from Mexican to Anglo ownership was fairly complete by the following decade.[24]

The loss of private land by Mexican rancheros and farmers was paralleled by the loss of communal lands traditionally used by the pobladores. While members of the mestizo working class were able, for the most part, to retain their individual residential plots in the pueblos during the second half of the nineteenth century, they did not retain access to pueblo communal lands. During the 1850s and 1860s in San Diego, Santa Barbara, San Salvador, and in Los Angeles as well, municipal authorities sold the public lands that had provided subsistence farming and livestock pasturage for generations of Mexicans. The "early Trustees [municipal board of trustees] handled their trust [pueblo lands] like a card giveaway game," concluded a historian of San Diego.[25] Pueblo lands throughout southern California were rapidly purchased by land speculators and other Anglo capitalists. For San Salvador, another historian added that, "in one way or another—through ignorance of the laws and language, timidity or racial discrimination or all of these—the Spanish speaking people generally could not or did not obtain public land."[26]

The Salvadoreños, in fact, had to struggle just to retain title to their private property. Beginning in 1852 and for the next thirty years the Salvadoreños' title to the land originally granted them was contested in court after court. The original grantor, Juan Bandini, was himself the first to contest the grant, because he needed cash to settle his own financial troubles. Thereafter residents of San Salvador fought for the preservation of their community against successive Anglo claimants to their lands. Finally, in the 1880s the California Supreme Court handed down a judgment favorable to the Salvadoreños, thus rebuking the Anglo claimants, the townbuilders of neighboring Riverside. However, by the mid-1880s most of the original San Salvador settlers had relinquished ownership of the hard-fought titles to their land. They were confronted with costly court cases and

denied access to their traditional pueblo grazing lands. In addition, they were faced with strict enforcement of the 1872 No-
Fence Law, which delivered a final blow to the devastated
cattle industry throughout southern California. Under these
conditions San Salvador could no longer maintain itself as a viable community.[27]

Table 10 Total Chicano, white, and nonwhite population in selected
southern California cities, 1860–1890.

City and year	Total population	Chicano population	Nonwhite population (by county only) [a]		
Los Angeles [b]					
1860	4,385	2,565	C = 11	I = 2,014	
			N = 87		
1870	8,504	2,131	C = 234	J = 2	
			N = 134	I = 219	
1880	11,183	2,231	C = 1,169	J = 1	
			N = 188	I = 316	
1890	50,395	c	C = 4,424	J = 36	
			N = 1,817	I = 144	
San Diego					
1860	731	206	C = 0	I = 3,067	
			N = 8		
1870	2,300	190	C = 70	I = 28	
			N = 15		
1880	2,637	242	C = 229	I = 1,702	
			N = 13		
1890	16,159	c	C = 909	J = 13	
			N = 376	I = 478	
San Bernardino/ San Salvador					
1860	940/1,092	206/227	C = 0	I = 3,028	
			N = 19		
1870	3,064 [d]/560	112/395	C = 16	I = 0	
			N = 8		
1880	1,673 [e]/NA	125/207 [f]	C = 123	I = 658	
			N = 17		
1890	4,012/228	c	C = 682	J = 2	
			N = 313	I = 399	

Table 10   (continued)

City and year	Total population	Chicano population	Nonwhite population (by county only)[a]			
Santa Barbara						
1860	2,351	1,554	C =	0	I =	365
			N =	0		
1870	2,640	1,210/1,512[g]	C =	109	I =	153
			N =	38		
1880	3,460	932	C =	227	I =	88
			N =	63		
1890	5,864	[c]	C =	581	J =	5
			N =	26	I =	73

SOURCES: 1860–1890 published U.S. census population reports and unpublished manuscript census schedules, unless cited otherwise.

[a] C = Chinese, N = Negro, I = Indian, and J = Japanese.

[b] See Griswold del Castillo, "La Raza Hispano Americana," 66.

[c] The 1890 census manuscript schedules were destroyed by fire, so that population figures for Spanish-surnamed persons are unavailable. Although the figures cited for Chicanos are not adjusted upward, at least one historian (Oscar Martínez) argues convincingly that nineteenth-century population figures for Mexicans are underenumerated by 40 percent.

[d] San Bernardino precinct, including the town of San Bernardino.

[e] Town of San Bernardino only.

[f] Agua Mansa only.

[g] Including the adjacent suburb of Montecito.

The Process of Barrioization

The economic, social, political, and demographic changes brought, about by the Americanization of southern California during the three decades following annexation (see Table 10) significantly altered the life-styles of the Mexican people in each pueblo. A process of barrioization such as that which had negatively affected the Chicanos of Santa Barbara during the last quarter of the nineteenth century also affected Chicanos in the other towns of southern California. Faced with their new reality as an ethnic minority group in a dominant Anglo society, and in a disadvantaged position because of their political powerlessness and economic displacement, Mexicans everywhere struggled to maintain their communities; not all were successful. Those communities that persisted did so only after their Mexican citizens adapted themselves to the new existence in a residentially segregated, poverty-stricken barrio. Throughout southern California the Chicano people managed to keep alive the mestizo heritage of the region.

The larger pattern of barrioization was manifested in different ways in the several Mexican communities of southern California, depending on the speed and impact of Americanization. The barrioization that characterized the Santa Barbara Chicano community was similar in many ways to the process in Los Angeles. The major difference between the two pueblos was the accelerated pace of Americanization and urbanization in Los Angeles. This undoubtedly accounted for the more rapid process of barrioization that took place there. Essentially the same forces that had changed the nature of the Santa Barbara pueblo—Anglo immigration, establishment of transportation and communication networks, tourist/real estate booms, residential and business expansion, shift in the economy—changed Los Angeles.

In this rapidly growing city the non-Spanish-surname population increased from under 300 in 1850 to nearly 9,000 by 1880. Consequently, the Chicano population fell rapidly from majority to minority status (82 percent of the total population in 1850 to 19 percent in 1880).[28] As early as 1860 a pattern of residential segregation began to emerge. The vast majority of Spanish-surnamed property owners, and approximately 70 percent of the total Chicano population (2,565 persons in 1860 and 2,131 in 1870), inhabited two enclaves in the city. The larger one corresponded to the core area of the original Mexican pueblo in the central part of Los Angeles adjacent to the plaza; the smaller was located in an area just south of the old pueblo. During the late 1880s Chicanos continued to be highly segregated in the old pueblo area (which by this time had expanded slightly in a northern and eastern direction from the plaza) and in the less segregated area to the south. As Richard Griswold del Castillo has noted in his study of Chicanos in Los Angeles, "By the

North Main Street, Los Angeles, 1883. Courtesy of the Bancroft Library, University of California, Berkeley.

1880s the barrio was a well-defined enclave within the heart of the city surrounded by Anglo suburbs."[29] Commenting on the barrio, or "Sonoratown" as the Anglos called it, an old Yankee pioneer in Los Angeles claimed that it "was an area almost untouched by the American influence . . . as truly Mexican as though it had been transported bodily from Old Mexico."[30] It was also the poorest section of Los Angeles, lacking the public services that other Angelenos enjoyed. But the barrio, with the old plaza as the center of its social existence, became the area that preserved the Chicano presence in a bewildering urban environment. Griswold del Castillo concluded:

The barrio gave identity and a feeling of being at home for the dispossessed and poor. It was a place, a traditional place, that offered some security from the city's social and economic turmoil . . . In a sense the creation of the barrio was a means of cultural survival. Proximity of residence reinforced the language, religion, and social habits of Chicanos and thus insured the continuation of their distinctive culture.[31]

Indeed, the Chicanos of Los Angeles developed mechanisms that guaranteed their ethnic and cultural persistence. Mutual aid societies, "juntas patrióticas" (which sponsored Mexican patriotic celebrations), political clubs, cultural groups, and a number of Spanish-language newspapers all contributed to the reinforcement of ethnic consciousness and solidarity among Chicanos. These new avenues of communication allowed Chicanos to reestablish their mutual social relations during a period when their society was reacting to the tremendous changes wrought by Americanization and urbanization.[32]

Two additional patterns of social change that affected Chicano society in Los Angeles were similar to those that manifested themselves in Santa Barbara. First, a trend toward matriarchal family structures occurred. The percentage of female heads of household had significantly increased by 1860 and remained stable through 1880 (15 percent in 1844 and 30 percent by 1880). The greater number of Chicanas assuming responsibility for the family may have been the result of premature male fatalities, abandonment, or seasonal migrations by males to procure employment. A second pattern, common to both communities but more prevalent in Los Angeles, was the high frequency of Chicano movement in and out of the barrio. Both California-born and Mexican-born residents tended to move more often between 1860 and 1880 than in the pre-1860 period. The Mexican-born group, however, did not evidence as marked a decline in population as it did in Santa Barbara. The non-California-born Mexicans in Los Angeles comprised 27 percent of the Spanish-surnamed population in 1860 and 20 percent in 1880.[33]

In contrast to Los Angeles and Santa Barbara, significantly different patterns of barrioization emerged in the two smaller pueblos of San Salvador and San Diego. Developments there resulted more from the rise of neighboring Anglo towns than from internal changes within the communities. This pattern of barrioization, which eventually led to the demise of San Salvador and the stagnation of San Diego, can be characterized as geographic isolation and political-economic strangulation.

In the entire San Bernardino Valley during the 1850s there were only two small settlements, San Salvador township (essentially the pueblos of Agua Mansa and La Placita) and the town of San Bernardino, which had been established originally as a Mormon colony in 1853. In 1860 the area was still thinly populated; San Salvador township contained slightly over a thousand inhabitants and San Bernardino somewhat less. By the early 1870s the situation had dramatically changed. The prospect of a major railroad line through the valley had increased Anglo immigration, expanded the agricultural economy, and spurred town building. San Bernardino increased in size, and the thriving new towns of Colton, Riverside, and Redlands were established. As the Mexican population of San Salvador declined, the neighboring Anglo towns experienced rapid growth (San Bernardino's population, for example, increased from 940 in 1860 to 3,064 by 1870).[34]

The gradual decline of San Salvador, which lasted over forty years, had begun in 1862 when the Santa Ana River flooded and destroyed most of the community. Although some residents sought temporary employment in nearby mining areas, most labored to restore their small farm parcels. "They do not seem inclined to wander far," Judge Benjamin Hayes remarked in 1864, "but prefer to pick up here and there where they can, patches of a few acres amidst the sand."[35] Although San Sal-

The pueblo of San Diego in 1850 (H. T. Powell sketch, February 8, 1850). Courtesy of the San Diego Historical Society, Serra Museum Library.

vador survived the flood, it had been left weakened and unable to resist Anglo economic and political encroachment during subsequent years. From the 1870s on, Salvadoreños were increasingly denied access to established grazing lands by squatters and farmers who fenced off the open range. Political harassment from Riverside authorities, who strictly enforced proagrarian laws, added to their difficulties and resulted in the confiscation of livestock and the levying of fines—acts that inflamed racial conflict and antagonisms. By 1880 the population of San Salvador had been reduced to slightly over two hundred persons and, according to at least one historian, "even subsistence ranching and farming was becoming impossible."[36] More and more frequently during the last two decades of the century the Chicanos of San Salvador, incapable of eking out a living in their own pueblo, moved to other valley towns (principally San Bernardino, Riverside, and Colton). With each departing family additional San Salvador land was absorbed into the encroaching farms and ranches of Anglo owners. Historian Donald S. Miller claims:

The nearly total disintegration of the remnants of the old New Mexican communities between 1884 and 1895 came as the final blow to the valley's earliest permanent Mexican inhabitants . . . The fact that Agua Mansa settlers retained a strong community cohesiveness almost into the twentieth century despite Anglo pressures provides one of the valley's historical anomalies . . . The true history of the nineteenth-century Mexican American is neither a romantic Spanish legend nor a tale of Mexican obstructionism [to Anglo progress]. Rather it is the deeply human story of a people's struggle for survival in the face of the ravages of an implacable nature and the depredations of an avaricious, insensitive Anglo tide.[37]

By the early twentieth century only a handful of Mexican families remained in the San Salvador area. Economic, political, and racial pressures, toether with the forces of nature, had combined to destroy the only community of nineteenth-century Mexicans in the San Bernardino Valley. Despite the disintegration of their community, the Salvadoreños had forged historical links between the pueblo society of the mid-nineteenth century and the barrio society of the early twentieth century.[38]

The same geographic isolation and political-economic strangulation affected San Diego, although this pueblo did not suffer as complete a decline as San Salvador. The Mexicans, who had lost control of the economic and political destiny of their pueblo by the early 1850s, nonetheless felt secure living in the dominant Mexican ambiance of San Diego. Richard Henry Dana, author of the famous *Two Years before the Mast,* had visited San Diego in 1834 and upon his return thirty-four years later, he concluded:

The little town of San Diego has undergone no change whatever that I can see. It certainly has not grown. It is still like Santa Barbara, a Mexican town. [39]

Others writing during the 1860s shared essentially the same impressions of San Diego. Even by 1860 the small pueblo population of over 700 was almost equally divided between Mexicans, Indians, and Anglos. [40] Anglos, however, particularly the commercial interests, were not content with remaining in the pueblo.

The first attempts to develop a new San Diego, commercially and residentially separated from the old Mexican pueblo, began in the early 1850s. The first two efforts failed; the third attempt was a success. Hoping to profit from the post–Civil War immigration and commercial development in California, a Connecticut entrepreneur attracted the attention of San Diego's leading Anglo merchants with his promotion of a "New San Diego" located on the bay. He encouraged the relocation of business establishments from Old Town to New Town by attracting settlers and investors and built several improvements, including hotels and a wharf. "The general feeling among enterprising San Diegans that Old Town was irreclaimably a Mexican pueblo led a group to attempt the foundation of a new town that should not be handicapped by too much historical background," observed one historian. [41] Within a few years after the establishment of New Town in the late 1860s, the old pueblo had been nearly abandoned by Anglo merchants and residents. Anglos either physically moved their homes and shops from the pueblo or constructed new ones in New Town. After the 1872 fire in Old Town, which destroyed the businesses of several remaining Anglo merchants, mercantile life in the pueblo virtually came to an end. The commercial growth, physical expansion, improvements, and population increase that New San Diego experienced during the boom of the early 1870s was repeated in an even larger boom of the 1880s.[42]

Cut off from any meaningful socioeconomic and political contact with New Town, the small population of Chicanos in San Diego remained intact. Left in isolation, the Mexican community continued its traditional social and cultural life patterns and, in fact, reinstituted and added others. By the mid-1870s the Spanish-speaking residents had established a Spanish-language newspaper. They also revived the traditional bullfights in the plaza, which had been outlawed several years before. Other social phenomena, such as the celebrations of Mexican patriotic holidays, led the pueblo correspondent for the New Town *San Diego Union* to write in 1874 that "upon the whole, now and then, Old Town is as it was twenty-two years ago."[43]

The social and cultural persistence of Mexican society in Old Town could not, however, forestall the gradual economic and physical deterioration of the old pueblo. Throughout the last quarter of the nineteenth century fewer and fewer descendants of the pueblo's families lived in Old Town and, as a result, many of the venerable adobes began to decay. By the 1890s there were only remnants of the once lively little pueblo. "The houses around the Plaza," recalled a former school teacher of Old Town, "were in good repair and the ruins one sees at the present time (1890) were thrifty looking places and were filled with people. Such a change!" she concluded. "It makes one sad to contemplate."[44] To an increasing number of Anglo tourists, as one recalled in 1899:

Old Town, San Diego, can never fail to be of interest. The dozens of ancient adobe houses, all crumbling to ruins, . . . aid in lending a peculiar charm to the place. Dusty, dirty, strewn with litter, roofs half off or entirely gone, adobe walls prostrated or tottering with age—all is a Pompeii of ruins.[45]

Ironically, visitors from the growing city of San Diego (2,637 residents in 1880 versus 16,159 in 1890) saved Old Town by

Old Town San Diego, circa 1874. Courtesy of the San Diego Historical Society, Serra Museum Library.

Old Town San Diego, circa 1905, with the ruins of several adobe structures in the foreground. Courtesy of the San Diego Historical Society, Serra Museum Library.

patronizing it as a "picturesque" tourist attraction. The community of Mexicans that once existed had, for the most part, declined beyond recognition by the early decades of the twentieth century.[46]

The barrioization that occurred in both San Diego and San Salvador was much more destructive than that which took place in Santa Barbara and Los Angeles. But the Mexican presence in these southern California cities, although weakened by the process of barrioization, would be strongly reinforced throughout the twentieth century.

The Proletarianization of the Chicano Working Class

The barrioization of southern California Chicano communities in the second half of the nineteenth century was the product of other socioeconomic and political patterns that had already evolved—political powerlessness, expropriation of land, economic transformation, legacy of racism—and that had negatively affected the lives of Mexican people. The subsequent incorporation of Mexicans into the Anglo labor market as an unskilled/semiskilled, immobile, manual laboring work force completed a structure of subordination for Chicanos in southern California society. The occupational structure of subordination, characterized by racial and class stratification, would continue to shape the lives of Spanish-speaking workers in the twentieth century.

Two developments accounted for the entrance of Chicanos into the labor market of southern California cities. First, the burgeoning urban economy (tourism and related services, construction, and incipient industrialization) and the growth of large-scale agricultural production in the hinterlands created the need for a large, cheap unskilled/semiskilled work force. Second, Mexican ranchers, farmers, and workers, who had been displaced as their traditional occupations in the pastoral economy disappeared, were compelled to work for Anglo employers. But for Chicano workers, unlike Anglo members of the working class in southern California, entrance and status in the labor market were determined by both class and race. They experienced class exploitation and an occupational stratification that placed them alongside others at the bottom of the socioeconomic ladder. Whereas white members of the working class could move beyond unskilled/semiskilled occupations to skilled or white-collar positions, the great majority of Chicanos could not. Most Mexicans were restricted to only the menial labor sectors of the work force. Forced out of the declining rancho economy and into the capialist labor market, displaced Chicanos fell victim to an occupational status that they shared with other racial groups such as the American Indians and Chinese. Mexican workers increasingly became a larger segment of the general working class, as other racial and ethnic workers were reduced in numbers or excluded from the labor market.

The proletarianization of Chicano workers in southern California occurred between the 1860s and the 1880s. Prior to that time the Mexican pastoral economy, although in a post–cattle-boom depression since about 1855, still supported the many occupations associated with the cattle trade. Most of the large ranchos and small Mexican farms remained intact. Unsold pueblo lands, in addition, still provided a means by which family subsistence farming and livestock grazing could be maintained. Most important for Mexicans—whether laborers, skilled artisans, or ranchers—was the continuation of their life styles, occupations, and employer-employee relations, which were steeped in tradition and which formed a vital part of the cohesiveness in Mexican society.

As seen in Table 11, the Spanish-surname occupational structure in 1860 revealed both continuities and change in Mexican society. In Santa Barbara, San Salvador, and San Diego, Mexican pastoral economic pursuits were still quite evident; ranchers and farmers accounted for 30.5 percent, 30.3 percent, and 24.3 percent of their occupations in these respective communities. The percentages of professional, proprietorial, and white-collar occupations remained traditionally low. The percentage of skilled workers (harness makers, shoemakers, saddlers, silversmiths, and vaqueros, for example) who were directly tied to the pastoral economy ranged from a low of 4.2 in San Salvador (where farming was more prevalent than ranching) to 39.1 in San Diego. The laborers who lived in the pueblos and

Table 11 Occupational structure for the total Spanish-surnamed (SS) and non-Spanish-surnamed (NSS) male head-of-household populations, southern California, 1860 (in percent).

Occupation	San Diego		San Salvador/ San Bernardino		Santa Barbara		Los Angeles	
	SS	NSS	SS	NSS	SS	NSS	SS	NSS
Pastoral/agricultural								
Rancher	29.0	6.4	3.4	1.3	9.2	5.6	7.0	NA
Farmer	1.5	7.5	26.9	48.8	15.1	13.6	2.0	NA
Professional	1.5	8.6	0.0	2.3	3.1	12.4	5.0	NA
Proprietorial	0.0	10.8	0.8	2.3	1.4	16.8	NA	NA
White-collar	1.5	7.5	0.0	0.3	0.7	2.5	NA	NA
Skilled	39.1	19.4	4.2	10.6	9.9	16.8	16.0	NA
Semiskilled	2.8	26.9	2.5	8.3	1.4	5.6	NA	NA
Unskilled								
Laborer	15.9	9.7	55.5	20.9	47.9	14.9	70.0	NA
Other	5.7	1.1	0.0	0.7	5.5	5.6	NA	NA
Unknown or unlisted	2.9	2.1	6.7	4.3	5.8	6.2	NA	NA
Number in population	69	93	119	301	292	161	863	NA

SOURCES: Federal manuscript census schedules, 1860. The figures for Los Angeles are from Griswold del Castillo, "La Raza Hispano Americana," 85; his study does not provide information on occupations of the Anglo population.

who engaged in subsistence farming and livestock grazing were important part-time and full-time workers in the cattle industry; they worked during the seasonal matanzas and rodeos.[47] Unlike the other three pueblos, Los Angeles had experienced a more rapid pace of Americanization and resultant economic change during the 1850s. Between 1850 and 1860 the percentage of Spanish-surnamed ranchers and farmers had been reduced from 20 to 7. In addition, the percentage of skilled workers increased slightly (from 11 to 16) and the percentage of unskilled workers increased significantly from 55 in 1850 to 70 in 1860.[48] These trends would characterize the Chicano occupational structure in other pueblos during the next decade.

Throughout southern California by 1870 the steady decline of the pastoral economy was reflected in a significant decrease in the numbers of Mexican workers and in a dramatic loss of property ownership, especially in Los Angeles and Santa Barbara.[49] The occupations of Spanish-surnamed heads of household also revealed the economic changes taking place. Although the occupational structure in San Diego and San Salvador—far less important areas of the pastoral economy than Santa Barbara and Los Angeles—did not change significantly until during the 1870s, the trends in the two largest towns were portents of tremendous change that inevitably affected all of southern California. From Table 12 it is evident that in Santa Barbara by 1870, for example, the percentage of ranchers and farmers had greatly declined since 1860 (from 24.3 to 6.4). Likewise, the percentage of skilled artisans declined, while the percentage of unskilled workers significantly increased from 53.4 in 1860 to 66.0 in 1870. In Los Angeles, too, the trend toward fewer skilled workers (from 16 percent to 5 percent) and the gain in unskilled workers (70 percent to 79 percent) occurred between the 1860 and 1870 census periods. By 1870 the process of proletarianization—the creation of an unemployed/underemployed, displaced, and unskilled/semiskilled Chicano working class— had clearly begun in Santa Barbara and Los Angeles (71.4 percent and 79.0 percent unskilled/semiskilled manual workers, respectively). Throughout southern California the process was nearly complete by 1880.

New Town San Diego, 1873 and circa 1890s. Both photographs reproduced by permission of the Huntington Library, San Marino, California.

Table 12 Occupational structure for the total Spanish-surnamed (SS) and non-Spanish-surnamed (NSS) male head-of-household populations, southern California, 1870 (in percent).

Occupation	San Diego		San Salvador/ San Bernardino		Santa Barbara		Los Angeles	
	SS	NSS	SS	NSS	SS	NSS	SS	NSS
Pastoral/agricultural								
Rancher	26.5	0.8	0.0	0.9	2.5	4.5	7.0	NA
Farmer	14.3	22.4	27.8	29.3	3.9	12.2	3.0	NA
Professional	2.0	9.3	0.0	6.8	2.0	9.1	6.0	NA
Proprietorial	2.0	17.6	5.1	7.1	3.4	11.7	NA	NA
White-collar	0.0	8.2	2.1	3.2	3.0	5.5	NA	NA
Skilled	24.5	25.3	8.2	13.8	6.4	24.6	5.0	NA
Semiskilled	6.1	9.8	7.2	25.9	5.4	12.4	NA	NA
Unskilled								
Laborer	2.0	3.5	48.5	11.5	64.0	11.9	79.0	NA
Other	6.1	2.0	0.0	1.3	2.0	3.3	NA	NA
Unknown or unlisted	16.3	1.0	1.0	0	7.4	4.8	NA	NA
Number in population	49	766	97	840	203	419	468	NA

SOURCES: Federal manuscript census schedules, 1870. The figures for Los Angeles are from Griswold del Castillo, "La Raza Hispano Americana," 85; his study does not provide information on occupations of the Anglo population.

Table 13 illustrates that in San Diego, Santa Barbara, and Los Angeles (with the exception of San Salvador) the Mexican ranch and farm-owning group had been generally dispossessed by 1880 (1.8 percent, 4.7 percent, and 9.0 percent, respectively). Similarly, the number of skilled workers in San Diego, San Salvador, and Santa Barbara had declined since 1870); only Los Angeles deviated from this pattern, as there the number of Chicano skilled workers increased. The percentage of professional, proprietorial (merchants), and white-collar (clerks, salesmen, bank tellers) occupations remained low in all the communities. The great bulk of Chicano workers in 1880 were either unskilled laborers or semiskilled manual workers, who had been displaced from traditional occupations in the pastoral economy. By 1880 nearly 88 percent of the Chicano work force in San Diego, 65 percent in San Salvador, 82 percent in Santa Barbara, and 65 percent in Los Angeles occupied the bottom of the socioeconomic structure.

Clearly, a racial and class division in the occupational structure of southern California cities had evolved during the period 1860–1880. Whereas Chicanos were increasingly confined to the lowest levels of the occupational hierarchy, the non-Spanish-surname population increased its concentration in the upper levels of the occupational and property ownership structures. By 1860 Anglos were already economically dominant in real and personal property holdings in Los Angeles and had made significant progress in Santa Barbara.[50] By 1880, however, Anglos undisputedly controlled the wealth in every southern California community. As the economy changed from one based on cattle raising to one tied to large-scale capitalist agricultural production and urban development, Anglos successfully entrenched themselves as the dominant political and economic force in the region.

A comparison of the non-Spanish-surname and Spanish-surname occupational structures between 1860 and 1880 (Tables 11 to 13) illustrates the continuing economic dominance of Anglos and the economic subordination of Chicanos. As early as 1860 Anglos, although a minority of the population in nearly every community, had made major inroads as large property-owning

Table 13 Occupational structure for the total Spanish-surnamed (SS) and non-Spanish-surnamed (NSS) male head-of-household populations, southern California, 1880 (in percent).

Occupation	San Diego SS	San Diego NSS	San Salvador/San Bernardino SS	San Salvador/San Bernardino NSS	Santa Barbara SS	Santa Barbara NSS	Los Angeles SS	Los Angeles NSS
Pastoral/agricultural								
Rancher	0.9	1.7	1.8	0.8	4.7	2.5	9.0	NA
Farmer	0.9	5.1	25.5	40.3	0.0	9.2	4.0	NA
Professional	2.9	11.0	1.8	7.3	1.6	14.5	7.0	NA
Proprietorial	0.9	12.0	0.0	9.7	2.3	16.3	NA	NA
White-collar	0.0	11.3	0.0	3.8	3.1	10.3	15.0	NA
Skilled	4.8	27.0	5.4	15.4	3.1	19.7	NA	NA
Semiskilled	6.7	17.5	5.4	13.4	2.3	9.0	NA	NA
Unskilled								
Laborer	80.9	11.3	60.0	8.5	79.7	8.4	65.0	NA
Other	0.0	2.2	0.0	0.4	0.0	2.3	NA	NA
Unknown or unlisted	1.9	0.9	0.0	0.4	3.1	7.7	NA	NA
Number in population	105	584	55	766	128	477	566	NA

SOURCES: Federal manuscript census schedules, 1880. The figures for Los Angeles are from Griswold del Castillo, "La Raza Hispano Americana," 85; his study does not provide information on occupations of the Anglo population.

ranchers and farmers (13.9 percent in San Diego, 50.1 percent in San Bernardino, and 19.2 percent in Santa Barbara).[51] Anglos had also begun to dominate the commercial life of these towns as merchants (except in San Bernardino, where mercantile activity was minimal until 1870). The Anglo occupational structure from the beginning was heavily concentrated in the upper levels; occupations in the skilled trades and in white-collar, proprietorial, professional, and pastoral/agricultural occupations accounted for 60.2 percent in San Diego, 65.6 percent in San Bernardino, and 67.7 percent in Santa Barbara (see Appendix 2 for a listing of occupations). Conversely, Anglo semiskilled (teamsters, deliverymen, waiters) and unskilled workers constituted 37.7, 29.9, and 26.1 percent of the total non-Spanish-surname occupations in these same communities in 1860.

The 1870 and 1880 censuses illustrate how the Anglo occupational structure stabilized with the great majority of persons fairly evenly distributed within the ranks of skilled workers, white-collar workers, proprietors, merchants, professionals, and farmers.[52] In addition, during this same period of the proletarianization of Chicano workers, the small percentages of Anglo unskilled workers further declined. By 1880 Chicano unskilled workers constituted between 60.0 and 80.9 percent of the total Spanish-surname work force in the various cities, while the percentage of unskilled Anglo workers ranged between 8.9 and 13.5 percent.

The Chicano and Anglo occupational structures from 1860 to 1880 depict the economic and occupational changes that characterized southern California society during the period. Yet quantification of Chicano occupational stratification cannot illuminate the social changes among Spanish-surnamed workers as a result of their proletarianization. Several important social developments were part of the new reality that characterized Chicano society in southern California—a reality of the last quarter of the nineteenth century that continued into the twentieth century.

The decline of the pastoral economy between 1860 and 1880 affected ranchers and farmers most severely, but skilled and unskilled workmen were also being displaced from traditional occupations. These displaced Chicanos were not immediately incorporated into the new labor market and remained a peripheral work force within the growing agricultural and urban economies. For Los Angeles between 1850 and 1880, for example, Griswold del Castillo concluded that "the Chicanos were effectively excluded from Los Angeles' growth." The dominant pattern for Chicano workers was toward "economic subjugation, occupational stagnation, and social conflict"; Griswold also states that while their old occupations declined, Chicanos did not enter new occupations. The same patterns emerged in Santa Barbara, San Diego, and San Salvador.[53]

Many Chicano workers reacted to their worsening economic situation during the 1870s by securing whatever traditional, pastoral-related work remained. Throughout southern California many found part-time, seasonal work as vaqueros in the dying cattle industry and as sheepshearers in the only traditional employment that had not declined throughout the region. This seasonal work, however, was too infrequent and often necessitated migrating even outside the state. Other workers, such as those in San Salvador, continued to eke out a living through subsistence farming and grazing; these activities, too, became increasingly difficult as Anglos encroached upon traditional pueblo lands.[54] For the most part, Chicanos were unable to secure full-time work at occupations in which they had once been employed. Nor were they able to find employment in occupations in the new economy. At first Chicanos resisted the menial occupations opened to them by Anglo employers. But as they faced increasing unemployment during the late 1870s (for example, in 1880 74.8 percent of the total Chicano work force in Santa Barbara and 46.6 percent in San Diego were unemployed during part of that census year) and as many non-Spanish-surnamed workers left the manual labor market, Chicanos entered the labor force en masse.[55] These last two circumstances hastened the proletarianization of the Chicano work force and reinforced a pattern of subordination for ethnic working-class people in California.

When the new Anglo economy was initially replacing the

Mexican pastoral economy, the need for a large pool of uns-killed labor did not exist. During the 1850s and 1860s, as small-scale agricultural production was established, Indians and some Mexicans were recruited as farm laborers. In the pueblos dur-ing the same period the modest demand for manual labor was often supplied by Indians and a few native-born Americans and European immigrants. By the 1870s, however, the increased pace of Americanization and the rapid influx of American capital investment changed the nature of labor market needs for Anglo employers. The dwindling resident population of Indians could no longer satisfy the demand for construction workers, tourist service workers, and farm laborers. Another ethnic working class group, the Chinese, was imported to fill the labor void. The Chinese became the first large group of farm laborers in the developing agribusiness (citrus fruit industry, especially) of southern California, and they filled practically every manual and service worker job in the urban areas (domestics, hotel workers, laundry workers, cooks, vegetable and fish peddlers). They were also imported as laborers for railroad construction in nearly every city in southern California. In addition, the Chin-ese established their economic influence as fishermen (abalone) and as vegetable farmers. It is not surprising that Chinatowns were located adjacent to the barrios in Los Angeles and Santa Barbara. (San Salvador never had a sizable Chinese population, but neighboring San Bernardino as well as San Diego had a small group of Chinese by 1880.) The Chinese—like the Chi-canos—experienced racist hostility from Anglo society. In fact, a racist xenophobia, together with economic and political harass-ment, eventually drove most of the Chinese from southern Cali-fornia cities during the last two decades of the century. The decline in the Chinese population and the increasing impover-ishment of Chicano workers, who could no longer support fami-lies on income from seasonal, pastoral-related employment, pro-vided the impetus to push Chicanos into the labor market by the late 1870s and early 1880s.[56]

The patterns of employment established at this time would persist well into the following century. Chicanos were recruited as farm workers and as laborers in other agriculture-related work (canneries and packing sheds). They were employed as construction laborers, as workers in the devloping transportation companies (street graders, pick-and-shovel laborers), in the utility companies (ditchdiggers and teamsters), and in a host of other menial, manual laboring jobs within the growing cities and expanding agricultural areas.[57]

Beyond the change in employment patterns during the late 1880s, other developments affected the composition of the Chicano working class throughout southern California. First, Chicanas entered the labor market in increasing numbers during the 1880s and 1890s. This new pattern of Chicana employment undoubtedly modified the Chicano family structure, since women were becoming wage earners and assuming dual roles as workers and mothers. Chicanas found employment as domestics, fruit cannery and packing shed workers, seasonal farm laborers who migrated with their children and husbands, and laundresses. Some also worked as seamstresses and dressmakers, but few ever acquired higher than skilled status. Chicanas were frequently finding employment outside the home and were assuming a new head-of-household status. Although this pattern was more evident in some barrios than in others, it was clearly increasing with each passing decade. For example, between 1880 and 1900 the percentage of employed female Spanish-surnamed heads of household and adult residents increased 118 percent (from 33 to 72) in San Diego and 375 percent (from 20 to 95) in Santa Barbara, while the percentage of male Spanish-surnamed heads of household only increased by 39 percent and 69 percent, respectively. This trend toward increasing matriarchal families manifested itself earlier in Los Angeles, where the female head-of-household population increased significantly (from 52 to 166) between 1850 and 1870 while the male head-of-household population declined.[58]

The second major pattern affecting the Chicano working class in the late nineteenth century involved the addition of large numbers of Mexican immigrant laborers, both free and under contract. During the 1890s the major railroad companies imported thousands of Mexican workers from Mexico and from along the U.S. border. In Los Angeles, Santa Barbara, and San

Chicana laundresses and their family in Santa Barbara in the late nineteenth century. Courtesy of the Santa Barbara Historical Society Library.

Bernardino by the first decade of the twentieth century Mexican workers constituted the principal manual work force for the Santa Fe and Southern Pacific railroad companies. Others who migrated to southern California cities on their own after 1890 found employment opportunities limited to the same types of jobs Chicanos were already performing.

During the last quarter of the nineteenth century the practice of restricting Mexicans to menial occupations in the labor market, thus closing the opportunities for them to acquire new skills, became a dominant pattern in the Chicano working-class experience. The vast majority of both native-born and foreign-born Mexicans continued to toil at unskilled jobs that supplied scarcely enough income for the survival of the Chicano family. "They [Anglos] treat them badly," declared a Los Angeles Spanish-language newspaper, "with despotism and humiliation."[59] Another Spanish-speaking observer similarly characterized the status of native-born Salvadoreños in 1902:

The passing years have wrought many changes to the people [Mexicans] and to the State. Most of the old pioneer settlers have passed away. Their descendants are scattered, some of them having fallen on evil days, [and] are the victims of distressing poverty; but many of them, in spite of the disadvantages under which they labor, still maintain the traditional virtues of their fathers.[60]

The 1900 census confirms these impressions and also profiles the pattern of restricted occupations for Mexicans. As seen in Table 14, Spanish-surnamed workers were grossly overrepresented in low blue-collar manual occupations (such as semiskilled teamsters and service workers, and unskilled laborers) throughout southern California cities—67.1 percent in San Diego, 80.8 percent in San Bernardino, 73.1 percent in Santa Barbara, and 80.0 percent in Los Angeles. In comparison to the non-Spanish-surname occupational structure, the percentage of Anglo low blue-collar workers ranged between 26.2 and 30.9 percent. The distinction between Chicanos and Anglos is even more striking in the low white-collar jobs (salespeople, clerical workers, and semiprofessionals such as accountants, musicians, and draftsmen) and high white-collar positions (professionals such as doctors, lawyers, teachers, dentists, as well as proprietor/merchants). The percentages of Spanish-surnamed persons holding these types of occupations ranged from 4.2 percent to 10.2 percent, while the percentages for non-Spanish-surnamed persons ranged from 40.9 to 46.6 percent.[61] Clearly, Chicanos continued as a proletarianized, ethnic working class in the lowest stratum of the economic order.

Summary and Conclusion

If Chicanos throughout southern California at the turn of the century had looked back over the preceding fifty years in an attempt to understand their situation, they would have discerned several interrelated historical developments. The process of barrioization from the 1860s to 1890s had established the socially and residentially segregated, impoverished barrios in which they lived. The racial conflict during the period 1850–1880 and the resultant legacy of racism had indelibly stamped social relations between Chicanos and Anglos. They had also inherited the political powerlessness that an earlier generation of Mexicans

Table 14 Occupational structure for Spanish-surnamed (SS)[a] and non-Spanish-surnamed (NSS)[b] male heads of household, southern California, 1900 (in percent). Appendix 1 discusses the occupational classifications.

Occupation	San Diego		San Bernardino		Santa Barbara		Los Angeles	
	SS	NSS	SS	NSS	SS	NSS	SS	NSS
High white-collar								
Professional	4.1	10.3	1.7	6.3	3.7	13.2	0.5	NA
Proprietorial	2.7	17.0	0.8	23.4	2.3	18.3	6.0	NA
Low white-collar								
Sales/clerical/semiprofessional	3.4	17.7	1.7	11.2	3.7	15.1	NA	NA
High blue-collar								
Skilled	10.3	19.3	5.0	21.1	10.2	20.3	10.5	NA
Low blue-collar								
Semiskilled	13.0	15.5	7.5	15.0	15.7	12.8	7.0	NA
Unskilled	54.1	10.7	73.3	15.9	57.4	14.0	73.0	NA
Unknown or unemployed								
Unlisted	2.7	9.5	0.8	2.0	3.7	6.3	3.0	NA
Unemployed (part of census year)	9.6	0.0	9.2	4.9	3.2	0.0	NA	NA
Number in sample	146	865	120	445	216	508	727	NA

SOURCES: Federal manuscript census schedules, 1900. The figures for Los Angeles are from Pedro Castillo, "Mexicans in Los Angeles, 1890–1920" (Ph.D. dissertation, University of California, Santa Barbara); his study does not provide information on occupations of the Anglo population.

[a] 100 percent of head-of-household population.
[b] 40-percent sample of head-of-household population (excluding nonwhites).

first experienced. Their proletarianization as an ethnic working class created a restricted status for them in the labor market, with the opportunity for upward mobility and a better life closed to the vast majority of them. But Chicano people preserved important elements of their society and culture despite the social and political changes resulting from the Americanization of southern California and the corresponding growth of a new capitalist economic order.

Mexican Immigration and the Expansion of the Santa Barbara Chicano Community

6.

The large-scale migration of Mexicans into the newly annexed area of the southwestern United States began during the California gold rush period. Later in the nineteenth century another intensive period of Mexicano northern migration began. But unlike the migrations before and after the Mexican War, in the 1890s Mexicans came to Santa Barbara and other cities in the United States in far greater numbers and had a more dramatic impact on the existing society. And whereas the Mexicans who had emigrated during the mid-nineteenth century or before had relocated in what were still Mexicans pueblos, the Mexicans of later migrations entered a predominantly Anglo society. Their renewed migration, evident by the early 1890s in Santa Barbara, greatly increased during the first two decades of the twentieth century to reach a peak in the 1920s. As these new Mexican residents began to settle permanently in the city, they developed a second barrio geographically distinct from the old pueblo barrio. Within this new barrio Mexicans established a rich social, organizational, and cultural life that was reinforced by the subsequent migration of more Mexicanos through the late 1920s.

Ironically, economic factors had attracted most Mexican workers to the United States and to Santa Barbara in particular, and it was also an economic factor, supported by social and racial rationales, that later led to the deportation of thousands of Mexican people in the Great Depression. During the late nineteenth century and early twentieth century the steady growth of the local economy necessitated Mexican labor, both free and contractual. Mexican workers formed the backbone of the labor-intensive sectors of Santa Barbara's prosperous agricultural hinterlands and its urban building and construction trades. Mexicans, however, benefited little from this increasing prosperity, since the vast majority were relegated to low blue-collar occupations. During the late 1920s and early 1930s, when both local economy and national economy became stagnant, the Mexicans were viewed as an expendable population who only aggravated the already adverse economic conditions.

Growth of the Lower Eastside Barrio

The Mexicanos who arrived in Santa Barbara during the late nineteenth and early twentieth centuries unknowingly entered a society in which their socioeconomic position was already fixed. The experience of the Mexican community since the 1870s had determined the subordinate status that Spanish-speaking people would continue to hold in Anglo society. Few non-California-born Mexicans had resided in the city since the departure of most members of that nativity group from Santa Barbara during the 1860s and 1870s. Not until the importation of Mexican section-gang workers by the Southern Pacific Railroad, beginning in 1893, was there a notable increase in the number of foreign-born Mexicans. Their arrival in 1893 initiated the first significant stage of modern Mexican immigration to Santa Barbara. This sizable influx of men, women, and children continued until approximately 1915, after which the volume and character of the migration began to change. The Southern Pacific continued to import its *"Cholo"* laborers in greater numbers as the completion of the San Francisco–Santa Barbara coastal route drew near. By the turn of the century, one year prior to the opening of the route, local newspapers often reported the arrival of hundreds of Mexicano railroad workers. "During the last few days," stated the *Morning Press,* "about 150 Mexicans have been added to the force at work on the coast railroad . . . Two cars containing 96 Mexicans, or 'Cholos,' as they are called," it later asserted, "came in [from Arizona] on the night train." Rationalizing the use of Mexican labor, the *Morning Press* further claimed that the "importation of this class of help is explained by the railroad people by the difficulty in getting other labor."[1] Except for the resident Mexican section gang located in the freight yards on the lower east side, most Mexican workers were quickly escorted to the large railroad camp a few miles north of the city, but they occasionally visited Santa Barbara. The Mexicanos at camp were continuously augmented by other important compañeros.[2]

The wages paid to the laborers at the camp were approximately $1.50 to $1.75 per day, from which the cost of room and board, $5.25 per week, was deducted. Under these circumstances one can understand why the Southern Pacific had difficulty in maintaining a large permanent work force. Many of those Mexicans who left camp before 1902—and, no doubt, many of those who were unemployed after completion of the coastal route—came to Santa Barbara to find work and shelter. The resident section-gang workers and the former railroad laborers who congregated near the freight depot constituted the origins of the lower eastside barrio. According to one observer, this group was concentrated in and near the section-gang houses along Quarantina Street (see map) and was made up of Mexicanos mostly from the states of Guanajuato, Zacatecas, and Michoacan.[3]

The railroad workers were not the only resident foreign-born Mexicanos in Santa Barbara before World War I. Mexican families began to settle permanently in the city during the 1890s. After one family situated itself, it would attract relatives and friends from the original home in Mexico: the familial migration network was very common.[4] By 1906 Mexican-born school-age children in Santa Barbara constituted the largest foreign-born element in the city. The Mexicano population was not experiencing a massive influx of new arrivals at this time, but rather a steady in-migration of nuclear and extended families. Most of the Mexicans who came during this period had left their homeland because of the worsening economic conditions, and after 1910 because of the destruction caused by the revolution.

There was also a small core of political refugees. The wealthy uncle and in-laws of Mexican President Francisco Madero, for example, sought temporary asylum in Santa Barbara. The relatives of Madero were, however, only a small elite group within the larger Mexicano working class.[5]

The demographic distribution of the foreign-born Mexican population was well established by the time the second large wave of immigrants arrived after World War I. Two pockets of Mexican population were located on the lower east side of Santa Barbara. Although a small cluster of Mexican families resided near the boundaries of Pueblo Viejo, they were physically separated from the historic barrio by a large marsh-like gully that was filled with water much of the year. The larger residential concentration of Mexicanos was situated near the Southern Pacific freight yard and fruit packing house on Quarantina Street. There was also a scattering of Mexicans throughout the lower east side. Few Mexicanos lived on Santa Barbara's west side (west of State Street).[6]

Prior to World War I much of the area on the lower east side was occupied by small-scale vegetable farming, marsh lands, the city dump, and vacant land. However, it was this area that by 1920 became the large Mexicano barrio (the approximately ten-block area bounded by Milpas, Ortega, and State streets). The Mexicanos there established an early pattern of work and residence based upon economic necessity and racial segregation. Mexicanos increasingly established residence near work opportunities (the railroad and lumber yards, the fruit packing house) in the least desirable and cheapest areas of the city. As Mexicano migration increased, the area of the barrio expanded and at the same time became more densely populated. The process replicated itself throughout the 1920s.[7]

The slow but steady influx of Mexicanos to Santa Barbara from 1893 to 1915 was followed by a much more intense migration from 1916 to 1927, especially during the period 1920 to 1924. The manpower shortages prevalent in the United States after World War I, and the chronically poor economic conditions in Mexico, produced a push-pull effect that brought hundreds of thousands of Mexicanos to this country. Thousands of Mexicans came to reside in the city and county of Santa Barbara during this time. This second phase of migration, like the earlier period, was basically familial, except that the arrival of families was much more frequent. By 1916 the local newspapers began acknowledging the increased volume of Mexican migration to the city and at least one, the *Daily News*, reported that there "is plenty [of work] in the city" for Mexicans.[8]

Prior to 1916 most Mexicanos apparently came in about equal numbers from the central and northern states of Mexico; during the later migration the people from the northern states were evidently in the majority (especially those from Durango, Sonora, and Chihuahua). A Mexican resident who arrived in Santa Barbara in 1916 vividly recounted the migration pattern:

One family comes from Durango and established itself here. From here it writes there and says come! come! come over it is good here. It brings others and others. Well, one was here . . . Juan Esparza—he brought twenty-eight families from Durango.[9]

Other principal areas from which many emigrated were the states of Jalisco, Guanajuato, and Michoacan. At least during the first years of residence in Santa Barbara, many Mexicans tended to associate primarily with others from their state of origin. This cohesive tendency, however, dissipated as Mexicans from various states lived side by side within the barrio over the years.[10]

The proliferation of the foreign-born Mexican population dramatically increased the residential concentration of Mexicans in the area of the lower eastside barrio. By 1930 Mexicanos densely populated the immediate lower eastside neighborhoods that bordered the Southern Pacific freight yard on all three sides (see map); the barrio resembled a horseshoe with an additional extension along Vine and Canal streets below De la Guerra Street. Although the lower east side of Santa Barbara was not exclusively inhabited by Mexicanos—a few Italian, black, and native-born Mexican families lived outside the core Mexicano areas—the barrio contained 85 to 90 percent of all foreign-born Mexican households.[11]

The formation of ethnic and immigrant group neighborhoods

was nothing new to Santa Barbara. Mexicans during the second half of the nineteenth century had, of course, experienced the barrioization that led to the establishment of the Pueblo Viejo barrio. Later in the nineteenth century and in the early twentieth century the Chinese, Japanese, and Italians also inhabited small ethnic enclaves.[12] But unlike the small number of non-Spanish-surnamed ethnic persons in the city, the foreign-born Mexicanos constituted a significantly large percentage (between 10 and 13 percent) of the city's total population (19,441 in 1920 and 33,613 in 1930) during the 1920s. The lower eastside barrio, like Pueblo Viejo in many ways, essentially became the second Mexican city within a city.

As the foreign-born Mexican population grew, the unique physical appearance of the barrio evolved. The small wooden frame homes of the Mexicanos dotted each block. Early in the century when the section gangs were laid off or fired by the Southern Pacific, for example, many families remained in the barrio and built humble abodes with the aid of the more established barrio families. In other cases Anglo entrepreneurs built cheap, low-rent single-room homes in the neighborhood. One such row of little red houses, for instance, became known to the barrio residents as El Chorizo (a Mexican link sausage). A few Mexicano-owned, family-operated markets and retail stores were also built to cater to the needs of the local residents. With the addition of a Catholic chapel in 1918, the barrio became a virtually self-contained Mexican community.[13] Other than for their employment, Mexicanos seldom had to venture outside its boundaries.

The Multifunctional Mutualistas

The two most important social institutions for the barrio residents were the family and the *mutualistas*. The latter incorporated the family and served several purposes, becoming a dynamic force in the sociocultural life and welfare of the Mexicano community. The formation of mutual-aid, benevolent societies by immigrant groups in Santa Barbara was not a novelty.[14] The vitality and activism of the Mexican mutualistas, however, far surpassed the mutual-aid societies that had been established by other groups. The several Santa Barbara Mexican mutualistas had four basic characteristics or functions in common: (1) mutual aid and insurance benefits; (2) fraternal association; (3) protection of the rights and privileges of Mexicans; and (4) promotion of cultural, social, patriotic, and recreational activities.[15]

One of the largest and most unique mutualistas to develop in Santa Barbara was the Club Mexicano Independencia (CMI). The CMI was the first mutualista to be established by foreign-born Mexicans in Santa Barbara. Unlike the other Mexican mutual-aid societies, the CMI was initially formed in 1917 by a junta or group of local Mexicanos rather than by a regional organization wishing to establish a local mutualista chapter in the city. The forerunner of the CMI (as indicated in the original CMI president's notebook) was named Club Hidalgo Benéfico Mexicano, an organization created by a group of about fifteen Mexicanos in 1914. The name was subsequently changed and the Club Mexicano Independencia was officially founded on September 15, 1917.[16]

The members of the CMI in 1917 appointed an eight-member Comisión Legislativa to draft a "Constitución y Reglamentos Interiores del Club Mexicano I." The original hand-drafted constitution explicitly described the purpose of the mutualista:

to bring closer together . . . the relations of the Mexicanos, especially among the members that form this Club in order that they extend to each other the hand of brotherly love for their protection, mutual benefits, and to procure through all the legal means the moral and material betterment of its members . . . to work without rest until the bonds of brotherhood and union may be an admirable deed, in order that in the future this Club establishes its power and the greater guarantee of its rights.[17]

The CMI hoped "to strive by all legal and just means," the final draft of the ratified constitution stated, "to honor, to elevate and protect this club and its members, so that in the future it may be the protection of our sons, brothers, and compatriots."[18]

The unique feature of the CMI, besides its being an independently organized local mutualista, was that membership was restricted to citizens of Mexico by birth or naturalization. The founding members of CMI, declaring themselves permanent residents of the United States, wanted to ensure that the mutualista remained a nationalistic Mexicano organization that would benefit only those who were actually Mexican citizens. It was also apparently a guarantee against the admission of the U.S.-born Mexican population and the second generation of foreign-born who might introduce a diluted Mexican culture into the mutualista. "I am Mexicano," the last surviving president of the CMI explained, but "my sons who were born here could not belong to the Club because they are American citizens by nationality; they are Mexicanos by blood, but by nationality they are Americans."[19]

The CMI offered a broad range of benefits to its working-class membership. Each member was entitled to weekly payments for sickness or in case of accident. If a member was permanently injured and unable to work, he/she was entitled to a pension for an indefinite period. The CMI also offered death benefit insurance, which provided for burial costs and at least $250 for the family, and an emergency fund for its members. Beyond the monetary benefits, sick or needy members were visited and their families cared for by other CMI members.[20]

The CMI was guided by an elaborate set of rules concerning the responsibilities and qualifications of its members. It had a detailed organizational schema, a formal initiation procedure, and a democratically elected or appointed officer hierarchy. The CMI was a nonsectarian and nonpolitical group.[21] Although the CMI was not involved in politics per se, it did assume responsibility as a politically oriented buffer group for the Mexicano community in Santa Barbara against racist elements in Anglo society. Protection for its members and for the Mexican community of the lower eastside barrio was a function occasionally performed by the CMI. The best example occurred in 1917. A Ventura County fire insurance company, apparently fearful of striking Mexican workers and aware of the history of Mexican rebelliousness in Santa Barbara, Ventura, and Los Angeles counties, issued a warning to its customers in the tricounty area. "Under no circumstances," the company insisted in a let-

The Club Mexicano Independencia on its tenth anniversary gathering, Santa Barbara, 1928. Courtesy of Federico López.

ter to its clients, "must you allow unemployed Mexicans to congregate on your premises; it is but a short step from discontent to an organized outbreak and outbreak means widespread ruin from fire."[22] No longer tolerant of such racist accusations, many Mexicanos, reported the *Daily News,* "are protesting over the insinuations against the loyalty of the Mexican people to the United States." Pablo Gonzáles (a cofounder of CMI) is a "leader here in a movement among Mexicans," the article concluded, "to put a stop to the public questioning of the stand taken by his people in the country."[23]

The defense of the Mexicano community was an important, though infrequently carried out, function of the CMI. Its most frequent and visible function was the provision of social-recreational activities. The CMI sponsored regular biweekly or monthly dances, as well as frequent picnics, barbecues, and Mexican national celebrations. With the possible exception of initiation fiestas or CMI anniversary celebrations, all activities were open to the entire Mexicano population.[24]

After 1925 many of the social festivites were planned and carried out by the Club Mexicano Independencia Femenil, the women's CMI group. In fact, the CMI Femenil became the main organizer of joint CMI social and fund-raising activities. Women had always attended meetings of the CMI, but not until 1925 did they form their own chapter. Mexicanas elected their own officers and conducted the business of their organization, in which the men had no voting rights. The CMI Femenil members were entitled to the same mutual benefits from the same general fund of the CMI.[25]

During the 1920s the CMI and CMI Femenil were composed of between 70 and 100 male members and a smaller group of women. With the members' families, the CMI probably numbered between 400 and 700 people at exclusive CMI functions. This mutualista maintained an important social cohesiveness for the lives of hundreds of Mexicanos in Santa Barbara.

The other popular mutualista was La Unión Patriótica Benéfica Mexicana Independiente (UPBMI), which had chapters throughout southern California. As early as 1913 the nearby Ventura County chapters helped the local Santa Barbara Mexicanos stage their Dieciséis celebrations. The Santa Barbara branch, eighth to be established in the region, was formally started in 1919; the leaders from the nearby Oxnard chapter and from two San Bernardino county chapters (Pomona and Colton) of the mutualista helped organize the Santa Barbara Mexicanos. The *Daily News* reported that the meeting took place "before a big and enthusiastic crowd" where officers were selected from the forty charter members.[26] One of the original cofounders of the UPBMI described this period of Mexican organizational activity (circa 1913 to 1925) as "el movimiento de sociedades." This organizational movement led to formation of the CMI and UPBMI and stimulated a great deal of interest in the Mexicano community.[27]

The UPBMI, unlike the CMI, did not have restrictions on membership. However, the members were predominantly foreign-born with the exception of a few native-born Mexicans from Pueblo Viejo and a few non-Mexican Latinos. The sons of foreign-born Mexican citizens were prominent in the organization. Notwithstanding its lack of citizenship qualifications, the UPBMI paralleled the CMI. The primary "object of the association," the *Daily News* reported, was "to protect the interests of the Mexican population."[28] The UPBMI also carried sickness and deaths benefits, and aided impoverished Mexicano families whether or not they were active members of the organization. Like most mutualistas, the UPBMI was composed of working-class Mexican people.[29]

The UPBMI, like the CMI, sponsored a wide array of social functions for the Mexican community. Monthly socials, such as dances and barbecues, as well as the Cinco de Mayos, were regularly organized by the group. Ofttimes the Oxnard and Santa Barbara chapters held joint activities. In addition, the UPBMI occasionally organized fund raisers, like the one in 1926 for the flood victims of Nayarit, Mexico. The mutualista fielded a local championship baseball team during the 1920s, which provided popular recreational activity for Mexicanos. The women members of the mutualista, like those in CMI, formed an auxiliary known as La Unión Femenil Mexicana, which was established in about 1926. The Unión Feminil organized cultural and social events for Spanish-speaking audiences. Together the women and men of the UPBMI constituted a membership that ranged from 80 to 150 throughout the 1920s.[30]

The CMI, CMI Femenil, UPBMI, and Unión Femenil Mexicana provided the lower eastside Mexican community with a variety of sociocultural and Mexican patriotic activities as well as with mutual aid and protection. Although the CMI and UPBMI were far the largest and most active of the mutualistas, there were many others. La Liga Protectora Latina, for example, established in 1924, was described as "a small club" that extended the same basic benefits to its members as did other mutualistas, but carried on few social activities; there was also a woman's auxiliary. Another mutualista, La Sociedad Internacional de Beneficios Mutuos No. 5, was formed in the late 1920s or early 1930s. This mutual-aid organization, which had several chapters throughout California, acquired a sizable membership during the 1930s (approximately 200), but unlike the CMI and UPBMI it deemphasized social activities.[31]

Other small groups of Mexicanos in Santa Barbara during the 1920s were organized for social and welfare activities. They were not, however, mutualistas. In 1922, for example, a small group of locals were encouraged by two out-of-state Mexicans to form a Mexican Masonic lodge in Santa Barbara (Mexicanos were excluded from the Anglo Masonic order in the city). Although Acacia Chapter No. 16 of the Mexico City–based Logia Nacional Mexicana consisted of no more than seventy individuals during its ten-year existence, it provided fraternal social activities for its members and also engaged in charity work among the poorest families in the barrio. Another group, which engaged only in charity work, was La Cruz Azul Mexicana. The "Mexican Blue Cross" recruited young girls and women to visit and care for sick barrio residents who could not afford doctors' fees. The organization also raised funds for those who could not pay medical bills or buy prescription drugs and medicines. Chapters were located throughout the southwestern United States, but remained affiliates of the Mexican national chapter. There were other small clubs in Santa Barbara such as the Club La Rosita, a group of thirty to forty young Mexican girls who promoted social activities, and the Mexican Ladies' Society de Josefa Ortíz de Domínguez, which sponsored Spanish-speaking entertainment for the barrio population.[32]

To help coordinate the large number of social activities sponsored by the many mutualistas, a confederation of organizations was established in 1927. La Confederación de Sociedades Mutualistas worked quite effectively in coordinating activities and maintaining communication among the Mexican mutualistas' members. Dances, barbecues, fiestas, and picnics sponsored by the umbrella organization throughout the 1920s often attracted crowds of 200 to 1,000 people. The various Mexicano organizations also united to coordinate the Mexican national patriotic celebrations. After 1917 a coalition formed under the name La Junta Patriótica. By the mid-1920s the junta was staging gala celebrations that attracted over 3,000 Mexicanos to Santa Barbara. In 1924, for example, the *Morning Press* reported that a three-day Mexican Independence Day celebration had attracted "practically every member of the Mexican colony in Santa Barbara."[33]

The activities of the many mutualistas and clubs provided continual social interaction and communication among the Mex-

The championship baseball team of the mutualista La Unión Patriótica Benéfica Mexicana Independiente, Santa Barbara, 1927. Courtesy of Yldefonso Osuna.

icans of Santa Barbara as well as with other Chicano communities in southern California where affiliated chapters were located. "There was so much going on all the time," recalled a longtime resident, "that there never was a dull moment."[34] By facilitating continued contact among Mexicanos, the organizations helped perpetuate Mexican culture, language, and cohesiveness in an otherwise foreign society. The mutualistas became the lifeblood of the lower eastside barrio community.

Employment

The social activity of the mutualistas gave the foreign-born sector of the Mexican laboring class temporary rest from work. Most Mexicanos came to the United States in search of employment and means to support their families. However, those who settled in Santa Barbara soon discovered that, with few exceptions, employment opportunities for Mexicans were limited to menial, manual laboring jobs. The earliest contingent of foreign-born Mexican laborers, the railroad workers, were the first to experience the closed occupational structure. When large numbers were laid off after the completion of the coastal route, the search for additional employment ended in their finding other types of manual day labor. Most Mexicanos who arrived during the next thirty years were also confined to the least desirable, poorest paying manual work.

Throughout the first three decades of the twentieth century, the expanding economy of the city and the agricultural areas near Santa Barbara became increasingly dependent upon Mexican labor. The opening of the coastal railroad route in 1901 started Santa Barbara on a course of steady economic development. The tourist trade now became a year-round industry instead of a seasonal business. The population of permanent residents was again steadily increasing after the stagnant period of the 1890s. After 1902 the Santa Barbara construction and related industries greatly expanded.[35] As Mexicanos began to enter the city in large numbers, they were recruited to fill the unskilled labor vacuum created by the sudden growth in building activity.

The construction of an electric urban railway system and the building of the Southern Pacific maintenance and freight yard in Santa Barbara during the first decade of the century created jobs for a sizable Mexican work force. In increasing numbers, however, Mexicanos left the railroad and entered other, more permanent employment. Many became pick-and-shovel laborers on the street-paving crews, which were paid wages of $1.00 to $1.25 per day. Yet even after Mexicans left the railroads, they were still stigmatized as "Cholo laborers."[36]

The demand for labor in the growing construction-building industry was not filled, even with the hundreds of foreign-born Mexican workers who came to Santa Barbara before World War I. "The common laborer is in demand in Santa Barbara," the *Morning Press* reported in 1911. "With the rush of street and sewer work and the general building prosperity," it stated, "it is becoming almost impossible to hire an able-bodied man."[37] But the immigration of large numbers of Mexicanos after 1916 evidently ended the pleas for more laborers. Thereafter, Mexicanos became the primary manual labor force in the various sectors of the construction industry. Several local and outside street-paving contractors, as well as the regional utility corporations such as the Southern Counties Gas Company, employed predominantly Mexicanos. A Mexicano who worked for a contractor who was paving Santa Barbara streets when he arrived in 1916 recalled that the construction crew comprised not less than 125 workers—trucker-teamsters, wheelbarrow men, cement workers, graders, pick-and-shovel men—of which "all were Mexicanos except the foreman." The daily wage now varied from $1.25 to $1.50, the amount paid to all Mexicans regardless of job function or skill. But the change from temporary railroad work to semipermanent street work was welcomed by Mexicanos wishing to settle in Santa Barbara.

They paid very poor salaries. But I thought it was good because where I came from I used to work ten hours for $1.25, 12¢ an hour. On the trains they used to pay only $1.00. Then I came here and they paid $1.25 for eight hours—it was good.[38]

A ready pool of Mexican surplus labor was always available to any contractor who merely went to the vicinity of lower State Street near Haley Street. Here the informal Mexican labor depot—an area where unemployed Mexicanos desirous of work assembled—provided the various contractors with all the labor they needed at low wages. Although many Mexicanos worked in the street-paving crews, others worked in different sectors of the urban construction and construction supply industry. Thirty or forty worked at the brickyard on the lower west side. Others loaded lumber at the wharf or at the lumber company on the lower east side. At building sites Mexicanos were hod carriers and common laborers. The expansion of light industrial development within the barrio during the 1920s created other unskilled jobs for incoming Mexicanos.[39]

The number of foreign-born Mexican workers in the construction-building industry was equaled by the number who worked in the agriculture-related industries. In both areas the type of employment open to Spanish-speaking peoples had been determined prior to the arrival of the majority of foreign-born Mexicanos; they continued the occupational patterns initiated by the native-born Mexicans of the late nineteenth century. The influx of thousands of Mexicanos throughout the first three decades of the twentieth century further solidified the poor, working-class status of the growing Chicano community. The expansion of agricultural production in the twentieth century, especially during the 1920s, increased the dependency upon seasonal, migratory labor. The incoming Mexicans became a major part of the resident and migrant farm labor work force. Walnut, lemon, and, to a lesser extent, perishable fruit and vegetable production attracted the largest numbers of men, women, and children.[40]

The annual migration of the Chicano family work force to the nearby agricultural areas was augmented by a growing number of foreign-born Mexican families in the early twentieth century. Together the native-born and foreign-born Mexican workers were picking, for example, over 2,225,000 pounds of walnuts by 1910 in the Goleta district just north of Santa Barbara. By the 1920s walnuts, one of the leading agricultural products of the county, was a million-dollar-a-year industry.[41] Each fall for about five or six weeks, hundreds of Mexican families migrated a short distance north of the city to camp out in the groves. The entire family was incorporated into the work force—the more family members, the more money the family could bring back to Santa Barbara. Although there were a few Anglos, Japanese, and other non-Chicanos picking walnuts, the vast majority were Spanish speaking. Men and boys generally worked in the groves, women and girls in the packing house. As one Mexicana recollected, "In the packing house there was only Mexicanos and del pais [native-born Chicanos] except for the foremen."[42] For parents and children (who usually missed the first part of the autumn school semester) the walnut season meant $200 or so added to the family income; but it was a difficult time in which the workers had to live in tents and toil long, tedious hours. Except for those who did not bring their own supplies and thus spent their earnings at the exploitive company store, Mexicanos became dependent upon the annual extra income. Some migrated as far north as San Jose and as far south as the

Imperial Valley to harvest other crops before returning home.[43]

The lemon industry employed the largest number of Mexicano workers. The increase in production after 1910 and especially during the early 1920s dramatically increased the number of Mexicanos picking lemons and working in the Johnston Fruit Company packing house in Santa Barbara.[44] Lemon picking and packing, unlike most agricultural work, was not seasonal and therefore provided full-time employment for many hundreds of workers. Men and women worked together in both operations. In the packing house males were principally employed in the washing and storage stages, while females predominated in the grading, packing, and labeling processes. Throughout the 1920s most Mexican males received $18 per 45-hour week; women received only $16 for a 50-hour week. The Johnston Fruit Company continued to pay low wages as long as recently arrived Mexicanos could be hired to replace the large turnover of workers seeking better employment.[45]

A survey in 1929 found that Mexicanos accounted for over 80 percent of the entire farm labor work force in Santa Barbara and other southern California counties. To the Santa Barbara Walnut Growers' Association, the Santa Barbara Lemon Exchange, the Santa Barbara Farm Exchange, and other agribusiness associations the steady supply of "cheap" Mexican labor guaranteed larger profits on their investments. The agriculture and construction industries provided needed employment for thousands of Mexicans, but at the same time constricted their ability to escape from their status as underpaid, often exploited laborers.[46]

Another survey undertaken in 1929–1930, a social welfare report, assessed the occupational distribution of Mexicano families in the city of Santa Barbara. The survey of 444 families with children attending school reported the following occupations of the heads of household: 264 laborers; 12 laundry workers; 25 gardeners; 5 carpenters; 5 truckmen; and 5 shoemakers, "among other occupations." Of the 316 Mexicanos who listed occupations, 95.0 percent were unskilled laborers; only 3.0 percent held skilled positions. The survey also pointed to the widespread unemployment facing Mexican workers in 1929. Of the 178 families (of which 143 were Mexicano) served by the East

Señor Escobar's Mexican Girls' Orchestra, Santa Barbara, circa 1926. Created from the need to promote the musical talents of barrio youth, the orchestra played at Mexican patriotic celebrations. Courtesy of Albert and Lydia Caballero.

Side Social Center, the survey claimed that "among the problem families, unemployment was a factor in 58 cases in 1929" and that more than half of the families received "intensive care." The survey of the Mexicanos concluded that given their unemployment and their occupational status, "this group represents an important problem."[47]

Impoverishment in the Eastside Barrio

By the late 1920s many Mexican workers faced increasing unemployment, which made family survival with the meager income of part-time work more difficult. Aid from friends, relatives, and mutualistas became insufficient as the material condition of Mexicanos deteriorated. Mexicanos had to contend, in addition, with inadequate housing, poor health care, and neglect by social agencies. The *Morning Press* in 1921 reported: "At present the great shortage of homes within the reach of the laboring man is causing more or less suffering among the poor."[48] The great majority of Mexicans in the lower eastside barrio could not afford to own their own homes, nor could they afford to pay $10 to $15 per month for rent. As a result, many were forced to live in overcrowded, unsanitary conditions. "The

S.P. [Southern Pacific railroad]," for example, "was bringing them all in and building section houses," recalled a woman who had worked for the East Side Social Center during the 1920s; "about ten families and one toilet."[49]

Poor health conditions were reflected also in the high incidence of infant mortality among the Mexicanos. In 1923 Santa Barbara boasted one of the lowest death rates in the United States; the death of babies was included in a different category in which "the infant mortality rate was highest among the Mexicans"—four times higher than for "white" infants.[50] By 1930 it was reported that "death among Mexican babies was five times as common as among others . . . Economic and social conditions," concluded the report, "were investigated and appraised as factors in these deaths."[51] Although the migratory pattern of work was cited as a problem in maintaining prenatal health care, the presence of the city's open dump in the eastside barrio did not improve the health conditions of the Mexicano community.

The stench from rotten refuse has become a nuisance to the householders in that portion of the city and fear of a contagion of disease resulting from the situation is general on the lower east side . . . Small Mexican children are permitted to play the part of scavengers on the dump of rotting, filthy debris. At almost all hours of the day they can be found playing over the dump, delving into its putrefying depths for food, playthings.[52]

Americanization Programs and Deportation

Soon after World War I, during the beginning of the peak period of Mexican immigration, the various social agencies in Santa Barbara began paying lip service to the "problems arising from the importation of Mexican . . . labor."[53] The general response from the social welfare agencies was to establish English-language and home economics courses for Mexicana wives. Other groups were more concerned about the presence of a large foreign population and the "Americanization problem" they constituted. The Native Sons of the Golden West, for example, were "astonished at the fact that there are over 2,000 residents of Santa Barbara who are recent arrivals from Mexico."[54] At a 1922 conference to discuss the unresolved "Mexican problem" in Santa Barbara, social welfare workers began to realize that the foreign-born were becoming permanent residents in the city. They failed to understand, however, that Americanization programs were not the answer:

The people [Mexicanos] are here and there is only one thing to do, and that is to accept the fact that they are here to stay, and the sooner they can be made to feel at home the sooner they will be willing to assume the responsibilities of citizenship . . . [We must] train people of their own race to work among them and carry the gospel of true American citizenship to them.[55]

Another social worker was able to view the problem more realistically and concluded that "Americanization to these people means exploitation—Whole families have been brought in for industrial purposes and then stranded—That, to them, means Americanization." But "they are doing remarkably well," observed several social workers after a tour through the barrio; "we have not given them enough credit for what they are doing for themselves."[56]

Americanization programs for Mexicanos were futile. From 1910 to 1927, only 0.7 percent of the 849 naturalization petitions on record at the Santa Barbara Court House had been filed by Mexican immigrants; this pattern of nonnaturalization continued throughout the 1930s. Americanization efforts, nevertheless, continued throughout the 1920s.[57]

Except for the services provided by the East Side Social Center and the Visiting Nurse Association's well-baby clinic for Mexican families, the various welfare agencies were unsuccessful. They failed to grasp the root of the problem facing most Mexicanos—few jobs and inadequate wages. Unable to earn sufficient money and faced with increasing unemployment, Mexicanos during the late 1920s found their standard of living deteriorating. When the programs to Americanize or assimilate the large number of Mexicanos failed, sending them back to Mexico was chosen as the solution. Prior to the concerted deportation drive beginning in 1930 in many U.S. cities where Mexicanos lived, several individuals and families had already been forcibly expelled from Santa Barbara. The first example of a program to rid the community of undesirable "indigent Mexicans" occurred in the summer of 1926. Its justification was the belief that Mexicanos created a serious burden on the welfare agencies. The district inspector of the U.S. immigration office, in conjunction with the Santa Barbara County Board of Supervisors, initiated the first repatriation efforts. Upon acquiring relief lists from the welfare agencies, the inspector had a ready list of deportable "indigent aliens." According to the *Daily News:*

The indigent rolls of Santa Barbara and Ventura counties are being materially reduced through the activities of Uncle Sam . . . In the last few months many indigents from Mexico, who in some cases have comprised entire families[,] have been sent back across the border . . . As fast as they are discovered they are being deported.[58]

The latest in a series of deportations, it was reported in 1926, involved a mother and her four small children.

The repatriation drive that began in 1926 was merely a prelude to the massive deportations of 1930–1933. The various claims that Mexicanos were *the* source of the welfare burden were, however, incorrect. In 1929 foreign-born Mexicanos accounted for 17.9 percent of the new welfare relief cases in Santa Barbara County, a figure only slightly higher than their percentage of the total population. In the city the largest social welfare agency, the Associated Charities, reported in 1926 that 62 percent of the relief cases were the elderly, "a fact which dispels," they concluded, "still another wrong impression, that foreigners are the bulk of the society's care."[59] Nevertheless, large-scale Mexicano deportations commenced. The U.S. immigration agents, aided by the interpreters of the East Side Social Center, enticed Mexicanos to return to Mexico. "Many of the people wanted to go back," a woman who witnessed the deportations recalled, "because things were so hard and they were promised [by the immigration officers] all the glory and everything else . . . A beautiful picture was painted . . . They went to Mexico," she added, but "then they tried to get right back in."[60] Others were untruthfully told that the Mexican government would provide them with land and supplies in a Baja California colonization project. By 1930 hundreds of Mexicano families were being deported. One observer recalled the scene at the Southern Pacific depot in Santa Barbara:

They [the immigration officials] had boxcars and they put all the people that went in boxcars instead of inside the trains . . . They sent a lot of people from around here too . . . A big exodus . . . They were in here illegally but the moral part of it, like separation and putting them in boxcars . . . I'll never forget as long as I live.[61]

It is impossible to determine accurately how many Mexicanos from Santa Barbara city and county were actually deported. A report published in 1935 gives some indication of the intensity of the local program:

Since 1930 there has been a large exodus of Mexican families from the United States. The Welfare Department of Santa Barbara County took an active part in encouraging Mexicans to return to their own country. A few hundred families were aided by the Welfare Department, with railroad transportation and otherwise, so that the number residing in the county has been appreciably reduced. We have no present means of knowing how many Mexicans there are here.[62]

Judging from personal accounts and from the few reports and articles published between 1926 and 1934, somewhere between 1,000 and 2,000 Mexicanos were repatriated from Santa Barbara—probably no fewer than 200 to 250 families.[63] According to several Mexicans who remembered the deportations, many of those who were deported, especially the native-born children of the deported families, eventually returned to Santa Barbara during the 1930s and 1940s.[64]

The repatriation movement not only affected the lives of those deported, it affected those who remained as well. The deportations removed friends and relatives who had contributed to the social vitality of the Mexicano community. The repatriations left the lower eastside barrio in a weakened sociocultural position because of the absence of a substantial number of barrio residents. The deportations also brought to a close an era of massive immigration from Mexico and thus temporarily halted the expansion of the Chicano community in Santa Barbara and in barrios throughout the United States.

Summary and Conclusion

Though distinct from the barrio of Pueblo Viejo, the barrio that formed on the lower east side of Santa Barbara resembled the older Mexican neighborhood in many ways. Residentially, socially, and occupationally, foreign-born Mexicanos followed patterns that had been established prior to their arrival. Much like the native-born Pueblo Viejo residents, the Mexicanos of necessity settled in an area of the city segregated from non-Mexicanos. Here they formed their own community where Mexican culture, social, and organizational life flourished. As workers, they occupied the same status as other Spanish-speaking people who were relegated to unskilled or semiskilled manual labor. But unlike their native-born counterparts, when the labor of foreign-born Mexican workers was no longer needed, they supposedly became welfare problems and many were deported. Those who remained behind, as well as those who were deported, contributed enormously to the Mexican heritage of Santa Barbara—a heritage of mestizo people who had migrated north from Mexico over the centuries and who would continue to come to Santa Barbara throughout the twentieth century.

Chicanos and the Labor
Market of the Early 1900s

7.

By the turn of the century, nearly a generation after Mexican
workers first had been incorporated into the capitalist labor
market, the fundamental patterns of Chicano employment were
established. Since the 1890s Chicanos had emerged as the backbone of the manual labor work force in Santa Barbara. During
the early twentieth century the local economy became even
more dependent upon a large pool of cheap, unskilled labor as
the urbanization of Santa Barbara and the development of agribusiness near the city steadily increased. The thousands of
foreign-born Mexicans who entered the city through the period
prior to the Great Depression provided the necessary additional
labor. They contributed to the expansion of the Chicano working class and shared the same low occupational status as those
Mexican residents who had lived in the community for many
years. Both native-born and foreign-born Mexicans were to remain at the bottom of the occupational structure in Santa Barbara for two principal interrelated reasons. An economic system
that benefited from the maintenance of a permanent low-paid
work force was evidently unwilling to allow upward occupational mobility for the great majority of unskilled and semiskilled workers. This class stratification was reinforced by a social and racial order that during the twentieth century
continued to relegate Mexican people to a subordinate position
as an ethnic minority group.

Patterns of Employment

The pastoral occupational tradition of an earlier generation of Mexican workers had virtually ceased to exist by the first decade of the twentieth century.[1] Most native-born Mexicans were now employed as day laborers in construction-related work and as seasonal agricultural workers. The increasing foreign-born worker population likewise was primarily tied to employment in construction and in agriculture. The latter industry employed, on a seasonal and permanent basis, the largest number of Mexicans—simply because it was dependent upon the labor of children and women as well as men. The same agricultural interests that employed the Chicano family members in the 1880s and 1890s continued to do so throughout the predepression period. As corporate agricultural production increased, so did the size of the work force. In the lemon industry, as an example, young Mexican men and women worked at the Johnston Fruit Company packing house in larger numbers after the increase of lemon production during the early twentieth century. After 1916 the work force at Johnston's was composed mainly of foreign-born; recent migrants were recruited throughout the period to fill the labor needs of the enlarged citrus fruit packing operation.[2]

Another source of agricultural employment from the late nineteenth century into the twentieth century was the annual walnut harvest. Native-born families, later joined by foreign-born families, migrated to Goleta each year and stayed from thirty to forty days, picking or processing walnuts. "The walnut season," one Chicano recalled, "was the only time of the year us poor people could get a little ahead."[3] Families worked in groups on a designated grove and were paid $25 per ton; a family could usually pick between six and eight tons during the first two pickings (each season lasted approximately four to six weeks). Women and children were the most important family workers in the walnut harvests. The amount any family could earn was largely dependent upon the number of children able to pick. The children were taken from school to perform this important family economic function. In 1911, however, the California labor commissioner began to cite the Santa Barbara walnut growers for illegal and exploitive use of child labor. After inspecting the workers in the groves and in the packing house, where mostly Mexicanas were employed, the commissioner found "conditions even worse than reported." He concluded that there were "so many children in the orchards that the schools were all but depopulated. One of the schools had closed down entirely."[4]

During the subsequent walnut picking season the president of the Walnut Growers Association threatened to use Japanese labor if an extension of summer vacation was not granted to the Chicano children. The association obtained a decision from the Superior Court, which in 1912 held that if a family pleaded hardship, the children could work. The walnut growers thus were able to employ children legally alongside their parents. The walnut growers, who had been dependent upon Mexican workers for nearly a generation, continued to rely almost exclusively on them. "In the past families would leave the city for the walnut groves," the *Morning Press* stated in 1912, "and in a few weeks derive quite a revenue. This, however, has largely been done by the poorer class of Californians," the newspaper concluded.[5] The availability of Chicano labor, especially child labor, was guaranteed to the Walnut Growers Association in 1921 after it made a pact with the county board of education. The agreement permitted local children to enroll temporarily in Goleta district schools during the picking seasons. Those who actually attended school helped their parents in the fields before and after school hours.[6]

The practice of hiring women and children in the walnut and lemon industries as a cheaper source of labor than men began in the 1880s and intensified during the twentieth century. Growers and packing-house superintendents realized that greater profits were earned when lower-paid women and children were utilized. Except for those women who held full-time positions in the Johnston Fruit Company packing house, most participated in family seasonal, migratory agricultural work. The native-born Chicanas who picked lemons, walnuts, apricots, and other agricultural products were joined by their foreign-born

counterparts during the early 1900s. Particularly in these agriculture-related industries the job functions of women were very
similar to those of men.[7]

While participation of women and children in agricultural
work grew during the early twentieth century, increasing
numbers of native-born Mexican men worked also as laborers in
the city's building and construction industries. During the
1880s and 1890s Chicanos first began to be employed in nontraditional (that is, nonpastoral) types of manual labor. During
the first two decades of the new century, county road crews and
private street-paving contractors began to recruit more and
more local Mexican labor for the greatly expanded activity related to grading and paving of streets in the city of Santa Barbara. The native-born made up the majority of these workers
prior to World War I, but thereafter were outnumbered by the
foreign-born. Some were fortunate enough not to become pick-
and-shovel laborers; by utilizing their knowledge of horses, they
became teamsters during the early period of nonmechanized
street work. However, the native-born Mexican teamster—even
though semiskilled—was paid little beyond the wages of the
common laborer. Whereas Anglo teamsters, who had formed a
local union in the early 1900s, were earning wages of $4.00 to
$4.50 per day in 1907, Chicano nonunion workers who used
their own horse teams earned only $2.00 to $2.50 as late as
1915; those without their own teams earned common laborer
wages—approximately $2.00 for an eight-hour day in 1913.[8]

The discriminatory practice of establishing wage differentials
between Chicanos and Anglos was complemented by the practice of job discrimination. Native-born as well as foreign-born
Mexicanos who worked among non-Chicanos or who worked as
segregated units were given the most difficult tasks. Within an
allocated job assignment, some employers would assign the easier tasks to Anglos and the most burdensome to Chicanos, especially, according to several observers, those who were dark
complected. Moreover, the opportunity for advancement was
decidedly far greater for Anglos. Within the Chicano working
class, the native-born had a slight advantage over the foreign-
born; ability to speak English and the experience of a few years

of schooling were more than most foreign-born Mexicanos possessed.[9]

The influx of large numbers of foreign-born Mexican workers into the manual labor market after 1916 drove many native-born Chicanos to seek other employment, especially if wages were depressed. This occurred most frequently in the construction industry and in the lemon packing operation. Most occupations for both native-born and foreign-born Mexicanos in agriculture-related work and in construction were temporary or seasonal. As the native-born began to pursue other types of manual labor, full-time employment became the objective. Although a large majority of native-born remained unskilled laborers and semiskilled manual workers throughout the period, by 1920 some had obtained other unskilled/semiskilled jobs as gardeners, deliverymen (auto and truck operators), teamsters, and janitors.[10] Gardening was probably the most popular job for those native-born Mexicans who were not laborers. Although gardening seldom paid more than common laborer's wages, working for a private party generally assured a gardener more permanent employment.[11]

Those native-born Mexican workers who were not so fortunate as to secure full-time jobs remained dependent upon seasonal work. Many supplemented their income with odd jobs, as well as the seasonal agricultural harvests. For example, the practice of selling home-made Mexican foods to help pay rent and taxes persisted after the nineteenth century. There were some men who periodically worked at the wharf or at the brickyard as loaders. Younger boys contributed to the family income by working as newspaper delivery boys. Women and girls also helped by taking washing and ironing into their homes.[12]

Labor Conflict

Together the native-born and foreign-born Mexicans formed the single largest group of manual laborers in the overall occupational structure of Santa Barbara. "We were all poor," a Chicana reflected about this period, "we were all in the same situation."[13] The fact that Chicano workers were limited to the most menial type of employment and received the lowest wages motivated many of them to contest the undesirable conditions in which they often worked. Chicanos throughout the first three decades of the century were shunned by the general labor union movement in Santa Barbara, but this did not deter them from creating Chicano worker solidarity when needed to confront oppressive working conditions. The Chicanos of Santa Barbara engaged in the earliest known strikes in every major area of work in which they were employed. The heritage of Chicano labor conflict in the Ventura–Santa Barbara county area began with the strike of Chicano and Japanese sugar beet workers in Oxnard. A labor association of Mexican and Japanese workers was formed to negotiate issues concerning labor contractors, the exploitive practices of the company store, and wages. After nearly two months of negotiation and violence the strike of the sugar beet workers ended on April 1, 1903, with an apparent victory for the biracial union.[14]

Less than six months after the Oxnard strike Chicanos at the Johnston Fruit Company packing house in Santa Barbara struck for shorter working hours and higher wages. The Chicano work force of lemon packers and graders had been refused their demands for reduction of the work day from ten hours to nine. When the Johnston Company board of directors refused to consider the workers' demands, the Chicanos walked off the job en masse. The Chicanos also protested the low wages they received: $1.50 and $1.75 per day to graders and packers, respectively. The demands of the strikers included the nine-hour work day and double pay for overtime. A reporter from the *Independent* concluded, after talking to the strikers, that "they are apparently unanimous in pressing their demands."[15] The workers refused to call off the strike until the board of directors heard them. The strikers had tactically planned to initiate the work stoppage at the height of the lemon packing season and thus paralyze company operations. The "vacationing" board of directors hurriedly assembled and agreed to a nine-hour day, but compromised on the overtime rate. "The men declare that they have gained a victory," reported one of the local newspapers, "as the primary object of the strike was to bring about a reduction in the number of hours which they worked."[16] The workers returned to the packing house following the settlement, but apparently no permanent union was established.

Although skilled Anglo workmen in the recently formed labor unions of Santa Barbara had threatened to strike in 1902 and 1903, Chicanos were the first workers who actually halted working operations in any one industry in the city. Native-born Mexican workers also conducted the second known strike in Santa Barbara in 1909. The small number of part-time, resident sheepshearers on Santa Cruz Island during the fall shearing castration season reportedly struck because of their overly burdensome working conditions. During the shearing seasons the men generally worked thirteen hours per day, seven days a week, for two to three months. They "demanded shorter hours," it was reported, "and an occasional holiday."[17] When their demands were not granted, the entire crew sailed to the mainland. The *Morning Press* reported that the strikers "included nearly all the men in this locality who understood sheep shearing."[18] The owners of the island sheep ranch were planning to hire strikebreaking sheepshearers from Ventura and other parts of Santa Barbara County. The outcome of the strike is unknown.

In 1913 street-paving work was curtailed for a short time as Chicano and other laborers went on strike. The fifty workers had been receiving 25 cents per hour; they demanded $2.50 per day, the wage being paid to laborers in other southern California cities. The private contractor settled the dispute by compromising on a wage of $2.25 per eight-hour day.[19]

The Chicanos of Santa Barbara were not a tractable work force. Perhaps the best characterization of them was provided in 1908 by Santa Barbara city councilman Caesar Lataillade, who reportedly was "in closer touch with the large body of laboring men of Latin-American extraction than any one individual in the community." He concluded that "no one can herd the Spanish and Italian laborers. They do their own thinking."[20]

The Chicano laborers of Santa Barbara thus contributed to a pattern of labor conflict that emerged throughout the region as well as throughout the southwestern United States during the early twentieth century.[21] But when Chicano workers organized themselves as strikers, they did so without the help of the established local unions. The labor union movement in predepression Santa Barbara was geared to organization of skilled Anglo workers. Even when Chicanos had the necessary experience as skilled workers, the more formal labor union locals, such as the carpenters' and plasterers' unions, admitted very few Mexicans, if any at all. For example, one Mexicano who desired to learn the carpentry trade during the 1920s in the closed-shop city recalled, "I wanted to be a carpenter in Santa Barbara but they wouldn't let me on account of my face—discrimination."[22] He subsequently moved to a city where he could learn the trade and join the parent union for carpenters, planning to return to the Santa Barbara local with his official union card; on his return, however, his union status did not assure him work with contractors as he had hoped.

The local union movement in Santa Barbara made no real effort to organize common laborers prior to 1922. Nevertheless, a small group of Chicano laborers, the hod carriers, began organizing their own union local in 1919 in order to "devise ways and means to better their working conditions."[23] Throughout the 1920s the hod carriers' local was the only formal union in which Chicanos participated; its rank and file were predominantly Chicano.

Chicano Occupational Structure and Mobility

Throughout the predepression period the great majority of Chicano workers remained nonunionized, predominantly manual, semiskilled and unskilled. Qualitatively, the occupational distribution of the Chicano work force did not change much from what it had been in the late nineteenth century. Quantitatively, the work force changed as a result of the large influx of Mexicanos, especially just prior to and during the 1920s. But relative to other workers in the city, Chicanos remained immobilized within the lowest occupational categories. The Chicano occupational structure of the first three decades of the twentieth century illustrates the continuity that existed from the time Chicanos were first incorporated into the labor market during the late nineteenth century.

Between 1900 and 1910 in Santa Barbara the overall occupational structure for Chicanos remained basically the same (see Table 15). The only notable changes in the distribution of workers were the increase of unknown occupations and the corresponding decrease in the percentage of low blue-collar unskilled laborers. These changes reflect the greater tendency of city directories to list nondescriptive occupations and to omit occupational designations altogether; the earlier census enumerations were more accurate in this regard.[24] Nevertheless, only minor variations occurred in the distribution of Chicano workers in the high white-collar, low white-collar, high blue-collar, and low blue-collar semiskilled occupations between 1900 and 1910.

In 1910 the bulk of the male head-of-household population still held low blue-collar jobs (64.2 percent). A total of only 10.2 percent of the Chicano work force was employed in low white-

Table 15 Occupational structure for the total Spanish-surnamed male head-of-household population, Santa Barbara, 1900–1930 (in percent).

Occupation	1900	1910	1920	1930
High white-collar				
Professional	3.7	1.4	0.7	0.4
Proprietorial	2.3	5.0	3.3	3.4
Low white-collar				
Sales/clerical/				
semiprofessional	3.7	3.8	5.9	5.6
High blue-collar				
Skilled	10.2	12.2	9.5	8.9
Low blue-collar				
Semiskilled	15.7	15.5	17.4	12.7
Unskilled	57.4	48.7	51.2	55.6
Unknown or unlisted	6.9	13.4	11.9	13.3
Number in population	216	419	545	973

SOURCES: Federal manuscript census schedules, 1900; Santa Barbara city directories for 1909–1910, 1920, 1929–1930.

collar and high white-collar occupations, with a slightly higher percentage (12.2 percent) employed as skilled blue-collar workers. The pattern of Mexican worker concentration in the lowest levels of the labor market was reinforced with each passing decade of the twentieth century. The percentages of Chicano low blue-collar unskilled workers, in particular, continued to increase after 1910.

Between 1910 and 1920, Table 15 shows that the slight percentage increase of low white-collar occupations held by Mexicans was offset by the percentage decrease of both high white-collar and high blue-collar occupations. The most significant occupational trend evident by 1920 was the increase of low blue-collar semiskilled (from 15.5 to 17.4 percent) and unskilled (from 48.7 to 51.2 percent) Mexican workers. In 1920 Mexican low blue-collar workers accounted for 68.6 percent of the entire Spanish-surnamed work force and 80 percent of those who listed occupations. Together, all blue-collar workers (both low and high) comprised nearly four-fifths (78.1 percent) of the Chicano work force; less than 10 percent of the Mexican male heads of household held low and high white-collar positions.

The 1930 Spanish-surname occupational structure reflected the sharp increase in Mexican immigration during the 1920s; this increase had reached its peak in 1926 before declining in the late 1920s.[25] The 1930 occupational structure also reflected the continuing overrepresentation of Chicanos at the bottom of the occupational hierarchy. Between 1920 and 1930 the percentage of unskilled low blue-collar workers increased from 51.2 to 55.6 percent. The percentage of all low blue-collar workers, however, remained essentially the same during the period (68 percent), as the percentage of semiskilled Mexican workers declined between the two decades. In addition, while the concentration of unskilled workers increased, the percentage of Mexicans in the high blue-collar and low and high white-collar positions declined slightly. Throughout the first three decades of the twentieth century, therefore, the occupational situation for the great majority of Chicano workers had not changed.

During the period 1900–1930 few Mexican workers ever experienced job mobility from one occupational level to another.

Table 16 Occupational mobility of the total male Spanish-surnamed head-of-household population between decades, Santa Barbara, 1900–1930 (in percent).

Occupational status at end of decade	1900–1910	1910–1920	1920–1930
In same occupational level	58.4	57.3	54.3
Mobility within same occupational level	10.6	6.1	9.0
(LBC semiskilled to LBC skilled)	(3.5)	(3.9)	(4.5)
(LBC unskilled to LBC semiskilled)	(7.1)	(2.2)	(4.5)
Downward occupational mobility	3.6	5.6	4.1
(HWC/LWC to HBC/LBC)	(1.8)	(2.8)	(2.9)
(HBC to LBC)	(1.8)	(2.8)	(1.2)
Upward occupational mobility	4.4	4.5	7.3
(LBC to HBC/ LWC/HWC)	(2.6)	(4.5)	(6.5)
(HBC to LWC)	(0.0)	(0.0)	(0.8)
(LWC to HWC)	(1.8)	(0.0)	(0.0)
Unknown or unlisted in one of the two decades	23.0	26.4	25.3
Number in population	113	178	245

SOURCES: Federal manuscript census schedules, 1900; Santa Barbara city directories for 1909–1910, 1920, 1929–1930.

LBC = low blue-collar; HBC = high blue-collar.
LWC = low white-collar; HWC = high white-collar.

Table 16 illustrates that the large majority of Spanish-surnamed workers who remained in Santa Barbara from one decade to the next were occupationally immobile. (If one were to take into

consideration the significantly high percentages of unknown occupations, the vast majority of which were listed as low blue-
collar jobs in either the preceding or the following decade, the
percentage of workers in the same occupational level after a decade would have been considerably higher.) Between the decades 1900–1910, 1910–1920, and 1920–1930, the percentage of
occupationally immobile or static workers was 69.0, 63.4, and
63.3 percent respectively. These figures include those who
moved back and forth between the low blue-collar unskilled and
semiskilled occupations, becaue these workers did not realize
true occupational mobility from one level to another. Only small
percentages of Mexican workers were mobile during the various
decades, and no significant patterns of mobility were manifested. The small number of workers, for example, who experienced downward occupational mobility during any decade were
offset by the small number of workers who registered upward
mobility.[26] The only consistent mobility pattern that Mexicans
experienced was within the low blue-collar occupational level.
However, the mobility trend was neither decidedly upward nor
decidedly downward between the unskilled and semiskilled
jobs. What occurred throughout the period, in fact, was a floating mobility of Chicano low blue-collar workers. It was common
for a worker to be employed in a semiskilled job in one decade
and in an unskilled job in the next decade and vice versa. This
pattern of floating mobility among Mexican low blue-collar
workers in early twentieth-century Santa Barbara leads one to
suspect that very little job differentiation existed between unskilled and semiskilled occupational functions.

Most Chicano workers, both native-born and foreign-born,
were locked into low blue-collar occupations for most of their
working years. Regardless of length of residence in the city or
longevity within a certain job, Chicanos could not break the pattern of low blue-collar occupational status. Older-generation as
well as younger-generation Mexicans were equally unable to
move from the bottom of the occupational structure in Santa
Barbara. Those Mexican male heads of household, for example,
who lived in the city in 1900 and still were residents in 1930
showed no apparent upward occupational mobility after thirty

Table 17 Occupational career mobility of worker group that persisted from 1900 through subsequent decades, Santa Barbara (in percent).

Year	Percent (and number) of persistent workers	Occupational level				
		High white-collar	Low white-collar	High blue-collar	Low blue-collar	Unknown
1900	100 (216)	4.4	7.1	9.7	70.0	8.8
1910	52 (113)	5.3	1.8	8.8	66.4	17.7
1920	29 (63)	4.8	3.2	6.3	63.5	22.2
1930	15 (32)	3.1	0.0	6.2	65.6	25.0

SOURCES: Federal manuscript census schedules, 1900; Santa Barbara city directories for 1909–1910, 1920, 1929–1930.

years (see Table 17). By following these persistent workers over time, it is evident that the vast majority who were unskilled and semiskilled workers in 1900 remained in low blue-collar jobs in 1930. Likewise, the high white-collar and low white-collar Mexican workers remained in their original occupations, though with less regularity than blue-collar workers. Although the percentage of workers in each occupational level declined relative to the increasing percentages of unknown occupations for each decade, occupational immobility is clearly the major trend.[27] Thus, the persistent Mexican workers who were tracked from 1900 to 1930, most of whom were native-born, rarely moved out of the occupational level which they had held in 1900.

Chicana Occupational Structure

The occupational experience of Mexican males during the period 1900–1930 was, to a large extent, shared by their female counterparts. Since the 1880s, when Chicanas first entered the labor market, they had been concentrated in two general areas of employment—domestic services and agriculture-related work. Throughout the first third of the twentieth century Mexican women continued to work with the rest of the family unit at harvest times. Although the main pattern of Chicana employment apparently remained seasonal and part-time, a growing number of females were acquiring full-time jobs. Financial necessity dictated a double role for many Chicanas as housewife and as wage earner.

In 1900 over two-thirds of the Chicana work force was employed in manual semiskilled and unskilled jobs (see Table 18). Chicanas predominated as full-time and part-time domestics, laundresses, servants, cooks, seamstresses, and waitresses. They were employed in Anglo homes and in the many tourist hotels in the city. In addition, many were hired as farm workers during the seasonal summer and fall harvests near Santa Barbara. Less than 6 percent of all Mexican women workers were in skilled, clerical, proprietorial, and professional occupations.[28]

Unlike the 1900 manuscript census, the city directories (1910, 1920, and 1930) failed to list part-time employed Chicanas, who constituted a large percentage of the work force. Notwithstanding this omission, the Chicana occupational structure, with one exception, did not change much from 1900 to 1930.[29] Throughout the period the high percentages of unskilled and semiskilled

Table 18 Occupational structure for total employed Spanish-surnamed female heads of household and adult residents, Santa Barbara, 1900–1930 (in percent).

Occupation	1900 [a]	1910	1920	1930
Professional	2.1	0.0	3.4	2.7
Proprietorial	1.1	0.0	0.0	2.0
Sales/clerical/ semiprofessional	1.1	14.8	28.8	28.8
Skilled	1.1	11.1	0.0	1.4
Semiskilled (manual)	30.5	7.4	30.5	11.0
Unskilled	35.7	66.7	37.3	54.1
Unknown or unlisted	10.7	0.0	0.0	0.0
Number in population	95	54	59	146

SOURCES: Federal manuscript census schedules, 1900; Santa Barbara city directories for 1909–1910, 1920, 1929–1930. The city directories did not list all working women as the federal manuscript census did. Thus the number of employed Chicanas is significantly less after 1900, since part-time employees were not enumerated.

[a] 17.9 percent unemployed, according to 1900 manuscript census.

women workers remained stable (66.2, 74.1, 67.8, and 65.1 percent respectively).

Chicanas continued to work in the same jobs in which they had been employed in 1900, particularly as laundresses and domestics. However, beginning in 1910 a new area of employment, sales and clerical jobs, began to be occupied by larger percentages of Chicanas. By 1910 nearly 15 percent of the Chicana work force was employed in these occupational areas; the percentage increased to 28.8 percent in 1920 and 1930. Clerical and sales job opportunities were opened to Mexican women as they began to be hired by the small but growing number of Mexican proprietors in the barrio, as well as by many Anglo merchants who needed bilingual employees for their increasing Spanish-speaking clientele. This significant upward occupational mobility of Mexican women after 1910 was an important change in what was otherwise a dismal occupational picture. Other than their mobility into the clerical/sales occupational level, few Chicanas were able to penetrate the ranks of the skilled and high white-collar occupations.

Non-Spanish-Surname Occupational Structure

The occupational structure for non-Spanish-surnamed persons in Santa Barbara from 1900 to 1930 was in direct contrast to that for male and female Spanish-surnamed individuals. The pattern established as early as 1860 continued; Anglos were underrepresented in low blue-collar occupations and evenly distributed in the high blue-collar and low and high white-collar occupations. Between 1900 and 1930 two notable changes affected the non-Spanish-surname occupational structure (Table 19). First, a sizable reduction in the percentage of high white-collar professionals and proprietors occurred. While the reasons for this decrease are not fully known, it may be partially attributable to the relative increase in the population of clerks, salespeople, and similar types of workers. The larger numbers in the low white-collar category reflect the significant population growth of Santa Barbara between 1900 and 1910 (from 6,587 to 11,659 persons), increasing commercialism in the city, and response to the expanding tourist industry. Secondly, within the

Table 19 Occupational structure for non-Spanish-surnamed male heads of household,[a] Santa Barbara, 1900–1930 (in percent).

Occupation	1900	1910	1920	1930
High white-collar				
Professional	13.2	4.3	5.3	7.6
Proprietorial	18.3	12.4	12.8	9.5
Low white-collar				
Sales/clerical/				
semiprofessional	15.1	21.9	22.2	26.8
High blue-collar				
Skilled	20.3	21.2	22.9	21.7
Low blue-collar				
Semiskilled	12.8	18.6	15.4	12.7
Unskilled	14.0	9.8	9.2	10.8
Unknown or unlisted	6.3	11.7	12.2	10.8
Number in sample	508	419	794	1,493

SOURCES: Federal manuscript census schedules, 1900; Santa Barbara city directories for 1909–1910, 1920, 1929–1930.

[a] 40-percent sample of head-of-household population for 1900 (excluding nonwhites); 20-percent sample of head-of-household population for 1910, 1920, and 1930 (excluding Chinese, Japanese, and Italian-surnamed persons).

low blue-collar occupations the percentage of unskilled workers declined after 1900, while after 1910 the percentage of semi-skilled workers began to decline also.

A comparison of the distribution of Spanish-surnamed and non-Spanish-surnamed workers in the labor market shows a clear and continuing occupational discrepancy throughout the early twentieth century. During the period 1900–1930 the percentage of Spanish-surnamed low blue-collar workers ranged between 64.2 and 73.1 percent while the percentage for non-Spanish-surnamed workers in the same occupational level ranged from 23.5 to 28.4 percent. Comparison of Tables 15 and 19 indicates that the occupational discrepancy between the two groups was even greater at the unskilled low blue-collar level (48.7 to 57.4 percent for Mexicans and 9.2 to 14.0 percent for Anglos). Greater occupational distance separated the groups in the high blue-collar, low white-collar, and high white-collar levels. The high and low white-collar occupations, in particular, illustrated that these areas of employment were virtually closed to most Chicanos. Whereas between 38.6 and 46.6 percent of the non-Spanish-surname work force were located in white-collar positions between 1900 and 1930, Mexican workers constituted only 9.4 to 10.2 percent in those same occupational levels.

Significant occupational distance existed not only between Mexicans and Anglos but, to a lesser degree, between Mexicans and Italians. The Italians, most of whom came to the United States during the late nineteenth century and early twentieth century, were one of the largest immigrant groups in Santa Barbara.[30] But unlike either native-born or foreign-born Mexicans, the Italians had a much more evenly distributed occupational structure (see Table 20). For example, the percentage of Italian-surnamed low blue-collar workers between 1900 and 1930 (ranging from 39.1 to 54.0 percent) was considerably lower than

Table 20 Occupational structure for Italian-surnamed male heads of household,[a] Santa Barbara, 1900–1930 (in percent).

Occupation	1900	1910	1920	1930
High white-collar				
Professional	0.0	3.8	0.0	2.7
Proprietorial	28.3	26.4	13.8	11.0
Low white-collar				
Sales/clerical/				
semiprofessional	8.7	7.5	10.3	11.0
High blue-collar				
Skilled	17.4	13.2	12.7	13.0
Low blue-collar				
Semiskilled	17.4	15.1	20.7	15.1
Unskilled	21.7	30.2	33.3	38.3
Unknown or unlisted	6.5	3.8	9.2	8.9
Number in sample	46	53	87	146

SOURCES: Federal manuscript census schedules, 1900; Santa Barbara city directories for 1909–1910, 1920, 1929–1930.

[a] 100 percent of head-of-household population for 1900; 33-percent samples for 1909–1910, 1920, and 1929–1930.

that for Mexicans. Furthermore, although the percentages of high white-collar professionals were negligible for both groups, the percentages of Italian skilled blue-collar workers were higher, and those for high white-collar proprietors were much higher (ranging from 11.0 to 28.3 percent). Overall, Italian immigrants had much greater occupational opportunity and more equitable distribution throughout the labor market than did Chicanos.

Summary and Conclusion

By 1930 Chicano workers comprised over 35 percent of the entire unskilled laboring class in the city of Santa Barbara. The percentage of Chicanos in agriculture-related work and in construction was considerably higher.[31] During the first three decades of the twentieth century, as the Chicano working class expanded, the occupational status of most Spanish-surnamed individuals remained much the same as it had for over two generations. The Chicano and Anglo working populations, for the most part, remained at the opposite ends of the occupational hierarchy, with the Chicanos remaining a poor, predominantly unskilled and semiskilled working class.

Both native-born and foreign-born Mexicans throughout the predepression era had few opportunities to advance beyond the position of an unskilled or semiskilled manual worker. Regardless of how long they remained in a particular job or how long they were residents in the city, most Chicanos could not break out of the lowest occupational strata of the labor market. In part, this was caused by job discrimination because of ethnicity. The low status of the Chicano workers did not foster docile behavior, however. When working conditions became too oppressive, Chicanos protested by striking against their employers. These isolated strikes achieved little qualitative change in the status of the Chicano working class as a whole. An economic system that necessitated a permanent, low-paid laboring class perpetuated the patterns of Chicano employment into the twentieth century. On the eve of the worst years of the Great Depression, the Chicanos had managed to gain little in the way of economic security as workers in Santa Barbara.

Race Relations in Twentieth-Century Santa Barbara

8.

Mexicans who immigrated to Santa Barbara during the early twentieth century soon discovered that they shared the same low socioeconomic and political status as the native-born Barbareños. Though they continued to occupy the same subordinate position vis-à-vis Anglo society, these two sectors of the Chicano community remained, for the most part, socially separate. For several reasons—proximity to employment, cheap land values, residential segregation, and desire to live with others of their same nativity group—the foreign-born developed their own community on the lower east side of Santa Barbara. The native-born remained within the historic barrio of Pueblo Viejo where their parents, grandparents, and great grandparents had once lived. Residential distance between the two nativity groups thus contributed to the social distance between them.

One additional factor that contributed greatly to the schism within the Chicano community was the resurgence of anti-Mexican attitudes in the dominant society. For most Anglos who did not personally interact with Chicano people, native-born and foreign-born held little distinction. The native-born Mexicans therefore were exposed to the same racism that had been revived as a result of the migration of thousands of foreign-born Mexicans into the city. By attempting to disassociate themselves from the newcomers, in order to avoid the possibility of being stigmatized as foreign-born Mexicans, the native-born added to the resentment between the two groups.

Mexican people in Santa Barbara during the twentieth century, like their predecessors during the second half of the nineteenth century, endured the institutional and individual racism that existed. Neither the threat of the Ku Klux Klan nor the mass deportations that would come with the Great Depression could erase the unique historical imprint made by the Chicanos on Santa Barbara society.

Pueblo Viejo in the Twentieth Century

During the early decades of the twentieth century, Pueblo Viejo still contained the majority of native-born Mexicans in the city. Tourists and writers of tourist literature would occasionally identify the historic barrio of Santa Barbara. "This section of the city," observed the author of a traveler's handbook in 1904, "is still largely inhabited by Spanish-speaking people who comprise about one-fifth or one-sixth of the city's population."[1] But for most tourists the romantic character of Pueblo Viejo had diminished by the turn of the century. Most of the once "picturesque" adobes had been destroyed or covered with wood, and only a few remained as models of the authentic historical architecture. "Often behind some cheap wooden frame house," another writer stated in 1904, "charming glimpses are caught of red-tiled roofs or deep verandas that make one regret the disappearance of this style of building."[2]

Within Pueblo Viejo the residential boundaries and the concentration of Spanish-surname households still closely resembled the pattern of the 1880s. The county assessor's Block Book for 1906, which indicated property ownership in the city, revealed that in the core area of the barrio (see map) 60.4 percent of all property owners had Spanish surnames. There was, however, a decrease in the total percentage of Spanish-surnamed property owners in the area between 1888 and 1906 (from 72 to 67 percent) because many were becoming renters. Not until the mid-1920s did Mexicans become a minority of the property owners in the barrio.[3]

Although the bulk of the native-born population remained in Pueblo Viejo, those who lived outside the neighborhood were scattered throughout the thinly populated areas east of the old barrio toward the foothills and on the lower west side of the city. There were also a few who relocated in the uninhabited hills above Santa Barbara. No doubt other native-born Mexicans moved because of the deterioration of the "Tenderloin" district located in Chinatown next to Pueblo Viejo, which consisted of fan-tan parlors, brothels, saloons, and opium dens. There were some who migrated from Santa Barbara altogether, but most remained in the city or settled in nearby areas in the county. The number of native-born Mexicans remained relatively stable, because those who departed prior to 1914 were partially replaced by Chicanos from nearby Montecito. After portions of the barrio in Montecito were destroyed by a flash flood in 1914, many of the displaced native-born relocated in the city.[4]

Pueblo Viejo still retained the conditions of poverty that had prevailed in the late nineteenth century. A long-time resident recalled that during the early 1900s "nobody had anything; just enough for existence and that's about all."[5] Part-time and seasonal employment and subsistence gardening often were not enough to provide sustenance. Some of the poorest families had to rely on grubbing lima beans after the seasonal threshings in nearby Carpinteria. According to one of those who participated in the lima bean harvests, "At that time [circa 1910 to 1916] people were just barely able to eat."[6] A barrio tradition of lending aid to the poorest families, which included the sharing of food, helped to alleviate destitution in Pueblo Viejo.

Though interfamily assistance was helpful, it did not lessen the dependency of several native-born Chicanos upon county welfare, a trend that had begun in the 1890s. During the first decade of the twentieth century some twenty-five Spanish-surnamed persons within the city of Santa Barbara and seventy-eight throughout the county, most of whom were senior citizens, were still on the indigent lists. Even through the 1920s, reported the Associated Charities, the area where the "most dense activity extends" was located in the old barrio near the "immediate region of De la Guerra and Santa Barbara streets." Here again, over two-thirds of those receiving charity assistance were the elderly.[7] The low standard of living for most native-born Chicanos was also reflected in the value of their homes. When compared with non-Spanish-surnamed homeowners in 1912, the Spanish-surnamed property owners possessed significantly less valuable real estate and dwellings. Spanish-surnamed homeowners with under $500 of assessed property value comprised 55.7 percent of all Chicano property owners. Conversely, over three-fourths of the non-Spanish-surnamed people possessed property valued over $500 and over one-half owned property valued at $1,000 or more.[8]

To help provide a modicum of security for themselves, many Pueblo Viejo barrio residents, like the Mexican residents of the lower east side, joined an organization that offered some financial aid during times of crisis; this mutualista-type organization also helped promote social activity within Pueblo Viejo. The native-born Mexicans established a second chapter of the Foresters of America, a national and international mutual-aid insurance association. The first chapter, which began in the 1890s in Santa Barbara, apparently shunned Mexican membership. Mexicans formed their own chapter of the Foresters, the Junípero Serra Court No. 147, in 1900. From the beginning the "Spanish Foresters," as the newspapers referred to them, comprised Spanish-surnamed working-class people and a few non-Spanish-surnamed individuals from intermarried families. The organization provided sickness and death benefits to its 100 to 150 members. The Foresters and its women's auxiliary also sponsored such social festivities as dances, fiestas, and barbecues for the Pueblo Viejo community. Throughout the first third of the century the Foresters remained an important organization in the barrio, until internal disagreement caused its demise in the early 1920s.[9]

Another native-born Mexican organization originally established by Anglos, the Eagles Club, evolved into a social-fraternal club. Shortly before World War I it began admitting a few Mexican members; by the 1920s the Eagles' membership was predominantly native-born Mexican, although several Anglo members remained. The Eagles sponsored social activities for its members and for the Pueblo Viejo barrio community at large.[10]

The social and economic activities of the Foresters and the

Eagles Club were complemented by familial recreation. The Sunday family barbecue, for example, was one of the few traditional pastoral pastimes that continued into the twentieth century. Extended families, neighbors, and friends regularly shared food, drink, and entertainment at these home-based activities. Sometimes groups of 50 to 100 people would organize a barbecue at some nearby secluded picnic spot. These occasions remain as cherished memories for many former residents of Pueblo Viejo.[11] Another nineteenth-century festivity, the celebration of Montecito's patron saint, continued into the early twentieth century. However, opposition from certain Catholic priests, as well as from many Protestants who viewed the celebration as sacrilege—together with the intrusion of Anglos in 1914 who hoped to make the affair a tourist attraction—caused the event to lose its significance for local Mexicans.[12]

Just as the residential and social patterns of the Pueblo Viejo Chicanos during the early twentieth century were continuations of the patterns established during the late nineteenth century, so too were the political practices. During the last two decades of the nineteenth century the Chicanos had become a politically powerless group. In 1904, however, Spanish-surnamed voters still constituted 15.3 percent of all registered voters in the city; and they continued to reelect Caesar Lataillade, the old político, to the city council from their ward. As a result of the Chicanos' persistence in registering to vote, by the late nineteenth century the practice of Anglo candidates courting the Mexican vote was established. But in time the Chicanos withdrew even more from the electoral process. "During recent years," the *Morning Press* reported in 1907, "there has been a decided falling off of the native California vote, the apathy growing more marked each year."[13] By 1920 Spanish-surnamed voters accounted for only 3.2 percent of the registered voters in the Santa Barbara city precincts.

Relations between Native-Born and Foreign-Born Mexicans

The political and socioeconomic position of the native-born Mexicans of Pueblo Viejo during the early twentieth century in

Santa Barbara was essentially analogous to that of their foreign-born counterparts in the lower eastside barrio. The native-born and the foreign-born, however, often viewed each other as two separate social groups. In part, the schism that developed within the Spanish-speaking community was caused by the external prejudices of Anglo society, which caused native-born Mexicans to react negatively against foreign-born Mexicans. The nineteenth-century legacy of racism against Mexicans was carried over into the twentieth century and revitalized by the mass media's derogatory emphasis on the Cholo immigrants from Mexico.[14] The migration and permanent settlement of large numbers of foreign-born Mexicans in the city rekindled many Anglo prejudices as the growing Mexican community became more visible in the larger society. In addition, during the second decade of the century, as repercussions of the Mexican Revolution—the Texas-Mexico border conflicts, the 1914 U.S. intervention in Mexico, and Pancho Villa's raid on Columbus, New Mexico—reached the United States, the anti-Mexican sentiment was reinforced. Native-born Chicanos, in most cases no different in appearance from the foreign-born, were subject to the same stigma as the Cholo Mexicans. A principal reason why many native-born residents of Pueblo Viejo kept their distance from the foreign-born was to try to avoid this negative association. The foreign-born Mexicans saw this aloofness as clannishness and rejection.[15] "They [the foreign-born] resented that we wouldn't say we were Mexican," a native-born woman recalled; "we always said we were Spanish." Her husband, a native-born son of foreign-born parentage, added that "they [the native-born] were ashamed to say they were Mexican."[16] Another native-born person remembered the derogatory way in which some Anglos used the term *Mexican:* "The word Mexican was a dirty word—'You're a damned dirty Mexican, you greaser.' This was a common thing."[17] As Carey McWilliams succinctly concluded: "A strong prejudice had existed in the region against Mexicans for many years . . . Generations had been steeped in the Mexican stereotype."[18]

Social interaction and marriage between native-born and foreign-born Mexicans in Santa Barbara during the first decades of the twentieth century did exist, but as the exception rather than the rule.[19] The number of foreign-born Mexicanos began to rise sharply toward the end of the second decade, and as a result their residential and social isolation from the native-born of Pueblo Viejo increased also. One individual, a native-born Barbareño of foreign-born parents who mingled with both groups, remembered the early twentieth-century pocho-cholo schism (pocho is a derogatory term used by foreign-born Mexicans in referring to the native-born):

Here in Santa Barbara you had two classes of [Spanish-speaking] people. The old time people [the native-born of Pueblo Viejo] . . . didn't want anything to do with Mexicans [foreign-born]. Mexicans never wanted anything to do with the "pochos."[20]

According to a former resident of Pueblo Viejo, another reason why the two groups of Mexicans seldom interacted was "because we segregated ourselves and kept away from them."[21] At least one Mexicano who immigrated to Santa Barbara in 1916 related painful memories of his experiences with the native-born Mexicans:

There was not much contact [between the native-born and foreign-born] because la gente del país here at the time that I came, at least to me, were a very standoffish people. They were very proud, those that lived here. They were angered at those who came from Mexico . . . We didn't like each other . . . and many difficulties began between us. Because those from here used to treat us as the gringos did—as "dirty Mexicans."[22]

Other residents of the lower eastside barrio also recalled that some of the Mexicans of the Pueblo Viejo barrio acted superior and considered themselves different from foreign-born Mexicanos. In the opinion of at least one individual, the apparent differences between the two groups were incomprehensible:

They are of the same Raza and they are Indios. Why did they used to behave like that? We did not come here to do harm or to ask for anything. We came to work and we were working to live.[23]

The rift between native-born and foreign-born Mexicans in Santa Barbara was not solely attributable to the external racial attitudes, which many native-born had internalized and which

had caused them to disassociate themselves from the stigma attached to the foreign-born. Nor was it only a product of their
residential and social isolation. There were, in fact, some internal (though minor) distinctions between the two Spanish-speaking groups. Certain linguistic features and some customs, for example, tended to make many aware of their different regional
origins. The native-born Barbareños, historically isolated from
the influence of Mexico, maintained certain provincial Spanish-
language anachronisms unfamiliar to the foreign-born Mexicans.
Conversely, the native-born often were unable to understand
certain words or idioms used by the foreign-born, although both
groups were able to converse easily with each other in Spanish.[24] Another language factor that added to the distinction between the two groups was the ability of many native-born Mexicans to speak English, an ability that most recently arrived
Mexicanos did not have. Certain customs and religious ceremo-
nies further differentiated the foreign-born from the native-
born. After moving from the native-born Chicano barrio of
Montecito to the lower eastside barrio of Santa Barbara, one
woman recalled: "It was like being in a part of Mexico . . . It
was just like going to a different country for my mother to move
down there to see all those people wearing rebozos [shawls]
which were very foreign to her."[25] Such things as *piñatas*, certain Mexican religious songs, and church *jamaicas* were novel-
ties to most native-born Mexicans in Santa Barbara.

Minor distinctions in language and customs, together with
the more important dominant negative racial attitudes toward
Mexicanos (which affected both native-born and foreign-born),
militated against cohesiveness of the Chicano community in
Santa Barbara. The desire to reside with one's most familiar
group perpetuated the physical and social isolation of the native-born in Pueblo Viejo and of the foreign-born in the lower
eastside barrio. The recurrent job recessions in the city and the
competition created by the steady influx of Mexican laborers
may have exacerbated the discord within the Chicano working
class. The rift within the Chicano community in the early twentieth century was not static; it changed over time and was most
obvious during the peak periods of Mexican immigration. After

the foreign-born remained as permanent residents for many years, the distinctions between the two groups began to blur, especially during the postdepression period.[26]

Mexicans in Anglo Society

Though many native-born and foreign-born Mexicans viewed themselves as members of two separate social groups in Santa Barbara, the dominant Anglo society seldom made this distinction.[27] Except for employer-employee relationships, personal contact between Anglos and Chicanos was minimal. But minimized contact did not mollify the resentment Chicanos felt toward Anglos; it was passed from one generation to the next and was fueled by personal experiences of discrimination, covert and overt. The historic Anglo-Chicano antipathy, emanating from the U.S. conquest of California, was carried over into the twentieth century. For example, the widespread Mexican use of "Yanqui" and "gringo" to refer to Anglos was perpetuated. Stories of injustices perpetrated against native Barbareño families during the nineteenth century also contributed to the legacy of resentment. A native-born Chicana, for example, recalled the lessons of mistrust of Anglos that her grandmother had instilled in her:

Grandmother would not trust any gringo, because they did take their land grants away and it still was a memory to her. She always used to say, "Stay with your race, stay with your own."[28]

Where contact between Anglos and Chicanos was most likely to occur, such as in the public schools, memories of mutual conflict or antagonism were most vivid. "There was a lot of discrimination in those days [the late 1910s and the 1920s] against the Spanish-American people as they called us," a native-born Chicano recalled. "The gringos never did like the Spanish."[29] Recalling the way in which many Anglos related to Chicanos with a sense of superiority, another Chicano concluded that "there is not a gringo who feels inferior to a Chicano . . . he can't help it, he's born that way."[30]

Contact between Anglos and foreign-born Mexicans occurred

even less frequently than between Anglos and native-born Mexicans. Nevertheless, the reduced contact did not decrease the bitterness many Mexicanos felt. One woman, reflecting on the past, noted that "the Americans never did like us . . . They didn't accept us . . . They never will, I don't think."[31] Another Mexicano compared the contemporary with the historic situation:

You know that discrimination still exists. Here we are in 1974 and still discrimination. Well how would discrimination be in 1916 [when he arrived in Santa Barbara]? Worse! More! You only have to think of putting yourself in the year that we are in; there is discrimination now in the schools, anywhere you [can] find discrimination against the Mexicanos. Well, how was it in 1916? In 1916 you were not a worker, you were a slave.[32]

Even though the dominant society generally made few distinctions between native-born and foreign-born Mexicans, subtle distinctions based upon color began to emerge as institutional racism developed during the early twentieth century. The color of one's skin was the easiest way to distinguish ethnic identity; the majority of mestizos were easily distinguishable as non-Anglos. However, within the physically heterogeneous Chicano population there were light-complected individuals, or *hueros*. Hueros were less likely to encounter discrimination than the darker-complected Chicanos. Fluency in English was also a factor that affected Anglo treatment of Chicanos. Thus, a huero native-born Mexican who was fluent in English probably did not experience the same degree of racial discrimination as did his/her darker-skinned counterpart, native-born or foreign-born, who spoke with an accent.

If you were huero you could associate with any gringo . . . the color of your skin is what mattered. That's what our impression was in those days; that's the way we accepted it then. If you were a little *prieto* [dark-skinned] you were an outcast.[33]

Few business establishments in Santa Barbara openly excluded Chicanos of any color, but as one person stated, "There were places that wouldn't make you welcome."[34] Most Chicanos knew which places did not welcome them. Two of these regularly singled out Chicanos for discriminatory treatment. The Bath House, or swimming pool located on the beach, excluded Chicanos, especially the darker-skinned ones. Some of the movie theaters required, by rule or by gentle persuasion, that "visible" Chicanos (the prietos) sit together with other people of color in a segregated section.[35] Given the racism against Chicanos—covert, overt, individual, and institutional—it is understandable why even today many Chicanos retain bitter memories of their past relations with Anglos. For several Chicanos still living in Santa Barbara painful experiences with racism have left indelible marks upon their lives. "You can't forget those things [acts of discrimination]," as one Mexicana evaluated her personal feelings. "You try to forget because . . . you should forgive and forget, but there is still a pain in there that another human being could do that to you."[36]

The Ku Klux Klan and Other Organizations

The institutionalization of Anglo racism against Chicanos and other non-Anglo-Saxon Protestants in Santa Barbara culminated during the 1920s in the formation of a local chapter of the Ku Klux Klan (KKK). A Santa Barbara chapter of the KKK had been established in 1897, but the klan of the nineteenth century remained a submerged, inactive small group. The KKK was reestablished in Santa Barbara in the early 1920s, this time with great enthusiasm. By 1923 an effective organizational effort in Santa Barbara and Ventura counties resulted in the initiation of over 400 new klansmen. The Santa Barbara city chapter was the most active, claiming that its "membership is of the highest standing, being composed of preachers, doctors, lawyers, bankers, merchants, in fact, men of every walk of life"; business executives, public officials, and policemen were also members.[37] The KKK boasted that it "is the only organization on earth that limits its membership to native-born Americans" and is a "100 percent Protestant organization." The KKK flaunted its success by parading down State Street (the central avenue in Santa Barbara) in hundred-car caravans. During these public displays of KKK activism "no masks were worn and no attempt

was made to conceal the identity of the members of the organization."[38]

The goal of the Santa Barbara klan, according to two local historians, was "to drive all the Jews, Negroes and Catholics out of
town."[39] Only the latter group, the majority of whom were
Chicanos, resided in Santa Barbara in large numbers. In hopes
of achieving this goal, klansmen called for " 'all white American
Protestants' to join in helping to stamp out the 'menace' of the
minority and religious groups in Santa Barbara."[40] Fortunately,
the threats of the KKK were seldom carried out, although there
was one exception. That instance involved an attack upon a
Chicano. In the first issue of the klan's newspaper, the *Ku Klux
Klarion,* a threat was issued to a native-born Barbareño who
allegedly was not taking proper care of his illegitimate family.
On Mexican Independence Day in 1923 a group of klansmen
confronted this Chicano, a descendant of a pioneer presidio soldier, whereupon the man allegedly drew a pistol in defense.
The klansmen fled; the Chicano shortly thereafter was arrested
by police, many of whom were rumored to be KKK members.
He was charged with carrying a concealed weapon and held in-
communicado by police for two days. Luckily for the Chicano,
an anti-KKK district attorney refused to prosecute him on the
charges of concealment and child neglect. Instead, the district
attorney issued a verbal attack against the klan's behavior,
which resulted in a ban against KKK membership within the
police force. As a result of public pressures and factionalism
within the internal organizational leadership, the local KKK by
1924 experienced a sharp decline in activism and influence. The
remaining chapter members maintained a low profile throughout the 1920s until the klan formally disbanded in the 1930s.[41]

Within the Chicano community few people realized the gravity of the Ku Klux Klan threat. Those few Chicanos who re-
member the KKK recall only the stories circulating during this
period. "People used to be afraid of them," a resident recollected, because "they heard rumors that they attacked Mexicans
. . . They didn't like the Mexicans."[42] Other persons circulated
the tale during the early 1920s that the anti-Mexican KKK in-
tended to kill every Chicano in Santa Barbara. Rumors about the

The Ku Klux Klan in Santa Barbara, circa 1921. Courtesy of the Santa Barbara Historical Society Library.

KKK in the Chicano community were discussed within the circle of the family or with neighborhood friends.[43]

The KKK as an Anglo institution had much less impact upon the Chicanos than another Anglo institution that attempted to infiltrate the barrios—the Protestant church. The KKK had wanted to drive the Catholics from Santa Barbara, but the Anglo Protestant missions wanted to coopt many Chicanos into their religious and cultural fold.

Protestant missionary work among Chicanos in Santa Barbara had begun as early as 1883, but for years it remained secondary to the conversion of the Chinese. After the successful conversion of many Asians, the missionaries during the first decade of this century turned their attention to the growing Chicano population. The proselytizers scheduled regular evangelical services in the Pueblo Viejo barrio. Some missionaries found that the Chicanos were "very responsive" and that they "willingly accept the work among themselves."[44] The Santa Barbara First Baptist Church established the first permanent missionary effort among

Chicanos in 1902, and by 1919 this mission had attracted enough native-born and foreign-born Mexicans to warrant its establishment as a regular church. The two Baptist churches in Santa Barbara throughout the pre-1930s, however, maintained segregation between the Anglo and the Chicano congregations.[45]

The Continuity of "Mexican Santa Barbara"

Although the Chicano community provided the largest field of missionary work for Protestants, most native-born and foreign-born Mexicans remained tied in varying degrees to Catholicism. Chicanos in the predepression era also maintained the major cultural-lingustic patterns of Spanish-speaking mestizo peoples, patterns that had persisted in Santa Barbara since its initial colonization. Without a doubt the most important ethnic-cultural influence in the development of Santa Barbara society over time has been that of people of Mexican descent. Certainly, the Italians and other foreign-born Europeans as well as the Chinese and Japanese, blacks, and others influenced local social history, but no ethnic group has had a greater cultural influence on Santa Barbara than the Chicanos.

The Chicano population throughout the early twentieth century remained stable vis-à-vis the total population of the city. By 1930, on the eve of the deportation drive in Santa Barbara, "Mexicans" alone—enumerated as "all persons born in Mexico, or having parents born in Mexico, who are not definitely white, Negro, Indian, Chinese, or Japanese"—comprised between 9.7 percent (3,279) and 12.3 percent (4,262) of the city's 33,613 inhabitants.[46] But the native-born Mexicans of native-born parents in Pueblo Viejo were not enumerated as Mexicans in the 1930 census. This sector of the Chicano population of Santa Barbara in 1930 probably ranged from 750 to 900 people.[47] Based on the number of Spanish surnames listed in the city directory, the average size of Chicano families, the census report, and the estimate for native-born, the total Chicano population in 1930 probably numbered between 4,600 and 5,100—or between 14 and 15 percent of the total city population. If one takes into consideration the omission factor for Spanish-speaking people in the census and other enumerations, the percentage of Mexicans in Santa Barbara could be even higher. Santa Barbara, the sixteenth most populous city in California in 1930, had one of the highest concentrations of Chicanos relative to non-Chicanos in the state.[48]

Summary and Conclusion

Although the two sectors of the Chicano community remained separated in their respective barrios, native-born and foreign-born shared the same status in Santa Barbara society. The Chicanos of Pueblo Viejo continued to live in their historic barrio throughout the early twentieth century, as did their foreign-born counterparts in the lower eastside barrio. Both internal and external factors accounted for the schism that existed between these two main elements of the Spanish-speaking community. Together, these Chicanos of Santa Barbara nevertheless established the foundations on which mestizo society would continue to develop during the postdepression decades. This generation of Mexicans constituted the historical link between nineteenth-century society and the contemporary community.

Urban Chicanos in Predepression Southern California

9.

The historical patterns that continued to mold the Chicano community in Santa Barbara were part of larger related developments unfolding in cities throughout the region. Chicano urban society in southern California during the first three decades of the twentieth century was, on the one hand, a combination of the continuing socioeconomic and political patterns established in the nineteenth century and, on the other, the product of more recent events. The migration north from Mexico of tens of thousands of people undoubtedly had its most dramatic impact within the barrios, but it had a great effect upon the larger urban society as well. Like other early-twentieth-century developments, the migration of Mexicans to California had deep roots in the nineteenth century, but was modified by the changing conditions of the new century. Similarly, the patterns of Chicano occupational stratification and barrioization, though they reflected their nineteenth-century origins, underwent significant changes in the twentieth century. Barrioization continued to be shaped not only by external factors associated with the rapid pace of urbanization in southern California, but also by internal changes within the barrio population. The process was an on-going dynamic one, especially in cities where the Mexican population was increasing rapidly.

Twentieth-Century Barrioization

Several modifications to the barrioization process were apparent in southern California cities between 1900 and 1930. Even as Chicanos continued to be concentrated within the historic pueblo core areas, newer barrios were established within the central city districts, close to places of employment. The creation of newer barrios sometimes resulted from the establishment of labor camps or railroad labor colonies and from the suburbanization of Chicano communities. Although unique factors were involved in each particular city, a general pattern was evident: the great majority of urban Chicanos continued to live in segregated and impoverished areas.[1]

Los Angeles provides a good example of the several different developments that were part of twentieth-century barrioization. Between 1900 and 1910 Los Angeles experienced a rapid urbanization and a tremendous population growth (from 102,479 to 319,198 inhabitants; see Table 21). Chicanos remained residentially concentrated in the historic pueblo-plaza area in the city's central district. But as the city began to change, so did the barrio. Historians Pedro Castillo and Ricardo Romo separately have shown how the development of the industrial and commercial zones near the barrio, together with the expansion of the transportation, service, and construction industries in Los Angeles, had a triple effect on barrio development. First, it created greater population density in the old barrio, as thousands of new Mexican residents came in search of employment. Second, population growth resulted in the expansion of the barrio from the old plaza area. Lastly, this expansion initiated a geographic dispersion of residents outside the barrio, whereupon new enclaves of Mexicans in East Angeles appeared after 1910. The old plaza area in the barrio, despite the expansion taking place around it, remained the social, cultural, political, and economic focal point of the community. Here Mexicans could socialize and be near Mexican business establishments and entertainment. They could also reside in the many house courts, hotels, and boarding houses that were located near sources of employment.[2] (House courts were single- and two-

story tenement-style buildings constructed around a central
courtyard.)

The thousands of Mexican-born persons who migrated to the
Los Angeles barrio-plaza area during the early 1900s soon obscured the smaller, yet identifiable population of native-born
Mexicans, many of whom were descendants of the nineteenth-
century pobladores.[3] Through this process of migration and set-

Table 21 Total Chicano, white, and nonwhite populations in selected southern
California cities, 1900–1930.

City and year	Total population	Chicano population	Nonwhite population [a]			
Los Angeles						
1900	102,479	3,000–5,000 [b]	C =	2,111	J =	150
			N =	2,131	I =	5
1910	319,198	9,678–29,738	C =	1,954	J =	4,238
			N =	7,599	I =	81
1920	576,673	29,757–50,000	C =	2,062	J =	11,618
			N =	15,579	I =	189
1930	1,238,048	97,116–190,000	C =	3,009	J =	21,081
			N =	38,894	I =	616
San Diego						
1900	17,700	638–893	C =	292	J =	14
			N =	313	I =	4
1910	39,578	1,588–1,595	C =	348	J =	159
			N =	597	I =	8
1920	74,683	3,563–4,028	C,J,I =	1,131		
			N =	997		
1930	147,995	9,266–20,000	C =	509	J =	911
			N =	2,723	I =	139
San Bernardino						
1900	6,150	411–575	C =	55	J =	4
			N =	84	I =	23
1910	12,779	1,300–1,600	C,J,I =	164		
			N =	177		
1920	18,721	2,586–2,766	C,J,I =	145		
			N =	269		
1930	37,481	6,839–8,890	C =	93	J =	124
			N =	518	I =	30

Table 21   (*continued*)

City and year	Total population	Chicano population	Nonwhite population [a]			
Santa Barbara						
1900	6,587	1,108–1,551	C =	224	J =	6
			N =	19	I =	0
1910	11,659	1,644–2,221	C,J,I =	416		
			N =	77		
1920	19,441	2,558–2,888	C,J,I =	399		
			N =	186		
1930	33,613	3,279–5,157	C =	213	J =	296
			N =	525	I =	13

NOTE: The estimated ranges for the Chicano population were computed by using one or more of the following procedures: (1) the 1900 manuscript census enumeration for Spanish-surnamed persons, plus a 40-percent upward adjustment to account for underenumeration (a formula used by Martínez, "On the Size of the Chicano Population"); (2) the total Spanish surnames listed in the 1910 city directories, multiplied by a 2.25 factor (a formula used by the city directories to include many women and children omitted from directory enumerations); (3) the 1910–1930 city directory enumerations of male Spanish-surnamed heads of household, multiplied by a 5.3 factor (a formula used by the 1929 *California Mexican Fact-Finding Committee* to include the wife and average number of children, 4.3, in Mexican households; (4) the 1910–1920 census figures for foreign-born Mexicans and the 1930 census listing of "Mexicans," plus a 30 percent upward adjustment to account for underenumeration (a formula used to arrive at a more realistic total Mexican population—see Bogardus, *The Mexican in the United States*); (5) estimates of the Mexican population from writers during the period and from contemporary scholars.

[a] C = Chinese, N = Negro, J = Japanese, I = Indian.
[b] Estimates taken from Castillo, "Mexicans in Los Angeles, 1890–1920."

tlement, Los Angeles in 1910 was well on its way to becoming the largest urban concentration of Mexican people in the United States. The residential density caused by the influx of new Mexican residents added to the already overcrowded and expensive housing in the central barrio. In their need for less costly housing, many new Mexican residents vied with other members of the growing working class for scarce lodging in the central city house courts and the remaining open spaces in the downtown area. In the latter location inexpensive dwellings could be built or rented within easy walking distance to employment. As more and more Mexicans and European immigrants occupied the low-rent house courts and hastily built shanties, new Spanish-speaking enclaves began to form not far from the old barrio. Low wages and high rents, together with a steady in-migration of workers, naturally led to overcrowding, unsanitary conditions, and poorly constructed housing. In 1906 Jacob Riis, well-known chronicler of tenement slum conditions in New York City's immigrant ghettos, toured central Los Angeles and de-

An old adobe home of the Sonoratown barrio, increasingly hemmed in by construction of downtown commercial buildings, Los Angeles, 1908–1909.

clared that he had seen slum conditions "of greater area, but never any which were worse than those in Los Angeles."[4] The Los Angeles City Council and other Anglo citizens evidently were shocked to discover "congested slum conditions, as bad . . . if not as extensive, as anything to be found in New York City." They found it difficult to believe that "the land of sunshine has any dark spots."[5] In this slum area where Chicanos were "the poorest of all minorities," noted Castillo, they "composed most of the inhabitants of tent and shack colonies and occupied many of the poorest house courts, often referred to as 'Cholo courts'."[6]

In 1906 the city council created the Housing Commission of Los Angeles and directed it to report on slum conditions. The commission was charged with determining whether house courts were conforming to the city sanitation and construction building codes, and it was empowered to order the demolition of nonconforming structures. In its 1908 report the commission attributed the city's slums to the mild climate, which "permits a primitive style of tent life," the availability of open land near downtown for the rental of ground space, an "impoverished Mexican wage," and the importation of Mexican workers by the railroads. The commission felt that "the peculiar growth of the Cholo court . . . apparently was an outlet for the congested Mexican population." It also reported:

Here we found filth and squalor on every hand. Miserably constructed houses, made of scrap sheet iron, old bagging and sections of dry goods boxes, were huddled together without any attempt at proper construction or order . . . The more Mexicans to the lot, the more money for the owner.[7]

The commission subsequently reported in 1913 that the Mexican colony in the house court slums was being removed owing to the construction of a warehouse. What the commission failed to note was that the encroachment of the downtown commercial and business zone was displacing Mexicans from the large central plaza barrio as well. This encroachment/displacement phenomenon would determine the course of barrioization for Los Angeles Chicanos for the next two decades and more.[8]

The expansion of the business and financial districts, the construction of new civic center buildings, railways, and railroad yards displaced hundreds of Mexican families from the historic central barrio as well as from the remaining downtown shanties. Many moved to dwellings in other areas of the barrio that were already overcrowded. Profiteering landlords contributed to this overcrowding by converting single-family dwellings into multiple units. Other displaced families, those who could afford it, moved across the river to eastside suburbs. These East Los Angeles Chicanos were the forerunners of a movement that grew steadily after 1910.[9]

Two additional circumstances influenced this suburbanization and formation of new metropolitan barrios. First, Chicanos

"A typical Cholo court," as it was termed by the Housing Commission of Los Angeles, 1909.

were not allowed to live in certain areas of East Los Angeles because of racially restrictive covenants that forbade the sale or rental of real estate to Mexicans. Anglos evidently feared the possible Mexicanization of their neighborhoods. Secondly, the suburbanization of many Los Angeles industries in directions east and south of the downtown area acted as a magnet to attract Mexican workers. Once this pattern of Chicano suburbanization gained velocity, the eastside barrios rapidly became overcrowded also. Conditions, however, were far more varied than in the central plaza barrio across the Los Angeles River.[10]

By 1920 the demographic pattern of Chicanos in Los Angeles had been established. Forty percent of the population (the official census estimated 30,000 Mexicans in 1920, but a more realistic estimate would be 50,000) resided in the central plaza barrio, with the second major concentration in the areas across from the old barrio on the east side of the river. Other enclaves of Chicanos were scattered throughout the metropolitan area of Los Angeles, particularly in the areas south and east of downtown. Between 1920 and 1930 the overall population explosion in Los Angeles coincided with the rapid growth of the Mexican population; the 1930 census enumerated nearly 100,000 Mexicans, yet other estimates ranged from 190,000 to 250,000. Even though the incoming Mexicans continued to reside in the two primary areas of population concentration, the process of suburbanization of the eastside barrios became increasingly pronounced with each passing year. Throughout the period 1900–1930 Mexicans in Los Angeles continued geographically to be highly mobile (only 30 to 40 percent of Chicanos remained in the city during any given decade). Irrespective of this migration of large percentages of the Mexican population, the cultural, social, and literary (Spanish-language press) components of Mexican society were constant.[11] A Mexican city existed within the heart of Los Angeles.

A historian who analyzed the residential patterns of Chicanos in Los Angeles between 1910 and 1930 succinctly described the types of barrioization that had occurred. "The majority of the modern Mexican immigrants who settled in Los Angeles in the period 1910 to 1915," Ricardo Romo noted, "were first attracted to the central or core section of the city by the presence of an existing Mexican colonia near the old Plaza and by economic opportunities within the industrial zone of that district." He concluded:

By the mid 1920's the Plaza community in the central district underwent a rapid economic transformation which eventually eliminated much of the inexpensive housing there . . . The increased commercialization of the central district drove Mexican residents to older neighborhoods and low-priced residential developments east of the center of the city. Throughout the 1920's, East Los Angeles (Boyle Heights, Lincoln Park, and Belvedere) absorbed the displaced residents of the central district and attracted the increasing influx of new migrants. Moreover, the increase of new manufacturers in the eastside and southeast of Los Angeles gave Mexicans an added incentive to relocate.[12]

The Los Angeles Mexican community had undergone a dynamic process of growth and expansion. Although the Los Angeles type of barrioization may prove to be a special case—because of its complexity and size—it nevertheless was part of the urbanization of Chicano society taking place elsewhere in southern California as well as throughout the United States.

In comparison to the Los Angeles metropolis, other cities in the region experienced more modest, though still significant, growth. Barrioization in these communities, less complex than in Los Angeles, still oftentimes resembled developments in the larger city. The San Bernardino barrio, for example, originated as a railroad labor colony. Although a small population of Spanish-surnamed persons (112) was residing in San Bernardino in 1880, an identifiable barrio did not form until the 1890s.[13] The city's barrio was the product of a Mexican colony established on the Santa Fe Railroad Company maintenance yards. Throughout the last decade of the nineteenth century and the first decade of the twentieth century, the Santa Fe transported hundreds of Mexican individuals and families to work in its San Bernardino yards. Other local foreign-born and native-born persons joined the colony as employment in the railroad yards expanded. By 1900 the small but growing railroad company barrio, referred to by Anglos as Cholo Hollow, contained over half of the city's Spanish-surnamed population. (The 1900 census enumerated 411 persons, 60 percent of whom were born in Mexico.[14]) In 1909, however, Santa Fe officials decided to relocate the entire colony to an area less conspicuous, yet adjacent to the company yards just outside the city limits. The local newspaper reported the plans to move the barrio:

The present location of the Cholo quarters[,] in the wye at the west end of the yards, is in full view of passengers on all trains leaving and arriving on not only the line to and from L.A. but Orange as well, and in consequence is passed by every train through this city. For years the camp has been an eyesore, marring the entrance to the city.[15]

Although the newspaper reported that Anglos living in the proposed new site were "uprising against the little brown toilers" and were "preparing to give the newcomers a hot reception"— one resident claimed he would "use a shotgun on these aliens if necessary"—the relocation proceeded. Santa Fe officials justified the relcation of Mexicans by claiming that "in their present locations . . . they distract from the surroundings at the entrance of the city."[16]

Between 1900 and 1910 the San Bernardino "Westside" barrio, as it came to be known, grew significantly as more and more workers were imported to meet the railroad's needs. It was not uncommon for two families of railroad section hands to share a one-room dwelling where, according to a local reporter, they could be "packed together like sardines as is the custom among peons."[17] By 1910, 67 percent of all Mexican households (approximately 800 to 1,000 people) were concentrated in the barrio. There was also indication of a small colony of workers forming near the Southern Pacific Railroad yards on the opposite end of town.[18] This trend toward greater concentration in the larger Westside barrio and in the smaller Meadowbrook barrio continued throughout the period; during the 1920s the two barrios contained at least 60 to 70 percent of all Spanish-surnamed families, and by 1928, 70 to 75 percent. The barrio residents (approximately 7,000 in 1930) experienced residential and school segregation, municipal neglect, and the poverty characteristic of the Chicano working class elsewhere in south-

A Mexican enclave located on city land near the old plaza barrio in Los Angeles, circa 1910.

ern California. They endured these disadvantages, however, and helped preserve the Mexican heritage that had been founded in the San Bernardino Valley by the nineteenth-century pobladores of San Salvador, some of whom now lived in San Bernardino.[19]

The barrioization in twentieth-century San Diego differed in some ways from the barrio development in San Bernardino and Los Angeles. "New" San Diego during the early twentieth century experienced significant population growth, from 18,000 people in 1900 to 40,000 by 1910. Within this expanding urban locale, characterized by one historian as "a middle class, homogeneous, commercial city with an overwhelmingly Anglo-Saxon population," two pockets of Mexican population existed. One was the Old Town pueblo, which had been isolated from New Town since the late 1860s. Here the small population stagnated further throughout the early twentieth century. The Old Towners nonetheless were able to maintain some semblance of identity among the increasing number of tourists who visited the historic pueblo. The second pocket of Mexican population, the more important in the barrioization process, was located in New San Diego, where as early as 1890 several Mexicans had located themselves in the downtown waterfront area.[20]

Just as Jacob Riis and the housing commission spotlighted slum conditions in early twentieth-century Los Angeles, the College Women's Club of San Diego in 1914 focused attention on conditions in their city. They reported that between 3,000 and 4,000 native-born and foreign-born Mexicans were living, together with some blacks and Anglos, in "distinctly slum conditions" along the downtown waterfront.

About them center the most definite problems in the social life of the community, such as overcrowding and unsanitary home conditions . . . It is difficult for poor Mexicans to secure cheap rents in San Diego, consequently they crowd themselves, several families into some old hovel or unsanitary shack. Some of these latter are presented to the view of the tourist on arriving.[21]

At the time of this survey the downtown barrio was in an early stage of transition. For over two decades Mexicans had entered this low-rent area to be near employment opportunities. But by 1910 the rising cost of rent, the demolition of condemned buildings, and the expansion of waterfront industries and business establishments had initiated a steady displacement of Mexicans and blacks. As in Los Angeles, nonwhite ethnic groups were limited by racially restrictive covenants to segregated areas in the city. In San Diego the area just southeast of downtown became the principal home of Mexicans and blacks. As early as 1914 approximately 25 percent of the Mexican population resided in this district "where crowding in cottages, shacks, and tenements," according to the social survey, was "at its worst."[22]

The Mexican migration into southeast San Diego increased dramatically after World War I and was nearly complete by the 1920s. Anglo residents in the area, originally known as Logan Heights, moved to newer subdivisions in the city and left the neighborhood to Mexicans and a small group of blacks. The addition of thousands of new residents into the Logan Heights barrio aggravated the existing overcrowded conditions as these workers helped fill labor needs in the nearby factories, fish canneries, laundries, lumberyards, and the construction industry in general. By the late 1920s an estimated 20,000 Mexicans were living in Logan Heights, the second largest such population concentration in southern California. There, according to a former Mexicano resident of the area, they were confined to a segregated barrio in "the midst of the cruelest kind of poverty."[23] A historian who studied the early Mexican community in the Logan Heights barrio confirmed this assessment:

The substandard conditions of the San Diego Mexican community, as reflected by their occupational status, living environment, and health problems, were magnified by their segregation. Separate schools, churches, and businesses existed for the Mexican community.[24]

San Diego's barrioization thus was similar to that which occurred in Santa Barbara with the development of a second, larger barrio that was geographically separated from the old pueblo barrio.

The Chicano Working Class

The dominant characteristics of the Chicano working class—an unskilled/semiskilled, impoverished group of men, women, and children at the bottom of the economic structure—had been firmly established during the last quarter of the nineteenth century throughout southern California. Native-born and foreign-born Mexicans in the first decades of the following century inherited the status of that earlier generation of Chicano workers who had been the first group of Mexican people incorporated into the new capitalist labor market. The subordinate position of Mexican workers was reinforced in the twentieth century by common use of the contract labor system, wage differentials determined by race and sex, labor conflict, and occupational immobility.

A report published in 1930 by California Governor C. C. Young's Mexican Fact-Finding Committee accurately profiled the status of the Chicano working class. The report verified that Mexicans were still heavily concentrated as laborers in the construction, service, transportation, and agriculture-related industries; it also indicated that Mexican workers could be found in every major sector of the economy, employed in a wide range of predominantly unskilled and semiskilled manual occupations. These new jobs had been created during the early twentieth century as industrialization and rapid urban expansion took place in southern California.[25]

The Los Angeles labor market for Chicanos during this thirty-year period was a microcosm of Chicano employment patterns in other cities throughout California. The tremendous population growth in the city had occurred along with dramatic economic growth. The expansion of nearly every major economic sector and the establishment of new manufacturing interests created the need for large pools of unskilled workers. The ever stronger tide of Mexican immigration, especially after 1910, coincided with the new demands for labor. In the railroad and newer electric railway system, in the construction and building supply industries, in the public works and utilities industries, and in the many service industries, Mexican labor predominated. After World War I, Los Angeles experienced another population, commercial, and industrial boom. As a result, Mexican workers were attracted by the rubber, steel, meat packing, food canning, and auto industries. The Chicana work force was employed in the downtown textile industries, in the wholesale and retail trade establishments, as well as in the laundries, domestic services, bakeries, and canneries. Throughout the period Mexican men and women constituted one of the primary sources of manual and factory labor in Los Angeles as they remained by far the largest ethnic and foreign-born group in the city. In fact, throughout California Mexicans constituted between 25 and 66 percent of the work force in most of the industries mentioned.[26]

Mexicans did not, however, benefit from their participation in the labor market as the masses of Chicanos remained an underpaid, racially segregated, low blue-collar, working-class group with very little hope for future improvement. "In Los Angeles and, indeed, in many communities," observed a journalist in 1929, "it is the Mexican [sic] who do the common

Downtown Los Angeles in the late 1920s, looking northeastward. Courtesy of Historical Collections, Security Pacific National Bank.

labor. In fact," he concluded, "we have imported them for that very purpose."[27] Another Los Angeles writer added that "all other races meet the Mexican with an attitude of contempt and scorn and they are generally regarded as the most degraded race in the city."[28] These reflections on the Chicano working class by members of the dominant society in Los Angeles extended beyond the limits of that particular city. In San Diego, Santa Barbara, and San Bernardino Chicanos faced similar experiences as they contributed their labor to the development of those cities too, but received little more than subsistence wages in return.

In many respects the Chicano working class in San Diego resembled the one in Los Angeles. Of course, San Diego was a much smaller city and never gained distinction as an industrial, manufacturing center. Yet Chicanos in San Diego were employed in the same sectors of the economy. They formed the largest group in the construction industry, where they accounted for approximately 90 percent of road and street laborers during the 1920s. They also formed large percentages of the laboring population in the lumberyards, the fish canneries, the laundries (principally Chicanas), the small factories, the utility companies, and the railway-railroad section gangs.[29] Chicanos were plagued with persistent unemployment and, according to a trade union spokesperson, were paid "wages that cannot possibly guarantee decent living." Not surprisingly, they constituted (according to a 1930 economic survey of Mexicans in San Diego) one of the poorest working-class groups in the United States.[30]

In Santa Barbara, Chicanos were limited to many of the same types of work in the same industries as in San Diego and Los Angeles. Unlike the situation in Santa Barbara and the other southern California cities, the Chicano work force of San Bernardino remained concentrated in railroad employment. San Bernardino's economy throughout the early twentieth century was dependent upon the Santa Fe Railroad and its large maintenance yards and shops. In the first two decades, for example, 60 to 80 percent of all Mexican workers were employed by the railroad, approximately 90 percent of whom were low blue-collar workers. Only after 1920, with increased agricultural production in the valley and diversification of the local economy, did Chicanos begin to leave the railroad for other work.[31]

Contract Labor, Racial Wage Differentials, and Labor Conflict   Two odious forms of exploitation, contract labor and racial wage differentials, added to the negative factors affecting Mexican workers. Contracting of Mexican workers by labor recruiters, employment agencies, and large corporate interests was commonplace in every city and agricultural area of southern California. Although the contract system provided employment for workers, it also kept thousands of Mexican employees in neocolonial-like servitude. In Los Angeles, for example, between the 1890s and the 1920s thousands of Mexican workers were recruited by the transportation and general construction

Mexican section-gang workers on the urban electric railway system in Los Angeles, circa 1903. Reproduced by permission of the Huntington Library, San Marino, California.

industries. Many such workers suffered under a system approximating debt peonage as from the meager employee wage employers extracted rent for company housing, provisions purchased (at highly inflated prices) from the company store, and other extra fees. "While contract labor exists," concluded the Los Angeles housing commission after investigating housing conditions of contracted workers, "decent living will be practically impossible for such workers without radical changes . . . The Mexican is condemned to a one-room shack," and for "temporary habitation old freighters and cattle cars are often used by railroad companies for the contract laborers and their families."[32] The domination and exploitation of contracted Mexican railroad workers included racial residential segregation—such as the removal and relocation of the Mexican railroad-worker colony in San Bernardino—and occupational segregation as well as abuses by labor recruiters or "coyotes." Contract labor was not limited to railroad work; other industries employing large numbers of Mexicans (such as the agricultural and construction industries) used this system for recruitment and retention of a large labor force.[33]

Another common practice of the contract labor system, frequently used for noncontract labor as well, was the establishment by employers of a Mexican wage differential. The creation of one wage rate for Anglo labor and a lower rate for Chicano workers apparently originated in the nineteenth century. The practice was common throughout southern California during the first third of the twentieth century. Wage differentials often ranged 20 to 50 percent less per day for Mexican workers performing the same jobs as other workers. Both the contract labor system and the establishment of wage differentials contributed to keeping Mexican workers poor and to the reinforcement of racial and class divisions in the labor market.[34]

Such exploitative labor practices were fought by many Chicano workers. Throughout the period 1900–1930 and after, workers' protests took the form of labor conflict or strikes. Virtually every industry in which Mexican workers were employed witnessed some form of labor conflict. Strikes against railroad and railway companies, agribusiness concerns, and the con-

struction, food canning, and packing industries usually pitted
Chicanos (and sometimes other workers) against large capitalist
interests. Labor conflict in southern California was part of a
larger trend occurring throughout the southwestern United
States wherever Chicanos were employed. However, Chicano
organizations were usually suppressed by economic reprisals
(firings or strike breakings), violence, deportation, and incarcer-
ation.[35]

When Chicano workers went on strike, they did so without
the aid of established labor unions like the American Federation
of Labor. Throughout the period unionization efforts of the national labor unions continued to shun unskilled labor. In some
cases even skilled Mexican workers were not permitted to join
local union chapters. The infrequent attempts by locals to organize Mexican unskilled workers during the period following
World War I were usually half-hearted efforts made only to establish better relations with labor unions in Mexico. The few
Mexicans in labor unions in southern California often were restricted to segregated locals of unskilled workers. In fact, when
the economy of southern California and the United States in
general began to show signs of stagnation and depression, local
labor unions (echoing the policy of the national union) were
among the first to condemn Mexican workers as a chief source
of the economic problems. A historian who studied the San
Diego Labor Council (AFL locals) accurately revealed the status
of Chicano workers within the labor union movement:

All these efforts [to organize Mexican workers] were short-lived and
had limited success due to the weaknesses and the racism that permeated the Labor Council . . . The Labor Council's campaign of 1926
revealed its constant vacillation between a racist position of blaming
Mexicans for all the problems faced by working people in San Diego
and a broader class-based interest in organizing all workers, regardless
of race, to fight the employer.[36]

Throughout the period 1900 to 1930 the Chicano working class
remained, for the most part, outside the sphere of organized
labor and therefore was particularly vulnerable to exploitation
by employers.

Occupational Structure, 1910–1930   Though the size of the Chicano working class expanded significantly in the twentieth century as a result of mass Mexican immigaration, there was little upward movement. Throughout the period from 1900 to 1930 Chicano men, women, and children continued to be locked into the bottom of the socioeconomic ladder.

In comparing the occupational structure of Spanish-surnamed male heads of household in southern California cities between 1900 and 1930, given in Tables 14 and 22, it is evident that the major pattern of Chicano employment was established by the turn of the century. In each decade thereafter there was no significant change in the vertical hierarchy of occupations. The only differences were in the total number of Mexican workers and the percentages of unknown occupations.[37] Only slight variations occur in each occupational level throughout the period, such as the small increase in the proprietorial and low white-collar occupations by 1910 (a product of Mexican immigration, the growth of the barrios, and the establishment of Mexican-owned businesses) and the small increase in the percentages of semiskilled, low blue-collar workers. However, the dominant patterns are unmistakable: throughout the period the great majority of Spanish-surnamed persons were low blue-collar, manual workers. Between 1910 and 1930, for example, the total percentage of Mexican male heads of household who were low blue-collar workers (primarily unskilled laborers) ranged from 68 to 73 percent in San Diego, from 74 to 81 percent in San Bernardino, from 65 to 69 percent in Santa Barbara, and a constant 79 percent (for 1910 and 1920) in Los Angeles. The percentage of Mexicans in high blue-collar, skilled positions remained quite low throughout the period, ranging between 4 percent (San Bernardino in 1928) and 12 percent (Santa Barbara in 1910 and Los Angeles in 1920). The combined percentages of Mexican workers in low white-collar and high white-collar occupations ranged between 5 percent (San Bernardino in 1920) and 12 percent (San Diego in 1910).[38]

Spanish-surnamed workers were not overrepresented in the low blue-collar occupations simply because unskilled and semi-skilled Mexican immigrants had become a majority of the

Table 22 Occupational structure for Spanish-surnamed male heads of household,[a] southern California, 1910–1930 (in percent).

Occupation	San Diego			San Bernardino			Santa Barbara			Los Angeles		
	1910	1920	1930	1910	1920	1928	1910	1920	1930	1910	1920	1930
High white-collar												
Professional	2	2	2	1	1	0	1	1	0	1	1	NA
Proprietorial	3	5	3	3	2	2	5	3	3	5	5	NA
Low white-collar												
Sales/clerical/semiprofessional	7	4	5	4	2	4	4	6	6	NA	NA	NA
High blue-collar												
Skilled	8	6	10	7	6	4	12	9	9	11	12	NA
Low blue-collar												
Semiskilled	22	10	14	11	10	4	16	17	13	7	6	NA
Unskilled	51	58	54	68	64	77	49	51	56	72	73	NA
Unknown or unlisted	7	14	12	6	15	8	13	12	13	3	3	NA
Number in sample	301	380	1,045	268	261	570	419	545	973	1,826	5,232	NA

SOURCES: San Diego city and county directories (1910, 1920, 1930); San Bernardino city directories (1910–1911, 1920, 1930); San Bernardino and Colton city directory (1928); Santa Barbara city and county directory (1909–1910); Santa Barbara city directories (1920, 1929–1930). The figures for Los Angeles are from Pedro Castillo, "Mexicans in Los Angeles, 1890–1920"; his study does not provide information on occupations for 1930.

[a] 100 percent of head-of-household population for 1910; 100 percent of head-of-household population for Santa Barbara, 1920 and 1930; 50-percent samples for San Bernardino and San Diego, 1920 and 1928/1930.

Chicano working class during the early twentieth century. Regardless of nativity, and regardless of whether one was a second-generation descendant of Mexican-born parents or a fifth-generation descendant of one of the earliest Mexican settlers in California, the likelihood of upward occupational mobility was almost nil. Throughout this period the vast majority of Chicano low blue-collar workers were unable to achieve skilled or higher occupational status.

Historian Richardo Romo discovered significant differences when comparing his occupational mobility study of Mexicans in Los Angeles between 1918 and 1928 to Stephan Thernstrom's study of other members of the working class in Los Angeles and in Boston for the same period (*The Other Bostonians*). White working-class populations in those two cities realized significant upward gains from low blue-collar to high blue-collar to white-collar occupations. "Mexicans in Los Angeles during the 1920's, however," concludes Romo, "encountered a far more 'closed' society; their movements from manual to non-manual employment categories were almost non-existent." Besides the fact that unskilled workers experienced negligible upward mobility, "Mexican skilled workers," Romo states, "suffered an unusual downward mobility compared to white workers in both Boston and Los Angeles."[39] Similarly, in Santa Barbara mobility from low blue-collar to high blue-collar or low white-collar positions for Mexicans was a rarity. The only mobility was within the low blue-collar unskilled and semiskilled occupations. However, between any two decades male heads of household experienced downward mobility as frequently as they experienced upward mobility within these low blue-collar occupations. The net effect was no real overall group mobility. In addition, in both Los Angeles and Santa Barbara native-born whites and even European immigrants (such as the Italians in the latter city) had a far more equal distribution in each occupational level than did Mexicans of the second, third, or later generations. Chicano male heads of household were cemented into the lowest levels of the occupational structure and could not expect to achieve a higher status for themselves or for their children.[40]

The occupational structure of female Spanish-surnamed heads

Adobe tile makers at the Angulo Tile Works, Santa Barbara, about 1920. This traditional occupation was carried on into the twentieth century. Courtesy of Alfred Domínguez.

of household and other employed Chicanas between 1900 and 1930 indicates that they too experienced the racial and class discrimination that affected their male counterparts. But women encountered a third form of discrimination in the labor market, sexism. Divisions of labor, wage differentials, restricted types of employment, and unequal treatment because they were women were part of the sexist practices carried on by employers.

Since their introduction as wage earners during the late nineteenth century, Chicanas had participated in the labor market in increasing numbers with each passing decade. In San Diego and Santa Barbara the large majority of Chicanas performed semiskilled and unskilled manual labor. Although many were employed full-time, a large percentage of Mexican women worked part-time or seasonally. For example, a 1930 occupational survey of 100 Mexican family households in San Diego indicated that 44 percent of the women worked in part-time and seasonal jobs; only one had a full-time occupation. Those who were part-time or seasonally employed workers were seldom listed in the city directories and, as a result, the total number of female Spanish-surnamed workers reported is misleading. Between 1900 and 1930 the percentage of manual semiskilled and unskilled Chicano workers ranged from 59 to 87 percent in San Diego and from 65 to 74 percent in Santa Barbara (Table 23).[41]

The vast majority of Chicanas were restricted to four general types of employment: (1) in the domestic services (maids, hotel laundresses, cooks); (2) in the cannery and packing houses (fish canners, food-processing-plant workers, fruit packers); (3) in the textile industry (factory operatives, seamstresses); and (4) in the agricultural industry (harvesters, pickers). By 1910 the dramatic increase in the Mexican population in every southern California city had had a significant effect on the Chicana occupational structure. It gave rise to a small Mexican merchant group that operated barrio retail shops. In addition, Anglo proprietors began to realize the potential profit to be had by attracting a Spanish-speaking clientele. Both of these developments opened the opportunity for Mexican women to find employement as clerks and salespeople in the barrio stores, and as bilingual clerks in Anglo-owned stores that catered to Spanish-speaking customers. As a result, between 1910 and 1930 from 16 to 30 percent of the Chicana work force in San Diego and from 15 to 29 percent in Santa Barbara were employed (full-time) in sales/clerical occupations. An unusual 60 percent of San Bernardino's female Spanish-surnamed workers were employed in these types of occupations, but this development was not evident until 1928. However, throughout the region the Chicana pattern of semiskilled and unskilled employment, much like that of the Chicano, was the dominant one. The female's dual role as mother and wage earner persisted and was reinforced in the twentieth century.

The female and male Spanish-surname occupational structures, when compared to the non-Spanish-surname occupational structure, dramatically reflect the class and racial differentiation between the two populations (see Table 24). Throughout the first third of the twentieth century, the non-Spanish-surname occupational structure remained basically unaltered with top-heavy distribution in the high blue-collar and low and high white-collar occupations. The percentages of Spanish-surnamed

Table 23 Occupational structure for total employed Spanish-surnamed female heads of household and adult residents,[a] southern California, 1900–1930 (in percent).

	San Diego				Santa Barbara				San Bernardino
Occupation	1900	1910	1920	1930	1900[a]	1910	1920	1930	1928
Professional	0	0	5	0	2	0	3	3	6
Proprietorial	1	3	5	2	1	0	0	2	6
Sales/clerical/ semiprofessional	1	20	16	30	1	15	29	29	60
Skilled	10	8	5	2	1	11	0	1	0
Semiskilled (manual)	7	10	8	9	31	7	31	11	3
Unskilled	80	49	61	56	36	67	37	54	24
Unknown or unlisted	0	10	0	1	11	0	0	0	0
Number in population	72	39	125	202	95	54	56	146	62

SOURCES: Federal manuscript census schedules, 1900; San Diego city and county directories (1910, 1920, 1930); San Bernardino and Colton city directory (1928); Santa Barbara city and county directory (1909–1910); Santa Barbara city directories (1920, 1929–1930). Part-time women workers were seldom enumerated in city directories; a large percentage of the Chicana work force was employed only part-time. Occupations for Chicanas in San Bernardino for the period 1900–1920 are not provided because either the employed Spanish-surnamed female population was negligible prior to 1930 or women's occupations were not enumerated in the 1900 census and city directories (fewer than 15 women were listed before 1930).

[a] 18 percent unemployed, according to 1900 manuscript census.

Cattle cars and freight cars used by the Southern Pacific Railroad to house Mexican workers and their families, Los Angeles, 1909.

persons in the low and high white-collar occupations between 1910 and 1930 ranged from 5 to 12 percent, whereas the percentages for the non-Spanish-surname work force in these same occupations ranged from a low of 36 percent (San Bernardino in 1910) to a high of 47 percent (San Diego in 1910). To illustrate another major structural difference between the two groups, during the same period low blue-collar jobs accounted for between 65 and 81 percent of the Chicano work force, but only for between 19 and 30 percent for non-Spanish-surnamed persons.[42] There were, however, two notable changes that affected the non-Spanish-surname occupational structure between 1900 and 1930 besides the large increase in the total number of workers in each successive decade. First, there was a general increase in the percentages of low white-collar workers in San Diego, Santa Barbara, and San Bernardino by 1910 (compare Tables 14 and 24). This change reflected the expanding urban economy, which necessitated larger numbers of salespeople, clerks, and semiprofessionals.[43] Second, there was a decrease in the number of non-Spanish-surnamed unskilled, low blue-collar workers, a change most likely attributable to the increasing numbers of Mexican workers who filled this occupational level.

Table 24 Occupational structure for non-Spanish-surnamed male heads of household, southern California, 1910–1930 (in percent).

Occupation	San Diego[a]			San Bernardino[b]			Santa Barbara[c]		
	1910	1920	1930	1910	1920	1928	1910	1920	1930
High white-collar									
Professional	8	7	4	4	4	3	4	5	7
Proprietorial	14	13	8	12	12	12	12	13	9
Low white-collar									
Sales/clerical/ semiprofessional	25	26	26	20	24	28	22	22	27
High blue-collar									
Skilled	19	19	16	27	27	26	21	23	22
Low blue-collar									
Semiskilled	14	15	21	17	19	13	19	15	13
Unskilled	5	7	9	7	5	7	10	9	11
Unknown or unlisted	14	13	16	12	9	10	12	12	11
Number in sample	1,318	3,001	4,370	867	885	782	419	794	1,493

SOURCES: San Diego city and county directories (1910, 1920, 1930); San Bernardino city directories (1910–1911, 1920); San Bernardino and Colton city directory (1928); Santa Barbara city and county directory (1909–1910); Santa Barbara city directories (1920, 1929–1930).

[a]20-percent sample of head-of-household population for 1910 and 1920; 10-percent sample for 1930 (excluding Chinese and Japanese-surnamed persons).

[b]20-percent sample of head-of-household population for 1910 and 1920; 10-percent sample for 1928 (excluding Chinese and Japanese-surnamed persons).

[c]20-percent sample of head-of-household population for 1910, 1920, and 1930 (excluding Chinese, Japanese, and Italian-surnamed persons).

Throughout the first third of the twentieth century Chicanos remained in occupational levels that reinforced their subordinate social and political status in the dominant society. Their concentration in the low blue-collar occupations, their occupational immobility, their exploitation by large capitalist interests and by other employers, their isolation from the established labor unions, and the suppression of their own organized labor activities were all part of the ongoing structure of subordination in which the Chicano working class lived.

The End of an Era

The massive migration from Mexico during the first three decades of the twentieth century reinforced the Mexican population density in the southern sections of California. By 1930 nearly 60 percent of all Mexicans in the state were located in the counties of Los Angeles, San Diego, Santa Barbara, and San Bernardino; nearly a third of the total Mexican population resided in the four cities selected for this study.[44] The Anglo response to the growing Mexican population in the cities of southern California occurred in several stages: from unconcern on the part of the general public, to approval by employers benefiting from Mexican labor, to the establishment of assimilation programs, to condemnation of Chicanos, and, finally, to deportation. These reactions reflected the ambivalent racial attitudes of many Anglos toward Mexicans. When their labor was needed, their social status was ignored; when their labor was no longer needed, they constituted a societal problem.

Prior to 1920 the dominant society focused little attention on the Mexican communities of southern California.[45] Only after the public began questioning the myth that Mexicans were here temporarily and would eventually return to Mexico did Anglos shift their focus to the "Mexican problem." Most of the early attention after World War I took the form of efforts to Americanize the Mexicans. Through Protestant missionary efforts and muncipal and charitable institutional programs, Mexicans became a favorite target for assimilationists: they were expected to shed their cultural distinctiveness and adopt Anglo standards (household and family care practices, "American" cooking, hygiene). These Americanization programs were generally unsuccessful, since they failed to deal with the hard economic and social realities faced by most Chicanos. The activities of San Diego's Neighborhood House in the Logan Heights barrio typified such efforts:

The Neighborhood House was one of the few institutions that responded to the plight of the Mexican community, yet its response to the Mexicans echoed the eagerness of San Diegans who remained aloof from the problems of the Mexicans to Americanize their foreign population . . . The efforts of the staff to shape the Mexican into the Ameri-

Students at the Vail Street School, Los Angeles, circa 1910. This was a school for children of Mexican families who worked at Simons Brick Company and who lived on the company grounds. Courtesy of Albert and Lydia Caballero.

can mold did not help the Mexican population. Twenty-five years of work in the Mexican community by the Neighborhood House had not resulted in any improvement in the status or condition of the Mexican.[46]

The outcome was similar for Americanization efforts in Los Angeles, Santa Barbara, and San Bernardino.[47]

The focus on the so-called Mexican problem changed by the mid-1920s because of the increasing economic woes of society as a whole. No longer was it simply a matter of the unassimilable and un-Americanized Mexicans, but of the well-being of the entire society. Increasingly throughout the 1920s Mexicans everywhere were identified as a welfare problem (a burden on welfare agencies) and a labor problem (a large, cheap labor source taking jobs away from Americans). By the second half of the decade, labor unions, community and municpal welfare agencies, chambers of commerce, local politicans, and others were joining the movement to restrict unlimited Mexican immigration.[48] As the Great Depression drew near, the destiny of hundreds of thousands of people was decided by federal and local anti-Mexican forces who sought to alleviate the problem. A federally sponsored drive to repatriate Mexicans, supported at the local level by county and city governments as well as by public welfare agencies, resulted by the early 1930s in the deportation from southern California cities of tens of thousands of Mexicans and their native-born sons and daughters. This traumatic blow to the barrios and significant reduction in the Chicano population in every community signaled the end of an era for Chicanos in southern California.[49]

Conclusion

The socioeconomic and political status of Chicanos in southern California at the beginning of the Great Depression was the product of a process that had begun at least eighty years earlier. Developments in the region during the second half of the nineteenth century determined the position that Mexicans would thereafter occupy in southern California society. Victims of the American conquest of their native land, the Mexicans of southern California witnessed the steady decline of their pueblos during the decades following the Mexican War. The destruction of the pastoral economy during the 1860s and 1870s and the establishment of a new economic order ushered in a period of occupational dislocation of Mexican workers. Their subsequent incorporation and proletarianization within the new capitalist labor market set a pattern that later generations of Chicanos could not break. The nineteenth-century Chicanos of southern California also witnessed the usurpation of their political and institutional power. Politically powerless and economically impoverished, Mexicans increasingly became residentially segregated in their original pueblo settlements as American cities expanded about them.

The racial and class subordination of Chicanos in the nineteenth century shaped the major experiences of Mexicans during the first third of the twentieth century. However, the tens of thousands of people who migrated north from Mexico in the early 1900s created dramatic changes within the existing Chicano communities and within the dominant society. The addition of these new Mexican residents resulted in the expansion of the old pueblo barrios and the formation of newer barrios. These people provided the labor necessary for the growth and profit of the local and regional economies. But their participation was limited for the most part to menial unskilled/semi-skilled jobs in which there was little hope for upward mobility. These exploited Mexican workers, who were considered an expendable labor force, were deported by the thousands during the economic depression of the 1930s.

While the period 1848–1930 is crucial for explaining the present status of Mexicans in southern California, it is only part of the history of a national ethnic minority group in the United States. To be sure, there are several historical patterns—such as the expropriation of Mexican-owned land, the loss of political power, racial and labor conflict, and the creation of new barrios—which were as evident in other parts of the United States as they were in southern California during the period.[50] What remains to be examined specifically is whether the processes of barrioization, Americanization, proletarianization, and racial-class stratification developed similarly in regions outside southern California. Fortunately, more and more scholars are focusing on new, intriguing questions in their research on Chicano history within the larger framework of U.S. history.[51] The challenging and difficult task of writing comparative Chicano urban history from a national as well as from a comparative ethnic-group perspective lies ahead. Only then will we be able to make specific, concrete comparisons between Chicanos and other groups in cities throughout the United States.[52] It is imperative that research into the Chicanos' past continue, for it is only from a basis of knowledge that we shall be able to understand the experience of Chicanos as an economically and politically disadvantaged ethnic group in the dominant, ever changing society. The roots of this Chicano experience can only be illuminated by understanding the history of those generations of Mexican people who lived through the profound change from Mexican pueblos to American barrios.

Appendixes

Glossary

Notes

Bibliography

Index

A Note on Sources and Methodologies

Appendix 1.

The primary and secondary printed materials utilized in this study are of seven general types: (1) local histories of southern California communities, including nineteenth-century "boom literature" as well as scholarly studies that focus on different topics of southern California history; (2) newspapers, in both English and Spanish, and other periodicals; (3) memoirs, diaries, and other personal accounts of Mexicans and Anglos; (4) doctoral dissertations, master's theses, and unpublished papers; (5) documents collected from oral history interviewees and from the archives of several county and city government agencies, university special collections libraries, and local historical society libraries; (6) oral history interviews; and (7) quantitative data from the United States census population reports for the period 1860 to 1930, federal manuscript census schedules for 1860 to 1900, and city directories for 1910 to 1930. This appendix focuses on the use and analysis of those sources that warrant further discussion, particularly the federal manuscript censuses, city directories, and oral history interviews.

Federal Manuscript Census Schedules for 1860, 1870, 1880, and 1900

The 1860 and 1870 schedules provided information on name, occupation, age, sex, color or race, value of real and personal property, and place of birth of the head of household and all household residents. Information on school attendance and literacy was also provided, but was not consistently recorded by enumerators. The 1880 schedules did not contain data on wealth, but included information on marital status, unemployment, and nativity of the respondents' parents. The 1900 census included, in addition to the 1880 information, data on home ownership and year of immigration of foreign-born persons.[1]

The breakdown of population for the occupational analyses was divided among Spanish-surnamed and non-Spanish-surnamed individuals. For all four census enumerations the Spanish-surname population was further differentiated by nativity (those born in California, Mexico, or elsewhere). American Indians with Spanish surnames were not included in the population analyses. The male heads of household constituted the vast majority of individuals for the occupational analyses—though in a few cases, where single adult employed males were listed as boarders or living with a family of different surname, these individuals were included. The analyses for Spanish surnames included all male heads of household and employed females after 1880. The same method was employed for selecting non-Spanish-surnamed persons. However, after 1880, samples of the non-Spanish-surnamed male heads of household were used instead of the entire population. Chinese, Indians, and the small number of blacks were excluded from the analyses of non-Spanish-surnamed individuals.

City Directories

The city directories provide an important data base for many of this study's findings on occupation and residence. The city directory house-to-house listings of residents in a given community were compiled almost every year in southern California cities during the twentieth century; few exist for the nineteenth century. The various city directories contain information on the name of heads of household, adult household residents, occupation, address, and ofttimes the name of the head of household's spouse (also widows and widowers). In addition, some of the

1920 and 1930 city directories included information on home ownership.

For the occupational analyses the following city directories were used: 1909–1910, 1920, 1928 (San Bernardino), and 1929–1930. These were selected as being the ones corresponding most closely to the decade intervals from 1900 to 1930. The procedure used for the selection of individuals in the occupational analyses of the manuscript census schedules was applied also to the city directories. However, Spanish-surnamed working women were also included for the period 1910 to 1930. The occupational analyses for Chicanas included women heads of household as well as all other women who listed an occupation (residents within nuclear families, live-in maids, and boarders).

The same selection procedures applied to the occupational analyses for non-Spanish-surnamed individuals, with the exception that occupations for women were excluded. The non-Spanish-surname analyses did not include individuals with Japanese or Chinese surnames; the occupations for Italians in Santa Barbara were analyzed separately for the period 1900 to 1930 (see Table 20). Chinese, Japanese, and Italian surnames, together with their ethnic forenames, were easily distinguishable from other non-Spanish surnames. Although a few ethnic surnames were somewhat ambiguous (similar Italian and Spanish names, for instance), their number was so small that they did not present a problem in selection procedures and they could not have distorted the findings. The surnames for blacks, however, could not be distinguished from other non-Spanish surnames in the city directories used for this study (Los Angeles and San Diego were the only cities that had a sizable black population by 1930; see Table 21). Twenty-percent samples for the non-Spanish-surname populations were used for most of the twentieth century; 10-percent samples, however, were used for the non-Spanish-surname populations in San Bernardino and San Diego in 1928/1930.

The city directories were an indispensable source for analysis of occupation, residence, and certain ethnic groups within southern California's work force from 1910 to 1930. In fact, there is no other source that offers a profile over time of the occupational structure and demographic patterns of the cities in the region. While the city directories offer valuable data for the researcher, one must be aware of their deficiencies. Omission of Chicanos and vagueness of occupational designation are two of the problems. Owing to Chicano migratory patterns of employment, language and cultural barriers, and segregated residential living, the city directory enumerators, like the U.S. census takers, no doubt omitted many Chicano residents from the directory lists. Stephan Thernstrom, in *The Other Bostonians*, has pointed to these deficiencies and others that confront those who use city directories in their new urban studies research.[2] Some of the more problematic areas that he describes are inconsistent listing of names (name changes, spelling errors, and the like), migration of individuals to suburbs outside directory boundary listings, incomplete and socially biased enumeration that often excluded the more transient persons in a community who were disproportionately members of lower socioeconomic and ethnic/racial groups. As city directories become more frequently used for urban studies, it is imperative that scholars analyze their accuracy, comprehensiveness, and selection biases. In the present study there is undoubtedly some margin of human error involved in the tabulation of census and directory data; but careful recording and analysis, it is hoped, has kept this margin to a level that has not distorted the findings. A representative city directory was compared with the corresponding federal manuscript census (which is considered to be more comprehensive) for the purpose of determining the inclusiveness and accuracy of city directories.

An analysis was made of the 1901 Santa Barbara City Directory (the 1900 city directory does not now exist) and the 1900 federal manuscript census for the same city. In order to compare the comprehensiveness and reliability of the listing of Spanish-surnamed persons in the city directory with the federal manuscript census, three procedures were used. The first comparison was made between Spanish-surnamed heads of household and their occupations as listed in the two sources. However, the 1901 Santa Barbara City Directory, unlike the 1900 manuscript census or the city directories for Santa Barbara after 1903, did not specifically designate the head of household. It was difficult, therefore, to determine the male head of household, especially when occupations are listed for more than one person in a given household. As a result, analysis of designated Spanish-surnamed heads of household between the two sources was not feasible. But by comparing the total number of males who listed an occupation in both the 1901 city directory and the 1900 manuscript census, an approximate comparison could be made between the total Spanish-surname employed male population and the listing of their occupations. In this first test for comparison between the city directory and manuscript census (see Table 25), there proved to be very little difference between the total numbers of employed male Spanish-surnamed persons found in both sources, and between the occupational distributions in each enumeration. Even though the city directory enumeration was taken probably several months to a year later than

Table 25   Total number of employed male Spanish-surnamed persons in Santa Barbara and their occupations, 1900 and 1901.

Occupation	1900 census		1901 city directory	
	Number	Percent	Number	Percent
High white-collar				
Professional	10	3.4	9	3.0
Proprietorial	5	1.7	7	2.3
Low white-collar				
Sales/clerical/				
semiprofessional	20	6.8	26	8.7
High blue-collar				
Skilled	24	8.2	30	10.0
Low blue-collar				
Semiskilled	44	15.1	38	12.7
Unskilled	171	58.6	175	58.5
Unknown or unlisted	18	6.2	14	4.7
Number in population	292		299	

the federal census enumeration, the number and occupational listings are strikingly similar.

A second procedure to test the reliability of the city directory against the manuscript census involved comparing the total Spanish-surname populations for both enumerations. Whereas tabulation of the total Spanish surnames in the 1900 census was a simple task, for the city directory it was more complicated. The directory listing of Spanish surnames usually only included adult males, females, and employed children. Therefore, the total Spanish-surname population in the 1901 city directory must be multiplied by a factor to account for the omission of unemployed minors. An omission factor can be determined by taking the average number of persons in Spanish-surname households listed in the 1900 census (4.3 family members) and multiplying this figure by the total number of individual Spanish-surname households listed in the 1901 city directory (284). Thus, the total number of Spanish surnames listed in the 1900 manuscript census is *1,108;* the computed total population for the 1901 city directory is *1,221.* Here again, if we take into account the difference in enumeration dates, Mexican immigration, and natural increase by birth, the two total population figures for 1900 and 1901 are quite comparable.

While the first two measures, which compare total listings between the 1901 city directory and the 1900 census, compare favorably, the third measure, which compares individual listings, is troubling.[3] An individual-by-individual check was made to determine what percentage of male Spanish-surnamed heads of household listed in the 1900 United States census were also listed in the 1901 Santa Barbara City Directory. This comparison between the two sources revealed that only 70 percent of the Chicano heads of household listed in the 1900 federal manuscript census were also listed in the 1901 directory. A very similar discrepancy was found by Thernstrom in his use of Boston city directories. The 30-percent omission of Chicano heads of household in the 1901 directory points to the problems in comparing different enumerations and raises questions about the degree of city directory inclusiveness for the Chicano population. The omission factor for heads of household in the 1901 city directory doubtless would have been much higher had cross checking of information not been examined. For example, while the United States census consistently supplied the full, formal names of each person, the city directory often included only nicknames, initials, and/or anglicization of Spanish forenames. Only after examining additional information on each head of household (such as address, other possible names or spellings, and occupation) were many included who otherwise would have been overlooked in the tabulations of the 1901 directory listings. Both enumerations were often guilty of misspellings and of different spellings of Spanish names; mispronunciation of Spanish names by English-speaking enumerators no doubt accounts for some of these problems.

The variations in enumeration listings between the 1900 United States census and the 1901 city directory are part of a larger problem—the exclusion of many Chicanos from the latter source. The 30-percent omission factor in the 1901 directory probably would have been less had the two enumerations been taken more closely together in time (as much as twelve months may have separated them). The U.S. census was recorded during the month of June, a peak period for Chicano migratory farm labor, and it is possible that the 1901 city directory listing was also taken during a time of seasonal migration of Chicanos from the city (either summer or fall harvests). These seasonal work-related migrations probably accounted for at least part of the high nonpersistence rates among Chicanos. Therefore, the time difference between the two enumerations together with the frequent in-migration and out-migration of many Mexican residents could have accounted for part of the omission of Chicanos reflected in the city directory. The city directories, unlike the census, probably excluded many transient workers in Santa Barbara (for example, most of the Southern Pacific Mexican railroad section-gang workers who were listed in the 1900 census were not listed in the city directory). The apparent aim of the private directory publishing company was to provide a listing of resident households in the city and, unlike the U.S. census, there was no attempt to enumerate every person who happened to be in the community at the time of the listing. In addition, as Thernstrom likewise discovered for Boston city directories, partial exclusion of the lower socioeconomic groups (unskilled and semiskilled workers) and of racial minorities was apparently operating in the 1901 Santa Barbara City Directory as well. If the hypothesized class and ethnic bias is in fact operating in the 1901 directory, the numbers excluded most likely would have further reinforced the conclusions presented on the low occupational status of Chicano workers. Although the total listing of individuals and occupations was comparable in both the census and the city directory, the dismal Chicano occupational profiles provided by these two sources probably erred on the optimistic side. Therefore, the problems inherent in both listings are not so serious as to call into question the major conclusions of this study.

The 1901 Santa Barbara City Directory is, in most respects, representative of the city directories published during the early twentieth century in cities throughout southern California (with the exception of the 1901 directory's nondesignation of head of household). Whether other early twentieth-century directories compare favorably in overall listings with the 1900 manuscript census or whether they too are as guilty of omission of individual Chicano householders as is the 1901 Santa Barbara directory awaits further analysis by scholars. While it is evident that city directories do not include all Chicano residents for any given period in any given city, their use will nevertheless become more important as researchers rely on them for occupational, demographic, and other significant information not available in other sources relating to urban society over time.

Occupational Structure and Classification

Since the publication over a decade ago of Stephan Thernstrom's pioneering study, *Poverty and Progress: Social Mobility in a Nineteenth Century City*, the focus of many urban studies has been on occupational and geographic mobility. Occupational mobility among workers is viewed as the key factor in measuring social mobility. The focus of the present study is on the occupational *structure* of the Chicano and non-Chicano population, rather than on occupational mobility per se. As a result, the occupational structure and classification here differs from one that might be constructed to facilitate a mobility study. In a provocative essay, Clyde Griffen perceptively concluded that "in theory and method there is a clear distinction between the study of occupational structure and the study of occupational mobility."[4] He further warns historians of the dangers they face in overrefining occupational classifications for analyzing mobility patterns; the socioeconomic variables employed by sociologists cannot be copied by historians because of the limitations of the quantifiable data available. "The preoccupation with stratification and mobility," instead of with "understanding the occupational universe" of any given number of workers, is in Griffen's opinion the major drawback of mobility studies.[5]

The purpose of this study is to profile the occupational universe of Chicanos, trace their general employment patterns over time, and compare their occupational structure with non-Chicanos in the same cities. In addition, the study analyzes Chicano worker response to a changing economy in the second half of the nineteenth century and to an altered work force and labor market during the twentieth century; these are areas of vital concern for understanding the historical development of the Chicano working class. For southern California it was far more important to explore the transition from a pastoral to a capitalist economy and its impact on the Chicano working class than merely to measure social-occupational mobility. Subsistence rather than mobility was the reality for most Chicanos throughout the period. Thernstrom pointed to the need for research that would reflect the differential opportunity among various ethnic groups; in one respect, this study does illustrate the range of occupational opportunities open to Chicanos in comparison to Anglos.

The examination of structure as opposed to mobility does not eliminate one's responsibility to establish a representative occupational classification. Although constructing such a classification is less complicated than constructing a mobility classification, which usually includes several socioeconomic variables, one is still faced with the problems inherent in quantifiable historical data (such as vagueness of occupational designations in census schedules and city directories, or occupations with the same basic job function but different designations).[6] Notwithstanding these deficiencies in data, the southern California occupational structures and classifications were set up with three main purposes in mind. First, an occupational structure was needed that would best profile the changes in the region's economy over time (for example, the decline of persons in pastoral and agricultural pursuits, and the addition of semiskilled workers within the expanding service-worker population in the urban economy). Secondly, an occupational structure was required that would best illustrate the occupational universe of southern California workers from 1860 to 1930, while maintaining the same basic schema or format as new occupations were incorporated into existing classifications—that is, an occupational structure flexible enough to accommodate easily new job descriptions and categories over a seventy-year period. Lastly, an occupational structure was needed that would show the relations between the Chicano and non-Chicano work forces throughout the period studied. Ideally, an occupational structure that would lend itself to regional and national comparative studies was desirable.

Thernstrom's later study (*The Other Bostonians*) served as a model for preparing the occupational structures in this study, especially for the twentieth century. The occupational structure used here was first organized by the usual technique of dividing nonmanual and manual occupations into two general classifications. These were then divided further into subgroupings that allowed for the general skill level of workers in the lower half of the structure (skilled, semiskilled, and unskilled) and for higher occupational classifications. For example, subgroupings for the semiskilled and unskilled categories were created in order to detail the distribution of Chicano workers in the lower levels of the overall structure. Likewise, the higher occupations were divided into professional, proprietorial, and low white-collar subgroupings. Additions to the subgroupings were included as new occupations began to emerge in the cities and as the capitalist economy expanded during the late nineteenth and early twentieth centuries. The small number of pastoral/agricultural occupations in the twentieth century no longer justified a separate subgrouping and they were, therefore, combined with the high white-collar proprietorial category.

The somewhat different subgroupings (high white-collar, low white-collar, high blue-collar, and low blue-collar) used for the period 1900 to 1930 include many of the same types of occupations found in the nineteenth century. However, this revised nomenclature best reflects the changing occupational situation in the cities of early twentieth-century southern California.

The tracing of occupational mobility was limited to only one dimension—movement from one occupational classification to another. Other variables for measuring social mobility—such as data on wealth (except for 1860 and 1870), value of property holdings, and wages—were only occasionally available for the period 1860 to 1930.[7] But the analysis of the mobility of Chicanos in Santa Barbara was concerned with the general *occupational* mobility patterns or frequencies, rather than with the wide range of factors used to measure vertical *social* mobility. These frequencies provided the outlines of occupational change in Santa Barbara. They also gave clues to the meanings of certain imprecise occupational designations.[8] "The shape of a community's occupational structure," as Thernstrom points out, is "obviously a prime determinant of the range of occupational mobility opportunities there."[9] This proved to be the case in analyzing the occupational structure of Chicanos in southern California from 1860 to 1930.

Oral History Interviews

The importance of Chicano oral historical research becomes increasingly evident as historians begin to fill in the gaps of twentieth-century Chicano history. The dearth of traditional sources of documentation on Chicanos necessitates the use of other source material, and quantifiable data and oral history are two main sources to be tapped. Fortunately, in recent years individuals have signaled the need for Chicano oral history, and a growing number of practitioners have responded by incorporating oral history into their research priorities.[10] The potential is great for creating new sources of information on Chicanos and other similar socioeconomic groups that have left few written records. It is especially urgent to record the oral testimonies of the older generation. One oral history practitioner correctly concluded that the tradition of the lower socioeconomic groups "is basically an oral tradition that lives within the family group or the locality for a generation or two and then slowly disappears."[11] The Chicano oral tradition must be preserved and it must be incorporated into the writing of Chicano history. This study has attempted to accomplish both of these tasks.

Many generally acknowledged procedural techniques of research preparation, questionnaire format, and interviewing guidelines used in oral history research have been incorporated. But the lack of adequately standardized interviewing procedures and the particular focus of this study necessitated the adaptation of certain techniques.[12] Oral history, as utilized in this study, served many purposes. To begin with, the oral interviews provided supplemental source material to corroborate information found in newspapers or in other printed materials; they also supplemented the analyses made from the quantifiable data (such as occupational and residential information). Although some practitioners claim that the only real function of the oral history interview is its supplemental source value, the interviews conducted for this study contributed information about Chicanos in the Santa Barbara community that was otherwise unobtainable. Oral history, therefore, became an important source for the reconstruction of certain aspects of local history (Chicano racial attitudes, the functions of mutualistas, repatriation, and many other subjects) for the period 1910 to 1930. Oral history, in addition, was the only source by which to record Chicano family life histories. In this way the oral interview can, as claimed by other oral historians, provide "a deep and sensitive exploration of how one individual has seen and reacted to the world about him," as well as "capture certain aspects of society which are difficult to display."[13] It was an indispensable source for understanding the internal dynamics of the Santa Barbara Chicano community.

Prior to selecting interviewees, a thorough survey was made of materials that related to Santa Barbara local history, and of the topics to be investigated for the history of the twentieth-century community. Interviewees were selected from both sectors of the Chicano community, the native-born and the foreign-born. Consultation with two individuals who had long-time associations with both sectors of the Santa Barbara Chicano community (Ida Cordero, a social worker for the Eastside Social Center–Catholic Welfare Service for over forty years, and Russell A. Ruiz, a local native-born historian) supplied an initial list of prospective interviewees. After these people were contacted and interviewed, other prospects were supplied by each of the interviewees. An interview format was constructed prior to the series of interviews. The questions were constructed to gain information about family background, personal life experiences, and recollection of certain events in local Santa Barbara Chicano history; each interviewee was asked essentially the same questions, except for the questions on background that necessarily differed when questioning native-born and foreign-born Chicanos.

Twenty-eight oral interviews were recorded, not counting the many interview sessions with the two consultants. Those interviewed included eleven women and seventeen men (thirteen native-born and fifteen foreign-born). The ages of the interviewees ranged from 62 to 88 years, with the average 72.3 years (excluding the two consultants). As required for the study, all interviewees were either born and raised in Santa Barbara or had migrated there from Mexico or other southwestern states between 1900 and 1930; all have resided in Santa Barbara since this period. All interviewees were bilingual, although some spoke only Spanish.[14] Most of the interviews were conducted bilingually, but some were exclusively in Spanish or in English.

It was impossible to determine how many Chicanos in Santa Barbara fit the age, residence, and time period requirements for prospective interviewees and thus one cannot measure the representativeness of the sample interviewed. The information contained in this study from the oral history interviews is based not on responses of any one or two interviewees, but on opinions common to most. Only when patterns of similar information from a series of interviews manifested themselves were they included here. By using this procedure a cross check of information from the many interviews was feasible. Also, by using information from newspapers whenever possible, the most reliable type of information from oral history resulted. These data were essential for writing the twentieth-century history of Chicanos in Santa Barbara.[15]

Occupational Categories

Appendix 2.

Pastoral/Agricultural

Apiarist	Fruit grower	Rancher (stock raiser)
Dairyman	Orchardist	Vegetable grower
Farmer	Poultryman	

High White-Collar

Professional

Architect	Engineer (electrical,	Officer (military)
Banker	civil, etc.)	Pharmacist
Capitalist	Geologist	Physician
Chemist	Governmental official	Psychiatrist
Chief of police	(major offices)	Publisher
Clergyman	Judge	School principal
Company president	Lawyer	Schoolteacher
Dentist	Newspaper editor	Veterinarian
Editor		

Proprietorial (major and minor proprietors)

Art store	Hotelkeeper	Peddler/huckster
Brewery	Landlord/apartment	Piano dealer
Confectionery store	owner	Real estate office
Contractor/builder	Leather goods	Restaurateur
Dry goods store	Liquor store	Saloonkeeper
Feed store	Livery keeper	Trader/dealer
Furniture store	Manufacturer	Vintner
Grocer	Merchant	

Low White-Collar

Semiprofessional

Accountant/bookkeeper
Actor
Artist
Assayer
Auctioneer
Auditor
Author/writer
Aviator
Chiropractor
Company vice president
   (or secretary-
   treasurer)
Conductor
Court reporter
Dispatcher
Draftsman
Health officer
Inspector
Interior decorator
Interpreter

Inventor
Investigator
Lecturer
Librarian
Manager/foreman
Messenger
Motion picture director
Music teacher
Musician
Newspaper reporter
Nurse
Optometrist/optician
Photographer
Postal inspector
Postmaster
Pugilist
Sea captain
Sculptor
Sexton
Speculator

Superintendent
Surveyor
Taxidermist
Technician (medical,
   dental, etc.)
Undertaker
Wharfinger

Sales/Clerical

Agent
Bank teller
Cashier/checker
Clerk/salesperson
Collector/solicitor
Mail carrier
Notary public
Operator (telephone)
Secretary
Stenographer
Timekeeper

High Blue-Collar (skilled)

Baker
Bicycle repairman
Blacksmith
Boat builder
Boilermaker
Brewer
Bricklayer
Butcher
Cabinetmaker
Carpenter
Carpet layer/weaver
Carriage maker/painter
Cement finisher
Cigar maker
Compositor/printer
Cooper
Coppersmith

Dressmaker
Engineer (stationary and
   locomotive)
Electrician
Floor layer
Forest ranger
Glassblower
Glazier
Gunsmith
Harnessmaker
Hatter
Horse trainer
Jeweler
Jockey
Lather
Leather craftsman
Linotype operator

Lithographer
Locksmith
Machinist
Mechanic
Midwife
Miller
Painter
Paperhanger
Piano tuner
Plasterer
Plumber
Potter
Roofer
Saddler
Sailmaker
Sausage maker
Sawyer

High Blue-Collar (skilled) *continued*

Sheetmetal worker
Shipsmith
Shoemaker
Silversmith
Stonecutter
Stonemason

Tailor
Tanner
Telegraph operator
Tile setter
Tinsmith
Upholsterer

Vaquero
Vulcanizer
Watchmaker
Welder
Wheelwright
Wood-carver

Low Blue-Collar

Semiskilled

Apprentice
Barber
Bartender
Bill posterist
Bottler
Box maker
Brakeman
Butler
Cable splicer
Chainman
Conductor
Cook
Deputy sheriff
Drayman/hack driver
Elevator operator
Factory operative
Fisherman
Foundryman
Horseshoer
Lineman
Longshoreman
Lumberjack
Marble worker
Meatcutter
Metalworker
Milkman
Miner
Molder
Night watchman
Nurseryman

Pantryman
Pattern maker
Pipefitter
Policeman
Pruner
Rattan worker
Sander
Sailor/soldier
Seamstress
Service station worker
Shepherd/herder
Stevedore/steward
Switchman
Tamale maker
Teamster
Telephone repairman
Trucker/driver
Waiter/waitress
Warehouseman
Well driller
Zanjero (ditch digger)

Unskilled (primarily laborers)
Boiler washer
Bootblack
Busboy
Cannery worker
Carwasher
Concrete worker
Dishwasher

Domestic/maid
Farm laborer
Fruit packer
Fruit picker
Gardener
Handyman
Helper
Hod carrier
Hostler
Hotel worker
House mover
Hunter
Janitor
Kitchen helper
Laborer
Laundry worker/
    laundress
Millhand
Oil worker
Porter
Restaurant worker
Scavenger
Section-gang worker
Servant
Street sweeper
Window cleaner
Woodchopper
Yardman

Glossary

Alcalde   Mayor.

Ayuntamiento   Equivalent to town or city council in municipal government.

Bandido   Bandit.

Barbareño   Santa Barbara Mexican.

Barrio   Segregated Chicano neighborhood.

Barrioization   Process by which nineteenth-century and twentieth-century segregated Chicano neighborhoods formed and changed over time as the result of many socioeconomic, political, cultural, and demographic factors.

Caballero   Horseman.

Californio   Mexican and Spanish ranchero or land grantee, usually of the upper classes; in other studies the term has been used to refer to any nineteenth-century Mexican in California.

Chicana or *Mexicana*   Female Chicano or Mexicano.

Chicanito   Chicano child.

Cholo   Derogatory term usually applied to recent Mexican immigrants, but used to refer to native-born Mexicans as well.

Cinco de Mayo   Fifth of May: a patriotic holiday that celebrates the Mexican victory over the French army in the Battle of Puebla, 1862.

Compadrazgo   System of godparent relationships.

Compañero   Friend, companion, countryman.

Dieciséis de Septiembre   Sixteenth of September: a holiday that commemorates Mexico's war of independence from Spain beginning in 1810.

Estero   Tideland, swamp.

Gente del país   Literally, the people of the country; the Mexican people of California.

Gringo A derogatory term used by Mexicans to refer to Anglo-Americans.

Huero Light-skinned or fair-complected person.

Jamaica Church-related (usually) charity fair or carnival.

Junta Group of people joined or united in some way, such as a council.

Madrina Godmother.

Matanza Cattle slaughter.

Mayordomo Foreman, boss, overseer.

Mestizo Individual of mixed Indian and Spanish heritage.

Mutualista Mutual-aid organization.

Nopal Cactus.

Padrino Godfather.

Patrón Influential patriarch of the community.

Piñata Colorful papier-mâché basket filled with nuts and candy, broken by a blindfolded person using a stick; commonly used at fiestas.

Poblador Settler in a pueblo.

Pocho Derogatory term used by Mexicans to refer to people of Mexican descent born in the United States.

Político Influential politician usually supported widely by his constituency.

Presidio Military garrison.

Prieto Dark-skinned individual.

Pueblo Municipality, town.

Ranchería Indian settlement.

Ranchero Stock raiser; usually recipient of a government land grant.

Rancho Tract of land devoted to stock raising.

Rodeo Cattle roundup for slaughter and/or branding.

Trasquilador Shearer, sheepshearer.

Tuna Cactus apple.

Vaquero Mexican cowboy.

Yanqui Yankee, American (often used derogatorily).

Notes

Introduction

1. For excellent reviews of the literature of Chicano history, see Juan Gómez-Quiñones and Luis L. Arroyo, "On the State of Chicano History: Observations on Its Development, Interpretations, and Theory, 1970–1974," *Western Historical Quarterly,* 7 (April 1976):155–185; Juan Gómez-Quiñones, "Toward a Perspective on Chicano History," *Aztlán—Chicano Journal of the Social Sciences and the Arts,* 2 (fall 1972):1–49; Arthur F. Corwin, "Mexican-American History: An Assessment," *Pacific Historical Review,* 42 (August 1973):269–308.

2. See, for example, Wayne Moquín and Charles Van Doren, eds., *A Documentary History of the Mexican Americans* (New York, 1971), 189; James M. Guinn, *Historical and Biographical Record of Southern California* (Chicago, 1902), 170; Robert G. Cleland, *The Cattle on a Thousand Hills* (San Marino, California, 1951), 166, 183; Joseph S. O'Flaherty, *An End and a Beginning: The South Coast and Los Angeles, 1850–1887* (New York, 1972), 200; Corwin, "Mexican-American History"; Moses Rischin, "Continuities and Discontinuities in Spanish-Speaking California," in *Ethnic Conflict in California History,* ed. Charles Wollenberg (Los Angeles, 1970), 55.

3. For writings that also support this thesis see, for example, Gómez-Quiñones, "Toward a Perspective on Chicano History," 35; David J. Weber, ed., *Foreigners in Their Native Land: Historical Roots of the Mexican Americans* (Albuquerque, New Mexico, 1973), esp. 203–260; Rodman W. Paul, "The Spanish-Americans in the Southwest, 1848–1900," in *The Frontier Challenge: Responses to the Trans-Mississippi West,* ed. John G. Clark (Lawrence, Kansas, 1971), 36–51; Leonard Pitt, *The Decline of the Californios: A Social History of the Spanish-Speaking Californians, 1846–1890* (Berkeley and Los Angeles, 1966), esp. viii.

1. The Mexican Pueblo of Santa Barbara

1. Sherburne F. Cook, *The Conflict between the California Indian and White Civilization* (Berkeley and Los Angeles, 1976), 7–8, 11–12, 56–90, 99–100, 188–191, 236, 255–329, 351; Maynard Geiger, O. F. M., *The Indians of Mission Santa Barbara in Paganism and Christianity* (Santa Barbara, 1960), 3–6, 9, 15–16; Hubert H. Bancroft, *History of California, 1801–1824*, vol. 2 (San Francisco, 1885), 530–536; Yda A. Storke, *A Memorial and Biographical History of the Counties of Santa Barbara, San Luis Obispo, and Ventura, California* (Chicago, 1891), 22–23; Sherburne F. Cook, *The Populations of California Indians, 1769–1970* (Berkeley and Los Angeles, 1976), 55.

2. Hubert H. Bancroft, *History of California, 1542–1800*, vol. 1 (San Francisco, 1884), 372–375, and *California Pastoral, 1769–1848*, vol. 34 (San Francisco, 1888), 278; Irving B. Richman, *California under Spain and Mexico, 1535–1847* (Boston, 1911), 138–139, 286; Edward S. Spaulding, *Adobe Days along the Channel* (Santa Barbara, 1957), 29. For population estimates see Bancroft, *History of California*, vol. 2, 573, 576–578, and vol. 3 (San Francisco, 1885), 649–650, 656. For visitors' descriptions of the presidio and pueblo during the 1830s and 1840s, see Richard Henry Dana, *Two Years before the Mast* (New York, 1959), 44; Alfred Robinson, *Life in California* (Santa Barbara, 1970), 28–29; Stella H. Rouse, *Santa Barbara's Spanish Renaissance and the Old Spanish Days Fiesta* (Santa Barbara, 1974), 12–19.

3. Cleland, *Cattle on a Thousand Hills*, 19–20; Richman, *California under Spain and Mexico*, 286; Bancroft, *History of California*, vol. 3, 649–651; John R. Southworth, *Santa Barbara and Montecito: Past and Present* (Santa Barbara, 1920), 74.

4. For a listing of rancho grants and land acquisitions for the Santa Barbara County area, see Bancroft, *History of California*, vol. 3, 655–656; Walter A. Tompkins, *California's Wonderful Corner* (Santa Barbara, 1962), 48–49; "Narración de Doña Teresa de la Guerra de Hartnell," *Pioneer Sketches*, no. 2 (University of California, Berkeley, 1875), 12. The only mention by Bancroft of private ranchos in the Santa Barbara County area prior to 1834 was the Ortega Rancho El Refugio and the rancho holdings of José de la Guerra y Noriega; see *History of California*, vol. 2, 172, and vol. 3, 770.

5. This analysis of the social class structure of Santa Barbara society before and after secularization was constructed from quantitative primary and secondary sources. See the following: Bancroft, *California Pastoral*, 278–279, 399–400, 493–494, and *History of California*, vol. 3, 653–655; *Assessment Roll for 1853*, Santa Barbara County Tax Assessment, Document of Santa Barbara County Courthouse; *Federal Manuscript Census Schedules*, Santa Barbara County, 1850 and 1860; Katherine M. Bell, *Swinging the Censer: Reminiscences of Old Santa Barbara* (Santa Barbara, 1931), 18, 29, 33, 41; Walter A. Hawley, *The*

Early Days of Santa Barbara, California (Santa Barbara, 1920), 82–83; Dana, *Two Years before the Mast*, 58, 60–61, 63 (Dana emphasizes the distinction between the upper-class Californios and the lower "caste" elements in California pueblos); William A. Streeter, *Recollections of Historical Events in California, 1843–1878* (University of California, Berkeley, 1878), 231; Storke, *A Memorial History*, 26–28; Nellie Sánchez, *Spanish Arcadia* (Los Angeles, 1929), 72. Carey McWilliams, in his *Southern California Country: An Island on the Land* (New York, 1946), 51–52, 54, offers a social-occupational hierarchic schema that applies in part to pre-1850 Santa Barbara; however, McWilliams impressionistically highlights the rift between the elite Californios and "Mexicans" without explicitly defining the latter group.

6. *Federal Manuscript Census Schedules*, 1850 and 1860; Bancroft, "Pioneer Register and Index," *History of California*, vols. 2–4; see also the 1860 Spanish-surname occupational structure in Table 3. Interpretations and research on the topic of social class stratification within pre-1848 Spanish-speaking California society are seriously lacking. Analyses based on race, class, and occupational-economic function in the pueblos and ranchos are needed.

7. *Federal Manuscript Census Schedules*, 1850 and 1860. Anglo visitors to Santa Barbara writing during the period were cognizant of the socioeconomic divisions between the "lower" or "poorer" classes and the "elite"; see Dana, *Two Years before the Mast*, 193, and Robinson, *Life in California*, 95.

8. Storke, *A Memorial History*, 22–23; Cook, *California Indian and White Civilization*, 236; *Federal Manuscript Census Schedules*, 1860; Bancroft, *California Pastoral*, 278. The employment of the Native Americans as servants for wealthy Californio families was still clearly a pattern in 1860, when some 43 of the 127 Indians in the town of Santa Barbara were servants in Spanish-surname households. Over 25 percent of the town's total Indian population (mostly children and adolescents) in 1860 lived within Mexican family households as either adoptees or boarders.

9. Dario Oreña, *Reminiscences of Early California* (Santa Barbara, 1932), 10; Bancroft, *California Pastoral*, 325, 332–333, 404; Cleland, *Cattle on a Thousand Hills*, 30–31, 56, 58, 60, 144; McWilliams, *Southern California Country*, 54; Pitt, *Decline of the Californios*, 9–10.

10. Bell, *Swinging the Censer*, 7–8. On the benevolence of Santa Barbara's leading patriarch, José de la Guerra y Noriega and other De la Guerra family members, see William H. Ellison, ed., " 'Recollections of Historial Events in California, 1843–1878,' of William A. Streeter," *California Historical Society Quarterly*, 18 (March, June, and September 1939):69, 168–169; Bancroft, *History of California*, vol. 3, 770; Fr. Joseph A. Thompson, O.F.M., *El Gran Capitan: José de la Guerra* (Los Angeles, 1961), 163–167; *Gazette*, 30 April 1857, 18 February 1858. (Newspapers referred to hereafter as *Gazette, Press,* and

the like are the *Santa Barbara Gazette,* the *Santa Barbara Press,* and so on unless otherwise specified.)

11. Jesse D. Mason, *History of Santa Barbara and Ventura Counties, California* (Oakland, California, 1883), 68–70; Pitt, *Decline of the Californios,* 33–34.

12. Storke, *A Memorial History,* 24–26, 63; Mason, *History of Santa Barbara,* 72–74; Pitt, *Decline of the Californios,* 35; Streeter, *Recollections of Historical Events,* 199, 203; Donald L. Stillman, "A Historical Survey of the Santa Barbara, California, Area during the Early Years of the American Period, 1846–1864" (Master's thesis, University of Southern California, 1948), 34–35, 99. For a discussion of the gang activity of Jack Powers, a former Stevenson's Regiment volunteer, see Pitt, *Decline of the Californios,* 106–107, 174, 177–178.

13. Racial conflict and Anglo racism against Mexicans had existed for a much longer period elsewhere in the present-day area of the Southwest. See, for example, Rodolfo Acuña, *Occupied America: The Chicano's Struggle toward Liberation* (San Francisco, 1972), 9–19.

14. William H. Ellison, ed., *Diary of "Judge" Charles E. Huse* (translated by Francis Price, University of California, Santa Barbara, 1953), 28 June 1857, 7 September 1857, 25 May 1865; Stillman, "A Historical Survey," iv, 99; Storke, *A Memorial History,* 63; see also the recollections of a Mrs. Graham in the *Morning Press,* 28 April 1894. The number of Anglos residing in Santa Barbara prior to 1846 probably numbered less than two dozen; see, for example, Mason, *History of Santa Barbara,* 44–49; Bancroft, *History of California,* vol. 2, 573, and vol. 3, 649.

15. In 1860 the non-Spanish-surnamed head-of-household population had increased to 35.4 percent of the total head-of-household population in Santa Barbara excluding the Chinese (who will be discussed later); see *Federal Manuscript Census Schedules,* 1860.

16. Ellison, *Diary of Charles Huse,* xiii–xvi. See also entries of 9 January 1854, 2 August 1855, 10 September 1855, 18 May 1856.

17. *Gazette,* 14, 19, and 28 June 1855. For Huse's influence in the *Gazette,* see Ellison, *Diary of Charles Huse,* xvi, 30 June 1855, 2 August 1855; Muir Dawson, "Southern California Newspapers, 1851–1876," *Historical Society of Southern California Quarterly,* 32 (March and June 1950):156; Walter A. Tompkins, "Santa Barbara Journalists, 1855–1973," *Noticias—Quarterly Bulletin of the Santa Barbara Historical Society,* 19 (winter 1973):1.

18. *Gazette,* 7, 14, and 28 June 1855; Dawson, "Southern California Newspapers," 156.

19. *Gazette,* 15 May 1856; see also 27 December 1855.

20. For background on public instruction in Santa Barbara during the early American period, see Lawrence L. Hill and Marion Parks, *Santa Barbara—Tierra Adorada: A Community History* (Los Angeles, 1930), 52–53; Southworth, *Santa Barbara and Montecito,* 201; Robert

N. Christian, "A Study of the Historical Development of the Santa Barbara School District" (Master's thesis, University of Southern California, 1963), 40–41. See also *Gazette*, 20 December 1885. For a discussion of the public school controversy in Los Angeles, see Pitt, *Decline of the Californios*, 226–228. Pitt, 135–136, also gives a good description of the Know-Nothing party and its effects on Mexicans in California; see also John W. Caughey, *California*, 2nd ed. (Englewood Cliffs, New Jersey, 1953), 282–283.

21. *Gazette*, 31 January 1856. See also Christian, "Santa Barbara School District," 41.

22. *Gazette*, 4 September 1856, 7 May 1857. See also Mason, *History of Santa Barbara*, 100–101; Christian, "Santa Barbara School District," 44.

23. Southern California Writers' Project of the Work Projects Administration, *Santa Barbara: A Guide to the Channel City and Its Environs* (New York, 1941), 88; Zephyrin Engelhardt, O.F.M., *Santa Barbara Mission* (San Francisco, 1923), 403–404; Christian, "Santa Barbara School District," 46.

24. 15 May 1856. Charles E. Huse most likely was the prime mover behind this type of editorial. He refers many times to the devout practices of the Spanish-speaking population, as well as to the disgust he felt for the Catholic religion. See Ellison, *Diary of Charles Huse*, 15 January 1854, 29 July 1855, 11 and 16 May 1856.

25. *Gazette*, 22 May 1856.

26. Ellison, " 'Recollections' of Streeter," 273; see also Maynard Geiger, O.F.M., *Mission Santa Barbara, 1782–1965* (Santa Barbara, 1965), 169–170; Pitt, *Decline of the Californios*, 148–166, 174.

27. Ellison, *Diary of Charles Huse*, 19 October 1855.

28. 31 May 1855, 22 November 1855; see also Ellison, *Diary of Charles Huse*, 10 September 1855, 18 October 1855; Weber, *Foreigners in Their Native Land*, 149; Stillman, "A Historical Survey," 58.

29. 14 and 28 June 1855, 17 and 24 April 1856, 6, 12, and 19 June 1856, 3 July 1856; see also Ellison, *Diary of Charles Huse*, xx; Joseph E. Cassidy, "Life and Times of Pablo de la Guerra, 1819–1874" (Ph.D. dissertation, University of California, Santa Barbara, 1977), 120–124. The Grand Jury investigation of the Californio Board of Supervisors evidently had little impact on the upcoming municipal election. Antonio María de la Guerra was elected mayor/chairman of the Californio-controlled city council; see *Gazette*, 8 May 1856. For further accusations against De la Guerra, see *Gazette*, 10 July 1856 and Walter A. Tompkins, *Santa Barbara's Royal Rancho: The Fabulous History of Los Dos Pueblos* (Berkeley, 1960), 145–149.

30. *Gazette*, 10 July 1856.

31. Pitt, *Decline of the Californios*, 174.

32. Streeter, *Recollections of Historical Events*, 211, 225–227.

33. Ibid., 229; Hill and Parks, *Santa Barbara*, 63–64; Ellison,

" 'Recollections' of Streeter," 171–172; Mason, *History of Santa Barbara*, 84; Owen H. O'Neill, *History of Santa Barbara County* (Santa Barbara, 1939), 153–154. Bancroft offers a factually incorrect account of Pico in his *California Pastoral*, 650. For a discussion of the Powers gang see Pitt, *Decline of the Californios*, 106–107, 174, 177–178. The case of Solomón Pico offers excellent research potential as an application of the Chicano social banditry thesis; see Pedro Castillo and Albert Camarillo, eds., *Furia y Muerte: Los Bandidos Chicanos* (Los Angeles, 1973).

34. For accounts of the Baldillo affair, see Cameron Rogers, *A County Judge in Arcady. Selected Private Papers of Charles Fernald* (Glendale, California, 1954), 115–122; O'Neill, *History of Santa Barbara County*, 177; Pitt, *Decline of the Californios*, 179–180.

35. Rogers, *A County Judge*, 114–115.

36. O'Neill, *History of Santa Barbara County*, 177.

37. Willoughby Rodman, *History of the Bench and Bar of Southern California* (Los Angeles, 1906), 48; Hill and Parks, *Santa Barbara*, 46–51; *An Outline of Historical Research with Excerpts from the Minutes of the Common Council of the City of Santa Barbara* (compiled under the direction of Mayor Harvey T. Nielson; Robert R. Heatke, research editor), 6 January 1851; *Gazette*, 27 September 1855.

38. Stillman, "A Historical Survey," 43–47; Pitt, *Decline of the Californios*, 135–136. For a discussion of the political power of the De la Guerra family, see Cassidy, "Pablo de la Guerra."

39. Ellison, *Diary of Charles Huse*, 12 August 1855, 128.

40. *Gazette*, 30 August 1855, 13 and 18 September 1855, 28 February 1856, 15 May 1856, 9 October 1856, 13 November 1856, 7 May 1857. See Pitt, *Decline of the Californios*, 137; Cassidy, "Pablo de la Guerra," 140–142.

41. Ellison, *Diary of Charles Huse*, 11 September 1855, 10 May 1856, 10 June 1856.

42. The grand jury letter was first published in the *San Francisco Herald*, 17 September 1859; it was reprinted in Bancroft, *Popular Tribunals*, vol. 1 (San Francisco, 1890), 483–484. See also Rogers, *A County Judge*, 114; *Gazette*, 18 October 1855, 10 January 1856, 17 July 1856, 14 August 1856; Mason, *History of Santa Barbara*, 95–96; Ellison, *Diary of Charles Huse*, 9 April 1855, 14 May 1855, 10 June 1855; Pitt, *Decline of the Californios*, 175.

43. Tompkins, "Santa Barbara Journalists," 1; Dawson, "Southern California Newspapers," 157; Guinn, *Historical and Biographical Record*, 169. The Californio who undoubtedly exerted pressure to have this act passed by the state legislature was State Senator Pablo de la Guerra. Copies of *La Gaceta de Santa Bárbara* exist only for the period 1879–1881.

44. Rogers, *A County Judge*, 113–114. See also *Morning Press*, 23 July 1901; Guinn, *Historical and Biographical Record*, 166; *Gazette*, 3 January 1856. The 1860 census reports listed 127 Indians living in

Santa Barbara; see U.S. Department of the Interior, Eighth Census: 1860, *Population of the United States* (Washington, D.C., 1864), 30. In the *Federal Manuscript Census Schedules* for 1860 the vast majority of the occupations for Indians were designated "servant."

45. McWilliams, *Southern California Country*, 55–56; Harris Newmark, *Sixty Years in Southern California, 1853–1913* (New York, 1916), 42, 62; Pitt, *Decline of the Californios*, 6–7, 53–54; *Federal Manuscript Census Schedules*, 1860; Sister M. Colette Standart, O.P., "The Sonoran Migration to California, 1848–1856: A Study in Prejudice," *Southern California Quarterly*, 58 (fall 1976):333–358. Marriage information is not specifically cited in the manuscript census; however, the name and age of the wife normally follow the name of the male head of household. Of the 46 non-California-born married Mexican heads of household enumerated in 1860, 38 had married women born in California.

46. *Federal Manuscript Census Schedules*, 1860. Based on the enumerator's listing of houses in order of visitations, the residential pattern clearly indicates clusters of Mexican-born households interspersed among the California-born families. Writers sometimes make distinctions between California-born and non-California-born Mexicans; see Charles E. Huse, *Sketch of the History and Resources of Santa Barbara City and County* (Santa Barbara, 1876), 26; *Gazette*, 14 February 1856; Angustias de la Guerra Ord, *Occurrences in Hispanic California*, translated and edited by Francis Price and William H. Ellison (Washington, D.C., 1956), 15, 55, 90; Oreña, *Reminiscences of Early California*, 76. In 1860 non-California-born Mexicans accounted for over 61 percent of the skilled workers and nearly 50 percent of the unskilled labor within the Spanish-surname work force.

47. Cleland, *Cattle on a Thousand Hills*, 39; Pitt, *Decline of the Californios*, 104–107.

48. Mason, *History of Santa Barbara*, 121–122. The non-Spanish-surnamed property owners indicated in Table 1 included several Anglo pioneers from the pre-1846 period, so that the total percentage of Anglos who had recently acquired property was substantially less. The tax assessments in Santa Barbara and other southern counties, when controlled by Californio tax collectors (as in Santa Barbara), generally reflect a sizable reduction from the real value of the property (perhaps 15 to 25 percent).

49. "Narracíon de Doña Teresa de la Guerra de Hartnell," 27. See also *Gazette*, 4 October, 1855, 31 January, 1856, 29 January, 1857. Pablo de la Guerra was the "silent partner-resident" of the highly successful land-claims law firm of Halleck, Peacy, and Billings. This relationship was evidently very important for Santa Barbara rancheros, who turned to the De la Guerra family influence in times of need. See Pitt, *Decline of the Californios*, 91–92.

50. The farmer group might be classified as a "middle class." Yet

this designation is misleading, since by comparison with the elite ranchero and lower occupational groups their property accumulation falls much closer to the latter. The farmers differed from the rancheros in that they managed their own lands, and they also differed from the more humble pobladores, who owned only a single town lot and dwelling. Moreover, the farmer class by surname did not contain the prestigious names of the rancheros; interfamily ties, however, may have existed between the two groups.

51. Camarillo, "The Making of a Chicano Community: A History of the Chicanos in Santa Barbara, California, 1850–1930" (Ph.D. dissertation, University of California, Los Angeles, 1975), 49–52.

52. *Federal Manuscript Census Schedules*, 1860, for the township of Santa Barbara. The manuscript schedules listed 2,235 individuals in the township, which included the adjacent pueblo lands. Spanish surnames totaled 1,554; but the 1860 *Population of the United States*, 30, listed 2,351, which may have been a corrected figure or an error. The county area in 1860 comprised what is today all of Ventura and Santa Barbara counties. The population of the city of Santa Barbara constituted over 60 percent of the entire region's population; see U.S. Department of the Interior, Tenth Census: 1880, *Population of the United States* (Washington, D.C., 1883), 382.

2. From "Mexican" to "American" Santa Barbara

1. *Bancroft Scrapbooks—California Counties*, vol. 4 (University of California, Berkeley), 311–312, clipping from *San Francisco Bulletin*, 1 May, 1867. See also *Morning Press*, 28 April 1894, 4 January 1900, 7 July 1907; Francis P. Farquhar, ed., *Up and down California in 1860–1864: The Journal of William H. Brewer* (New Haven, 1930), 56, 58.

2. Letter from Pedro C. Carrillo to Abel Stearns, 6 June 1861 (Stearn MSS, Huntington Library), cited in Cleland, *Cattle on a Thousand Hills*, 126; Pitt, *Decline of the Californios*, 108–109. Pitt also gives a good description of the effect of flood and drought in southern California; see 244–248.

3. Edward S. Spaulding, *A Brief Story of Santa Barbara*, (Santa Barbara, 1964), 59; Frank Sands, *A Pastoral Prince: The History and Reminiscences of J. W. Cooper* (Santa Barbara, 1893), 120; Hill and Parks, *Santa Barbara*, 69–70. The 1862 tax assessor estimated the number of cattle to be well over 200,000. The tax collectors of this time, however, generally calculated assessments at about 60 percent of the real figures.

4. *Bancroft Scrapbooks*, 310, clipping from *Alta California*, 14 October 1864. One local historian claimed that a $3,000 gift of charity from San Francisco was returned; see Mason, *History of Santa Barbara*, 126.

5. *Bancroft Scrapbooks*, 310, letter to the editor from C. Marshall, 15 October 1864; Rogers, *A County Judge*, 233.

6. Oreña, *Reminiscences of Early California*, 57. See also *Bancroft Scrapbooks*, 310, reprint of a letter published in *Alta California*, 14 October 1864.

7. Michael J. Phillips, *History of Santa Barbara County, California, from Its Earliest Settlement to the Present Time* (Los Angeles, 1927), 68; interview in 1922 with Mrs. Ysidora Domínguez.

8. James M. Guinn, "The Passing of the Cattle Barons of California," *Historical Society of Southern California*, 8 (1909–1911):59; Storke, *A Memorial History*, 44; Art Berman and Elaine Berman, "This Land Was Their Land," *West Magazine, Los Angeles Times*, 2 April 1972:7; Interview with Alfred Domínguez (20 August 1974); Walter A. Tompkins and Russel A. Ruiz, *Historical High Lights of Santa Barbara* (Santa Barbara, 1970), 63–65.

9. Guinn, "Passing of the Cattle Barons," 51. See also Walter C. McKain, Jr., and Sara Miles, "Santa Barbara County between Two Social Orders," *California Historical Society Quarterly*, 25 (December 1946):316; *Press*, 1 April 1871.

10. *Bancroft Scrapbooks*, 314–315; Hill and Parks, *Santa Barbara*, 70; *Santa Barbara Press*, 10 October 1870; McKain and Miles, "Santa Barbara County," 316–317; Cleland, *Cattle on a Thousand Hills*, 126.

11. *Bancroft Scrapbooks*, 316–317, 321–322. For New England architectural influence see John S. McGroarty, *California of the South—A History* (Los Angeles, 1933), 364; Spaulding, *A Brief Story*, 59. See also *Santa Barbara Post*, 31 November 1869; *Press*, 23 October 1869.

12. Tompkins, "Santa Barbara Journalists," 2. See also *Post*, 13 January 1869.

13. *Press*, 23 October 1869, 9 April 1870, 29 April 1871. See also Cleland, *Cattle on a Thousand Hills*, 230; Glenn S. Dumke, *The Boom of the Eighties in Southern California* (San Marino, California, 1955), 6.

14. John E. Baur, *The Health Seekers of Southern California, 1870–1900* (San Marino, California, 1959), 65–66. For promotion of agrarianism, see *Press*, 22 January 1870, 5, 13, and 19 February 1870, 9 April 1870. For tourism and immigration, see *Press*, 5 February 1869, 23 October 1869, 7 May 1870, 5 November 1870. For Johnson as a capitalist, see *Press*, 12 December 1872.

15. *Press*, 20 January 1873, 8 March 1873, 11 April 1873. See also Mary C. F. Hall-Wood, *Santa Barbara As It Is* (Santa Barbara, 1884), 9; *Bancroft Scrapbooks*, 328, clipping dated 22 November 1872; *Press*, 1 April 1871, 23 March 1872.

16. *Press*, 7 June 1873; Southworth, *Santa Barbara and Montecito*, 135–136; Storke, *A Memorial History*, 66. For the volume of city

real estate transactions reported by the recorder's office, see *Press*, 10 and 11 April 1873.

17. Nordhoff, *California* (New York, 1873), 111, 114; O'Neill, *History of Santa Barbara County*, 208; Baur, *The Health Seekers*, 66. See also *Press*, 7 September 1874, 14 November 1874.

18. Dumke, *Boom of the Eighties*, 223.

19. Guinn, *Historical and Biographical Record*, 161. For the influence of Hollister, see Tompkins, *Santa Barbara's Royal Rancho*, 197–202; Dumke, *Boom of the Eighties*, 162; *Press*, 9 April 1873. For background and the activities of Cook, see *Press*, 1 January 1872.

20. *Press*, 30 November 1872.

21. *Weekly Press*, 27 September 1873. See also *Press*, 24 September 1870, 10 June 1871. For improvements during the first boom, see Southern California Writers' Project of the Work Projects Administration, *Santa Barbara*, 41; O'Neill, *History of Santa Barbara County*, 203; Christian, "Santa Barbara School District," 36.

22. Letter reprinted from the San Francisco *Alta California*; see *Press*, 27 September 1873. See also *Federal Manuscript Census Schedules*, 1860 and 1870; Dumke, *Boom of the Eighties*, 8.

23. O'Neill, *History of Santa Barbara County*, 184–185. Richard Morefield, "The Mexican Adaptation in American California, 1846–1875," (Master's thesis, University of California, Berkeley, 1955), 50, claims that Mexicans failed to become a political power. This may be true at the statewide political level, but at the local level where circumstances directly affected most Californios, they constituted a potent political force. Santa Barbara is a case in point.

24. Streeter, *Recollections of Historical Events*, 241–243, 247.

25. Tompkins and Ruiz, *Historical High Lights*, 57–58. See also Pitt, *Decline of the Californios*, 206, 234–239; Mason, *History of Santa Barbara*, 144.

26. *List of Registered Names for the County of Santa Barbara, July 30, 1867, as they appear on the Great Register of the County for the year 1867* (San Francisco, 1867). See *Press*, 1 July 1869, for the town and county roster of elected officials. One often finds, in addition to Californios, the names of sons of Anglo families who married daughters of influential Californio families.

27. For the case against De la Guerra see *Press*, 20 November 1869, 4 December 1869; Cassidy, "Pablo de la Guerra," 192–195. On the assessment question see *Press*, 1 July 1869, 14 August 1869, 19 February 1870, 5 March 1870; Storke *A Memorial History*, 47.

28. *Press*, 10 September 1870. See also *Times*, 26 November 1870.

29. Letter reprinted from *San Francisco Daily Examiner* in *Press*, 21 October 1871. See also *Press*, 2 September 1871.

30. *Press*, 9 September 1871.

31. Letter from R. Espinoza of Santa Barbara, translated from Spanish, dated 4 September 1871, printed in *Press,* 9 September 1871. See also directory of town and county elected officials, 18 May 1872.

32. 23 August 1879. See also 29 May 1880.

33. 12 June 1873. See also *Great Register of the County of Santa Barbara, 1873* (Santa Barbara, 1873).

34. *Weekly Press,* 19 July 1873, 17 August 1873; *Press,* 2 and 20 August 1873.

35. 2 August 1873.

36. *Weekly Press,* 19 July 1873. See also *Press,* 2 August 1873.

37. *Press,* 9 August 1873.

38. 9 August 1873. See also *Times,* 23 August 1873; *Press,* 4 and 9 August 1873, 3 September 1873.

39. *Press,* 6 and 8 September 1873.

40. McKain and Miles, "Santa Barbara County," 318.

41. *Federal Manuscript Census Schedules,* 1870. The Spanish-surname population in the township of Santa Barbara was 1,210 and the total population listed was 2,640. The Spanish-surname population numbered 1,512 in the larger area in and near Santa Barbara. See also U.S. Department of the Interior, Ninth Census: 1870, *Population of the United States,* vol. 1 (Washington, D.C., 1872), 92; McKain and Miles, "Santa Barbara County," 312. In 1873 visitors swelled the town's population, whereupon the Mexican population probably accounted for about one-third of the total; for newspaper reports of the population increase, see *Weekly Press,* 27 September 1873; *Press,* 20 January 1873, 18 October 1873.

42. McKain and Miles, "Santa Barbara County," 315. The conclusions drawn from this article are based on small (12.5 percent) sample populations for the county of Santa Barbara in 1870 and are therefore open to question. However, the general changes in the economic-occupational structure that were analyzed in depth for the town of Santa Barbara were similar to changes occurring in other towns.

43. Camarillo, "Making of a Chicano Community," 92–94.

44. Ibid.

45. *Federal Manuscript Census Schedules,* 1870. Of the twenty principal industries in the town, for example, only one was operated by a Spanish-surnamed owner. For the continuation of the California-born and Mexican-born in traditional employment, see McKain and Miles, "Santa Barbara County," 313. The heritage of small, subsistence agriculture practiced by the Mexican community has often been overlooked, but it did play a role in the lives of most; see, for example, Jesse Francis, "An Economic and Social History of Mexican California, 1822–1846" (Ph.D. dissertation, University of California, Berkeley, 1936), 545–577. A small corps of Californio rancheros still operated their ancestral grants in 1873; of the eighty people owning over 500 acres of land in the county, nineteen had Spanish surnames; see *Press,*

22 November 1873. For newspaper ads calling for labor, see, for example, *Press,* 30 November 1872, 8 Janaury 1873, 3 March 1873.

3. Barrioization of the Chicano Community

1. *Weekly Press,* 17 January 1874; see also Rouse, *Santa Barbara's Spanish Renaissance,* 25–26.

2. Albert F. Webster, *A Sketch of Santa Barbara* (Santa Barbara, 1876). For other reprinted tourist accounts during the period 1874 to 1876, see *Weekly Press,* 24 October 1874; *Daily Press,* 23 January 1875; Mary Cone, *Two Years in California* (Chicago, 1876), 90–91.

3. *Daily Press,* 31 March 1877.

4. *Weekly Press,* 24 February 1877. See also *Weekly Press,* 5 February 1876; *All about Santa Barbara, California, The Sanitarium of the Pacific Coast* (Santa Barbara, 1878), 10–11.

5. Edith P. Cunningham, ed., *Letters and Journal óf Edith Forbes Perkins, 1908–1925,* vol. 4 (1931), 197.

6. Streeter, *Recollections of Historical Events,* 241.

7. 14 August 1886.

8. Edwards Roberts, *Santa Barbara and around There* (Boston, 1886), 75. See also Mary H. Wills, *A Winter in California* (Norristown, Pennsylvania, 1889), 96–97; *Morning Press,* 18 January 1890, 8 October 1890, letter reprinted from the San Francisco *Post;* Rouse, *Santa Barbara's Spanish Renaissance,* 26–27; Thomas M. Storke, *California Editor* (Los Angeles, 1958), 30.

9. McWilliams, *Southern California Country,* 61, 69.

10. *Federal Manuscript Census Schedules* for 1880 listed 932 Spanish surnames out of a total of 3,469 names. For estimates of the Spanish-surname population from 1881 to 1884, see Joseph J. Perkins, *A Business Man's Estimate of Santa Barbara County, California* (Santa Barbara, 1881), 25–26; Storke, *A Memorial History,* 51. See also U.S. Department of the Interior, Eleventh Census: 1890, *Report on Population of the United States,* pt. 1 (Washington, D.C., 1895), 73, 452; Clio L. Lloyd, *Santa Barbara* (Santa Barbara, 1892?), 12; Ernest J. S. Purslow, *Water Supply for Santa Barbara and Vicinity* (Santa Barbara, 1896), 13.

11. *Daily Press,* 4 March 1874, 12 April 1876; O'Neill, *History of Santa Barbara County,* 287; Rouse, *Santa Barbara's Spanish Renaissance,* 26–27.

12. S. E. A. Higgins, *La Casa de Aguirre of Santa Barbara, 1841–1884* (Santa Barbara, 1896), 28. For destruction of remaining adobes in the late 1880s and 1890s, see *Morning Press,* 26 June 1889, 21 May 1891. For construction of the public kindergarten and Santa Barbara Gas Works buildings near Pueblo Viejo, see *Morning Press,* 31 August 1894 and 11 December 1895.

13. Edwards Roberts, "A Santa Barbara Holiday," *Harpers*

Monthly Magazine, 75 (November 1887):834. Roberts was a Boston journalist who spent considerable time in Santa Barbara in the wake of the boom of 1886. His semifictitious article about a visit to Santa Barbara evidently recounted his own experiences on his first trip to the community and described the characters he met while there. The quote in the text reportedly was from the Chicano gardener at the main tourist hotel. See also Roberts' *Santa Barbara and around There.*

14. *Assessor's Block Book, Santa Barbara City, 1888* (Document of Santa Barbara County Assessor's Office, County Administration Building). There were few Spanish-surnamed property owners outside the geographic boundaries of the barrio in 1888. Pueblo Viejo contained well over 90 percent of the Spanish-surnamed property-owning population at this time.

15. *Daily Press,* 19 June 1873, 14 July 1874, 26 April 1875, 1 May 1875, 2 August 1877, 24 December 1883, 24 May 1886. For origins of the Mexican circus in Santa Barbara, see Bell, *Swinging the Censer,* 19, 25.

16. *Bancroft Scrapbooks,* 325, clipping of 8 March 1872; *Daily Press,* 1 July 1874, 24 November 1879; *Weekly Press,* 16 and 17 October 1874, 29 July 1876; *Morning Press,* 15 November 1896; Storke, *California Editor,* 41.

17. *Daily Press,* 4 October 1873; see also 3 October 1873 (this quotation was translated by the *Press;* the original speech was not available).

18. Streeter, *Recollections of Historical Events,* 241. See also *Daily Press,* 16 September 1874, 28 August 1876, 14 September 1880, 18 September 1883, 17 September 1884; *Weekly Press,* 19 August 1876; *La Gaceta de Santa Bárbara,* 13 September 1879.

19. *Morning Press,* 17 September 1892, 6 May 1893, 15 September 1896, 17 September 1898.

20. Engelhardt, *Santa Barbara Mission,* 404, 406. See also *Daily Press,* 4 June 1877, 28 May 1883, 12 June 1898.

21. Pitt, *Decline of the Californios,* 215.

22. Hall-Wood, *Santa Barbara As It Is,* 30.

23. 28 July 1877. See also *La Gaceta de Santa Bárbara,* 9 August 1879.

24. *Weekly Press,* 28 July 1877; *Daily Press,* 20 July 1883. See also *Weekly Press,* 26 July 1879; *Daily Press,* 18 July 1881; *Independent,* 21 and 23 July 1883; *Morning Press,* 21 July 1888, 16 July 1895, 2 July 1897; Rouse, *Santa Barbara's Spanish Renaissance,* 36.

25. *Press,* 22 March 1873; *Weekly Press,* 7 April 1877; *Morning Press,* 3 September 1895, 20 April 1888. In my interviews with descendants of nineteenth-century Santa Barbara Chicano families, many recalled the traditional family barbecues where everyone shared food and drink. The last reported community-invited Mexican wedding took place in 1878; see *Daily Press,* 12 October 1878.

26. Reverend A. W. Jackson, *Barbariana; or, Scenery, Climate, Soils, and Social Conditions of Santa Barbara City and County, California* (San Francisco, 1888), 19–20.

27. *Weekly Press*, 13 and 20 September 1879; *Daily Press*, 2 August 1881; *Morning Press*, 26 April 1893, 17 June 1896. Two Spanish-language newspapers appeared for a few years during the period 1879 to 1893. *La Gaceta de Santa Bárbara* was again published between 1879 and 1881; José Arzaga was the editor. Another paper, *El Boletín*, was published during the late 1880s and early 1890s before the editor left for Los Angeles.

28. *Weekly Press*, 9 October 1875; *San Diego Union*, 17 January 1875, 21 February 1875; *La Gaceta de Santa Bárbara*, 23 August 1879, 22 November 1879; see also Pitt, *Decline of the Californios*, 210–213.

29. *Federal Manuscript Census Schedules*, 1860, 1870, and 1880.

30. *Daily Press*, 8 February 1886; *Morning Press*, 25 July 1888, 31 October 1895, 11 February 1897, 13 October 1898. Most migrants left Santa Barbara to seek new employment opportunities.

31. *Santa Barbara County Board of Supervisors' Minutes*, Books C–H (Santa Barbara County Clerk of the Board of Supervisors, County Administration Building), 5 August 1878, 4 February 1880, April 1890, and July 1893. See also *Weekly Press*, 10 August 1878, 8 and 24 March 1879, 20 September 1879; *Daily Press*, 7 May 1881, 10 May 1882, 11 January 1883; *Morning Press*, 10 April 1890, especially 8 April 1897, 15 August 1897. The names of welfare recipients and the amounts received were printed in the Supervisors' Minutes books and often reprinted in the *Press*.

32. Storke, *A Memorial History*, 73. See also *Morning Press*, 15 December 1891, 8 August 1899.

33. *Morning Press*, 23 December 1892, 22 December 1893, 23 December 1894, 21 December 1897.

34. *Morning Press*, 5 May 1891, 29 August 1891, 18 May 1898.

35. *Daily Press*, 20 September 1876, 17 October 1876.

36. *Federal Manuscript Census Schedules*, 1860 and 1870; *Daily Press*, 23 July 1885.

37. *Daily Press*, 10 December 1877, 26 December 1885.

38. O'Neill, *History of Santa Barbara County*, 257, 289.

39. *Southern California Country*, 63.

40. L. Studdiford McChesney, *Under the Shadow of the Mission, A Memory of Santa Barbara* (London, 1897), 18. See also Webster, *A Sketch of Santa Barbara*, 4–5; Streeter, *Recollections of Historical Events*, 127–131; *Daily Press*, 8 January 1878.

41. Pitt, *Decline of the Californios*, 267, 269. For the education of Californio children, see Englehardt, *Santa Barbara Mission*, 412, 414; Geiger, *Mission Santa Barbara*, 194, 196; *Press*, 9 July 1870; *Daily Press*, 15 July 1882; *Morning Press*, 2 May 1897.

42. *Daily Press*, 8 and 15 July 1876; *Morning Press*, 6 July 1888, 6

July 1890. For Spanish clubs see *Daily Press*, 16 and 26 March 1878, 18 September 1878; *Morning Press*, 12 April 1891, 9 August 1899. See also Rouse, *Santa Barbara's Spanish Renaissance*, 33–41.

43. For intermarriage, especially of the De la Guerra family, see *Daily Press*, 4 May 1881; *Morning Press*, 6 July 1889, 26 June 1891, 18 April 1895, 1 July 1897. For references to mixed social functions between elite Californios and Anglos, see *Daily Press*, 23 April 1881, 18 July 1881.

44. *Great Register of the County of Santa Barbara, 1873*. Spanish-surnamed voters numbered 271 of the total number of 792 registered city voters. At the county level, those with Spanish surnames comprised 29.5 percent (483) of the 1,639 voters. Thus, the city of Santa Barbara in 1873 still contained 56.1 percent of all Spanish-surnamed voters in the county.

45. *Weekly Press*, 12 July 1879. See also *Old City and Election Information*, Office of City Clerk, Santa Barbara City Hall.

46. *Daily Press*, 3 and 7 March 1874.

47. *Outline of Historical Research*, from city council minutes P556 B-B, P594 B-B, and P595 B-B, P597 16 B-B, 16 April 1874, and 15 October 1874. See also Gidney, Brooks, and Sheridan, *History of Counties*, 121–122; *Daily Press*, 7 April 1874, 10 August 1874. Although two Anglos had temporarily presided over a Californio-majority board of trustees prior to 1874, the election of Cook marked the first time an Anglo presided over an Anglo majority.

48. *Daily Press*, 11 and 28 March 1878, 2 April 1878. See also *Weekly Press*, 26 January 1878.

49. 10 April 1880. One of the reasons why the Mexican vote was small, according to the *Gaceta* editor, was that "large numbers of them [were] absent [because of] the sheepshearing work in the countryside."

50. *Daily Press*, 2 and 6 April 1878; *Weekly Press*, 29 June 1878, 13, 15, 16, and 20 July 1878. Caesar Lataillade was reelected as the third-ward councilman in 1886 and retained that position into the twentieth century.

51. For the defeat of Spanish-surnamed candidates in municipal elections, see *Morning Press*, 14 September 1887, 2 March 1888, 8 April 1890, 7 April 1896, 15 November 1898. See also *Great Register of the County of Santa Barbara, California, 1890* (Santa Barbara, 1890).

52. *Daily Press*, 6 July 1875; *Weekly Press*, 7 August 1875, 4, 16, and 18 September 1875.

53. *Weekly Press*, 21 July 1877. For the case against Covarrubias see *Daily Press*, 19 June 1877, 9, 17, and 18 August 1877.

54. *Weekly Press*, 1 September 1877. See also *Daily Press*, 9 August 1877, 4 September 1877.

55. *Weekly Press*, 15 September 1877, 6 September 1879; *Daily Press*, 14 March 1878, 27 and 29 October 1878, 3 November 1878, 10 September 1879, 7 October 1880. For accusations against Covarrubias prior to 1877, see *Daily Press*, 21, 22, 23, 26, and 30 July 1875.

56. 11 September 1880.

57. *Daily Press,* 19 June 1882.

58. *Daily Press,* 19 and 26 June 1882.

59. *Great Register of the County of Santa Barbara, California, 1890.* For an 1894 listing of county and city officials, see W. Taylor Goodman, compiler, *Pacific Directory Company's Business Directory and Pocket Guide to Santa Barbara* (Santa Barbara, 1894), 68.

60. *Morning Press,* 23 June 1892; see also 8 and 9 April 1878. For arrest and conviction of Spanish-surnamed individuals see, for example, *Daily Press,* 12 September 1874, 4 January 1878, and 18 September 1878 for the 1870s; for the 1880s and 1890s see 13 October 1889, 21 November 1889, and 20 June 1893. For incidents of assault against Mexicans see 25 September 1876 and 18 October 1879.

61. *Daily Press,* 17 June 1886. See also Francis C. Kroll, *Memories of Rancho Santa Rosa and Santa Barbara* (Santa Barbara, 1964), 92; *Daily Press,* 10 February 1876, 14 October 1880; Storke, *California Editor,* 38; Tompkins and Ruiz, *Historical High Lights,* 66–67, 95–96; Webster, *A Sketch of Santa Barbara,* 3–4.

62. *Daily Press,* 25 April 1874, 2 and 9 May 1874, 6 June 1874, 16 and 18 July 1874, 30 March 1875, 27 and 29 January 1876, 28 February 1885.

63. For the best account of the 1886 boom, see Dumke, *Boom of the Eighties,* esp. 157, 163, 165, 173, 264, 276. See also O'Neill, *History of Santa Barbara County,* 282–283; *Daily Press,* 27 March 1886, 15 March 1887, 10 August 1887; Baur, *The Health Seekers,* ix.

64. *Daily Press,* 18 November 1874; *Bancroft Scrapbooks,* clipping from San Luis Obispo *Tribune,* 20 May 1876; *Daily Press,* 12 March 1883.

65. Caroline H. Dall, *My First Holiday; or, Letters Home from Colorado, Utah, and California* (Boston, 1881), 5, 7, 273.

66. Ibid., 255. See also R. A. Lang, compiler, *1897 Directory of Montecito, Summerland, Carpinteria, Goleta and Santa Barbara,* Press of W. H. Arne, 1897. The concentration of Spanish surnames was still confined to the area of Pueblo Viejo, primarily along Canon Perdido, Carrillo, De la Guerra, Anacapa, Santa Barbara and Garden streets (see map). There was a scattering of Spanish surnames in the area west of State Street, which probably represented a small migration of Chicanos to more isolated areas of the city, and a similar scattering in the lower east side. These residents most likely are the earliest contingent of Mexicano immigrants, those who began migrating to Santa Barbara in large numbers during the early twentieth century.

4. Origins of the Chicano Working Class in Santa Barbara

1. *Daily Press,* 1 July 1874; *Weekly Press,* 18 September 1875 and special issue September 1875 (undated, vol. 7, no. 11). See also *Daily Press,* 6 April 1876, 3 June 1880.

2. Dumke, *Boom of the Eighties*, 163; Hill and Parks, *Santa Barbara*, 96. See also *Daily Press*, 20 July 1886, 11 October 1886, 20 April 1887, 18 May 1887, 25 February 1888.

3. Sands, *A Pastoral Prince*, 158; *Daily Press*, 7 September 1875, 5 and 6 April 1877, 20 April 1881; Report of the County Assessor for 1878, see *Daily Press*, 1 July 1878.

4. U.S. Department of Interior, *Agriculture of the United States*, Eighth Census, 1860 (Washington, D.C., 1864), 10–11; U.S. Department of Interior, *The Statistics of the Wealth and Industry of the United States*, Ninth Census, 1870, vol. 3 (Washington, D.C., 1872), 104–105; U.S. Department of Interior, Census Office, *Report on the Productions of Agriculture*, Tenth Census, 1880 (Washington, D.C., 1883), 34, 106, 144; U.S. Department of Interior, Census Reports, vol. 5, *Agriculture*, pt. 1, Twelfth Census, 1900 (Washington, D.C., 1902), 62, 268; Reports of the County Assessor for 1878 and 1883, see *Daily Press*, 1 July 1878, 8 July 1883.

5. Dumke, *Boom of the Eighties*, 9.

6. Spaulding, *A Brief Story*, 60–61, and *Adobe Days*, 118–119; Department of Interior, Ninth Census: 1870, *Population of the United States*, vol. 1, 92; Storke, *California Editor*, 44–47; O'Neill, *History of Santa Barbara County*, 261.

7. Spaulding, *A Brief Story*, 61; Storke, *California Editor*, 44–46; O'Neill, *History of Santa Barbara County*, 260; Wills, *A Winter in California*, 53–54; McChesney, *Shadow of the Mission*, 62–64. See also *Daily Press*, 29 April 1876, 19 September 1878, 25 February 1884; *Weekly Press*, 3 August 1878; *Morning Press*, 30 April 1887; Phillips, *History of Santa Barbara County*, 185. For a good discussion of the early Chinese community in southern California, see McWilliams, *Southern California Country*, 84–95.

8. *Santa Barbara Index*, 30 April 1874. See also Kroll, *Memories of Rancho Santa Rosa*, 4; *Daily Press*, 11 October 1873, 26 December 1874, 8 December 1875.

9. 16 May 1876. See also *Weekly Press*, 20 and 27 May 1876.

10. *Weekly Press*, 5 and 26 July 1879, 6 September 1879. See also *Daily Press*, 19 June 1876, 13 and 25 September 1876; *Weekly Press*, 29 September 1877, 1 October 1877, 24 May 1879. For a general survey of the treatment of Chinese workers in California during this period, see Alexander Saxton, *The Indispensable Enemy: Labor and the Anti-Chinese Movement in California* (Berkeley and Los Angeles, 1971).

11. Storke, *California Editor*, 45–46. For pressure exerted against remaining laundries, see *Daily Press*, 12 and 19 September 1882, 25 August 1884. For police harassment of Chinese social activities, see *Daily Press*, 25 and 29 August 1883; *Morning Press*, 11 February 1890, 30 January 1894. For abolition of the Chinese abalone trade, see *Morning Press*, 21 April 1889, 4 and 6 October 1898, 17 February 1900.

12. Department of Interior, Tenth Census: 1880, *Population of the United States*, 382. For missionary endeavors, see *Press*, 21 March 1874; *Weekly Press*, 3 October 1874; *Daily Press*, 17 and 24 February 1874; *Morning Press*, 16 February 1896.

13. *Daily Press*, 31 July 1885, 5 February 1886.

14. The enumeration of individuals in the 1860 census created a problem in making comparisons with the 1870 occupational analysis for Spanish-surnamed workers, since the 1860 census did not specify the exact location of residents within the township of Santa Barbara. However, the town of Santa Barbara and nearby Montecito were the only two colonies of Spanish surnames in the township at this time. The 1870 census *did* specifically state the area in which all individuals resided. The analysis of occupation in this study for 1870 and 1880 is limited to the city of Santa Barbara. However, the omission of Spanish-surnamed workers (39 in 1870) in Montecito did not appreciably affect the percentages in the occupational structure of the city of Santa Barbara.

15. Because of the difficulties indicated in the preceding note, as well as the seasonal migration of Mexicans, the persistency and nonpersistency of the Spanish-surname population between 1860 and 1870 cannot be analyzed precisely. Notwithstanding these discrepancies in enumeration, approximately 18.8 percent or 55 of the 292 family male heads of household present in 1860 persisted into 1870; 78 percent of these were California-born.

16. Carey McWilliams alludes to a process of occupational erosion in *Southern California Country*, 65. The step-by-step occupational changes that he outlines do not, however, accurately reflect the changing Chicano occupational situation in Santa Barbara from 1870 to the 1890s.

17. O'Neill, *History of Santa Barbara County*, 267–268; C. M. Gidney, Benjamin Brooks, and Edwin M. Sheridan, *History of Santa Barbara, San Luis Obispo, and Ventura Counties, California*, vol. 1 (Chicago, 1917), 108; *Daily Press*, 14 June 1877, 13 July 1877, 23 October 1878; *Weekly Press*, 14 July 1877, 13 April 1878.

18. McChesney, *Shadow of the Mission*, 44–45.

19. *Daily Press*, 5 December 1877, 13 April 1878; Tompkins, "Santa Barbara Journalists," 5.

20. 21 July 1877.

21. *Daily Press*, 18 December 1877.

22. For descriptions of the occupations of caballero and vaquero, see the *Santa Barbara Index*, 16 April 1874; *Daily Press*, 18 May 1878, 10 July 1878; *Weekly Press*, 9 October 1875. For reference to sheep-shearers, see *Daily Press*, 16 and 22 April 1874, 5 June 1877, 25 March 1878, 29 September 1879; *La Gaceta de Santa Bárbara*, 12 March 1881. Pitt, *Decline of the Californios*, 254, also mentions sheepshearing activities in other areas of southern California during the 1870s. Rod-

man Paul in his article, "The Spanish-Americans in the Southwest," 45–47, alludes to the effects of job dislocation on rancho workers.

23. The 1880 *Federal Manuscript Census Schedules* listed information concerning unemployment of heads of household. The enumerator of Santa Barbara was diligent in consistently listing those unemployed part of the census year for both Spanish-surnamed and non-Spanish-surnamed individuals.

24. Judging from the seasonal-migratory nature of the work Mexicans performed, it is possible that the enumerator may have discounted a sizable number of workers and families who were not present at the time of the enumeration. One can only guess how many Chicano workers may have been omitted. But in July, when the census information was collected, many Chicano families were working in the hinterlands. Oscar Martínez makes a strong case arguing that the underenumeration of Spanish-surnamed people throughout the Southwest in the decennial censuses is 40 percent below real population figures. See "On the Size of the Chicano Population."

25. Ismael de la Rocha, "A Study of Social Mobility Patterns of Mexicans and Irish in Santa Barbara, 1870–1890" (unpublished paper, University of California, Santa Barbara, 1973).

26. Camarillo, "Making of a Chicano Community," 168.

27. *Federal Manuscript Census Schedules*, 1880. See also *Daily Press*, 3 December 1874, 17 December 1880, 19 September 1882, 7 and 16 November 1883. The mother of an interviewee also was employed part-time, and later full-time, as a home-based laundress beginning in the 1890s; interview with Veronica Medina (16 August 1974). Most domestics during this period were paid from $8 to $20 per month, depending upon age and capability.

28. Quoted in Mason, *History of Santa Barbara*, 175.

29. 20 August 1883. See also *Daily Press*, 31 July 1882, 22 September 1883; *Weekly Press*, 24 April 1880.

30. *Daily Press*, 24 May 1884; *Morning Press*, 26 July 1890, 5 March 1897.

31. *Daily Press*, 10 January 1884. For the almond harvests and other economic activities of Chicano children see *Santa Barbara Independent*, 11 November 1880; *Daily Press*, 29 November 1879, 11 November 1880.

32. Throughout the 1880s the school census of the city continued to record the largest absence of school-age children from the Chicano third ward district; see *Morning Press*, 29 May 1887. The Chicanitos of Santa Barbara were, no doubt, joined by their compañeros from Montecito for the seasonal harvests; see *Morning Press*, 16 November 1889, 20 February 1898.

33. *Morning Press*, 12, 13, and 22 November 1896.

34. *Morning Press*, 25 June 1897, 25 July 1897. Nearly every indi-

vidual interviewed who was born and raised in Santa Barbara either participated in the annual walnut harvests or knew families who did.

35. *Morning Press*, 23 December 1896.

36. W. H. Hoffman, *Catalogue of Natural History Goods* (Santa Barbara, 1886), preface, 7. For other Chicano leather workers see *Morning Press*, 28 October 1889, 28 January 1894.

37. For the sea lion trade, see *Daily Press*, 16 March 1880; *Morning Press*, 14, 21, and 23 May 1891, 13 July 1897, 15 February 1899. For references to vaqueros and shepherds, see Kroll, *Memories of Rancho Santa Rosa*, 48–49; *Daily Press*, 5 February 1881, 7 February 1884.

38. *Daily Press*, 23 August 1881, 23 November 1881, 22 September 1882; *Morning Press*, 6 September 1887, 26 April 1892, 5 May 1892, 14 September 1892, 26 March 1893, 23 August 1895; *La Gaceta de Santa Bárbara*, 10 April 1880.

39. Kroll, *Memories of Rancho Santa Rosa*, 60, 70; also interviews with Leo Cordero and Walter Cordero (19 and 20 September 1974). Leo's father, Walter's great uncle, was the mayordomo on many county shearing circuits during the 1890s and early 1900s.

40. Interviews with Miguel García and Russell A. Ruiz (12 September 1974, 20 August 1974). Mr. García, age 80, is probably the last surviving trasquilador in Santa Barbara. Mr. Ruiz's relatives participated in the western states migration.

41. For tamal and nopal vendors, see Kroll, *Memories of Rancho Santa Rosa*, 24; *Morning Press*, 9 September 1891, 3 November 1891, 2 April 1892; *Daily Press*, 20 August 1885. For bootblacks and hacks, see *Daily Press*, 20 April 1880; *Morning Press*, 16 September 1892, 12 May 1893.

42. *Outline of Historical Research;* also reported in the *Morning Press*, 27 and 30 January 1895.

43. *Santa Barbara County Board of Supervisors' Minutes*, Books G and H, April 1897 and January 1900. For earlier periods see Books C–F (1880, 1885, 1886, and 1891). For Chicano street workers, see *Daily Press*, 18 May 1885; *Morning Press*, 31 March 1893, 19 December 1893, 13 October 1895, 13 November 1895. For the employment of Chinese laborers, see *Daily Press*, 6 September 1875, 19 January 1876; *Morning Press*, 30 August 1877, 28 and 31 January 1888.

44. *Morning Press*, 1 October 1889, 13 April 1899, 17 and 20 August 1899.

45. 8 June 1894.

46. 29 July 1894.

47. 26 August 1899.

48. For reference to Santa Barbara as a year-round resort, see *Morning Press*, 4 and 26 March 1892 and 2 May 1896; Baur, *The Health Seekers*, 69–71.

49. See also Table 18 for the occupational structure of all Spanish-surnamed women between 1900 and 1930.

5. Mexican Society in Nineteenth-Century Southern California

1. These three cities, and Santa Barbara, were selected for several reasons. In the nineteenth century these pueblos were the centers of the Mexican population; they also controlled the economic resources and political power in southern California (particularly Santa Barbara and Los Angeles). Throughout the late nineteenth and early twentieth centuries these same locations developed into the principal cities in the region. They provide the historical backdrop from which to trace the development of Chicano society over time, as Mexicans remained a sizable population in each locality. These locations, furthermore, are geographically representative of the southern California region, which contains the large urban center of Los Angeles, smaller coastal cities like Santa Barbara and San Diego, and inland valley cities like San Bernardino. It should be noted that for the San Bernardino Valley, the pueblo of San Salvador will be discussed for the nineteenth century; however, since this pueblo did not persist after the turn of the century, the Chicano community in the neighboring city of San Bernardino will be discussed in Chapter 9 for twentieth-century developments.

2. This overview of the social class structure in the pueblos of southern California is based on analysis of traditional primary and secondary sources as well as quantitative sources (*Federal Manuscript Census Schedules* for 1850 and 1860). For individual citations on each of the four communities, see notes 8 through 14.

3. See, for example, Table 11 for the percentages of the groups designated *rancher* and *professional* within the pueblo occupational structures for 1860. The variations of occupation and social class in the different pueblos will be discussed later in this chapter. See also the percentages in Table 11 for the occupational groupings designated *skilled, semiskilled,* and *unskilled.* San Diego, however, varies from the other pueblos.

4. Between the 1830s and the 1850s the Native American population in the pueblos declined from an estimated high ranging from 10 to 25 percent in the earlier period to a low ranging from 3 to 10 percent during the latter period. By 1870 the Indian population in the growing towns and cities had been reduced to only a fraction of its earlier size. See Cook, *California Indian and White Society,* 236–239, and his *Populations of California Indians,* 55. Assimilation and intermarriage of Indians into mestizo society is evident when the federal manuscript census schedules for Santa Barbara and Los Angeles are analyzed; see also note 6.

5. In southern California, unlike central Mexico, a system of

peonage did not manifest itself among the mestizo people. The pastoral economic functions that pueblo residents traditionally performed were reinforced by social, religious, and familial ties and by employer-employee loyalties. For references to Mexican social cohesiveness in each of the pueblos, see the citations listed in notes 6 through 12.

6. Richard A. Griswold del Castillo, "La Raza Hispano Americana: The Emergence of an Urban Culture among the Spanish Speaking of Los Angeles, 1850–1880" (Ph.D. dissertation, University of California, Los Angeles, 1974), 20–35, 77–78; Camarillo, "Making of a Chicano Community," 18–24.

7. Federal Writers' Project, Work Projects Administration, *San Diego: A California City* (San Diego, 1937), 30, 32; Charles Hughes, "The Decline of the Californios: The Case of San Diego, 1846–1856," *Journal of San Diego History*, 21 (summer 1975):6–8; William E. Smythe, *History of San Diego, 1542–1908*, vol. 1 (San Diego, 1908), 124, 131–134, 148–156; George Tays, *Plaza in Old San Diego* (Berkeley, 1937), 1; Theodore S. Van Dyke, *The City and County of San Diego* (San Diego, 1888), 18; Clarence A. McGrew, *City of San Diego and San Diego County*, vol. 1 (Chicago, 1922), 62–65; Douglas Gunn, *San Diego: Climate, Resources, Topography, Productions, etc.*, etc. (San Diego, 1886), 7–8. The total population of the town of San Diego in 1860 was 731.

8. For primary and secondary sources that shed light on the social class structure of San Diego, see the following: Smythe, *History of San Diego*, vol. 1, 142; Lillian Whaley, *Old Times in Old Town* (San Diego, n.d.), 1–2; William Shaw, *Golden Dreams and Waking Realities; Being the Adventures of a Gold-Seeker in California and the Pacific Islands* (London, 1851), 15–16, 20–21; Tays, *Plaza in Old San Diego*, 2; *Federal Manuscript Census Schedules*, San Diego County, 1860. The occupational structure for Spanish-surnamed heads of household in the town of San Diego in 1860 (see Table 11) indicates that the percentage of ranchers there (29 percent) was the highest, compared to the occupational structure in the other southern California pueblos. The percentage of semiskilled and unskilled mestizo workers was the lowest. Another historian has estimated that the elite "rico" class was much larger (perhaps as high as 62 percent) in 1860 San Diego; see Mario T. García, "The Californios of San Diego and the Politics of Accommodation," *Aztlán*, 6 (spring 1975):77.

9. Several confusing names have been applied to this oldest pueblo settlement of Mexicans in the San Bernardino Valley. Actually, San Salvador comprised two adjoining pueblos separated by the Santa Ana River. On the northwest side of the river was the Agua Mansa pueblo, and directly across the river on the southeast side was La Placita (de los Trujillos). San Salvador refers to the combined communities of Agua Mansa and La Placita. It was also the name later given to

the voting district, school district, and parish church. See Joyce Carter Vickery, *Defending Eden: New Mexican Pioneers in Southern California* (Riverside, California, 1977), 3–4.

10. Vickery, *Defending Eden*, 9–30; H. F. Raup, *San Bernardino, California: Settlement and Growth of a Pass-Site City* (Berkeley, 1940), 16–17; John Brown, Jr., and James Boyd, *History of San Bernardino and Riverside Counties* (Chicago, 1922), 26–27, 31; George W. Beattie and Helen Pruit Beattie, *Heritage of the Valley: San Bernardino's First Century* (Pasadena, California, 1939), 59–61; Emily M. Knight, Arda M. Hoenszel, and Gerald A. Smith, "Historic Chronology of San Bernardino County," *Quarterly of San Bernardino County Museum*, 9 (summer 1962):3–5; Father Juan Caballeria, *History of San Bernardino Valley: From the Padres to the Pioneers, 1810–1851* (San Bernardino, 1902), 102–106; Tom Patterson, *A Colony for California: Riverside's First Hundred Years* (Riverside, California, 1971), 131–132.

11. Benjamin Hayes, *Pioneer Notes: From the Diaries of Judge Benjamin Hayes, 1849–1875* (Los Angeles, 1929), 268, 270, 272; see also the similar remarks of another Anglo pioneer—Horace Bell, *Reminiscences of a Ranger; or, Early Times in Southern California* (Los Angeles, 1881), 73.

12. Beattie and Beattie, *Heritage of the Valley*, 96–97, 106–107, 177; Vickery, *Defending Eden*, 17–20, 31, 50, 58–60; Patterson, *A Colony for California*, 130; Emma Maltsburger, *The Story of Colton, California* (Colton, 1974), 35–36; Brown and Boyd, *History of San Bernardino*, 34–35; *Federal Manuscript Census Schedules*, San Bernardino County, 1860.

13. Pitt, *Decline of the Californios*, 18–19. Racial conflict and Anglo antagonism toward Mexicans in southern California was part of the legacy evolving throughout the Southwest during the nineteenth century. See Acuña, *Occupied America*, esp. 1–123.

14. Pitt, *Decline of the Californios*, 30–31, 33–35; Donald S. Miller, "Guachama: A Place to Eat," in "The Bent Cross: A History of the Mexican American in the San Bernardino Valley," ed. Carlos E. Cortés (unpublished manuscript); Vickery, *Defending Eden*, 42–44, 47–49; Beattie and Beattie, *Heritage of the Valley*, 97–98; Federal Writers' Project, *San Diego*, 35–36; Hughes, "Decline of the Californios: San Diego," 9; García, "Californios of San Diego," 70.

15. Pitt, *Decline of the Californios*, 148–166; Griswold del Castillo, "La Raza Hispano Americana," 191.

16. Griswold del Castillo, "La Raza Hispano Americana," 200–205; Camarillo, "Making of a Chicano Community," 128, 134–135; Patterson, *A Colony for California*, 60–61, 117–118. Very little evidence was found to indicate that the San Diego case was similar to that of Los Angeles, Santa Barbara, and San Salvador. However, one local historian suggests that American military abuse and confiscation of

Mexican property during the war inflamed racial animosity in San Diego; see Hughes, "Decline of the Californios: San Diego," 9.

17. Patterson, *A Colony for California*, 118.

18. Griswold del Castillo, "La Raza Hispano Americana," 255–257, 260–270.

19. Beattie and Beattie, *Heritage of the Valley*, 98–100, 206; Bell, *Reminiscences of a Ranger*, 72, 275–279; Vickery, *Defending Eden*, 63–64.

20. Patterson, *A Colony for California*, 118; Miller, "Guachama," 73–77; Caballeria, *History of San Bernardino Valley*, 122; *Great Register of the County of San Bernardino, State of California*, 1867–1868, 1873, and 1880; Beattie and Beattie, *Heritage of the Valley*, 109–119. In contrast to the San Salvador township, Spanish-surnamed persons constituted only 11 percent of all voters in Riverside.

21. Miller, "Guachama," 74; see also Patterson, *A Colony for California*, 209–210.

22. García, "Californios of San Diego," 70–72, 79–80; Hughes, "Decline of the Californios: San Diego," 2, 19–22. *Great Register of San Diego County, California*, 1867, 1872, and 1879.

23. See, for example, Pitt, *Decline of the Californios*, chaps. 5 and 6; see also Cleland, *Cattle on a Thousand Hills*, and W. W. Robinson, *Land in California* (Berkeley and Los Angeles, 1948).

24. Mario T. García, "Merchants and Dons: San Diego's Attempt at Modernization, 1850–1860," *Journal of San Diego History*, 21 (winter 1975):69–70, Hughes, "Decline of the Californios: San Diego," 17–18; Cleland, *Cattle on a Thousand Hills*, 196–197; R. W. Brackett, *The History of San Diego County Ranchos* (San Diego, 1960), 51–52, 55–57, 62–64; Griswold del Castillo, "La Raza Hispano Americana," 77–79, 94, 96. Charles Hughes, in his article "The Decline of the Californios: The Case of San Diego, 1846–1856," concluded that the San Diego cattle industry never attained the same economic importance as in other southern California rancho areas. As a result, there were fewer wealthy ranchers in the county, and their economic decline did not parallel the losses suffered by the rancher class elsewhere in the region.

25. H. C. Hopkins, *History of San Diego: Its Pueblo Land and Water* (San Diego, 1929), 159, 162, 215, 223–258, quote on 243; U.S. General Land Office, *Pueblo Lands of San Diego: Exceptions to Survey Made by John C. Hays, July, 1858* (San Francisco, 1869), 5–7.

26. Patterson, *A Colony for California*, 117.

27. Beattie and Beattie, *Heritage of the Valley*, 109–119; Miller, "Guachama," 75–77; Patterson, *A Colony for California*, 60–61, 117–118; Vickery, *Defending Eden*, 80–82. For the effects of the No-Fence Law elsewhere in southern California, see Van Dyke, *City of San Diego*, 10–11; *San Diego Union*, 19 December 1871.

28. Griswold del Castillo, "La Raza Hispano Americana," 62–63, 66.

29. Ibid., 242–247, 250–253, quote on 276. See also McWilliams, *Southern California Country,* 64–67.

30. Quoted in Ricardo Romo, "Mexican Workers in the City: Los Angeles, 1915–1930" (Ph.D. dissertation, University of California, Los Angeles, 1975), 80.

31. "La Raza Hispano Americana," 255; see also 34, 219–220, 253–254; McWilliams, *Southern California Country,* 69.

32. Griswold del Castillo, "La Raza Hispano Americana," 213–228, 274–275.

33. Ibid., 69–70, 73–75, 205–211. Repatriation movements to Mexico occurred in Los Angeles as well as Santa Barbara.

34. Brown and Boyd, *History of San Bernardino,* 39, 46; U.S. Department of Interior, Eighth Census, 1860, *Population of the United States,* 31; Miller, "Guachama," 65–68; Raup, *San Bernardino,* 41; Vickery, *Defending Eden,* 76–78; U.S. Department of Interior, Ninth Census, 1870, *The Statistics of the Population of the United States,* vol. 1, 91.

35. Hayes, *Pioneer Notes,* 272; Beattie and Beattie, *Heritage of the Valley,* 107–108; Vickery, *Defending Eden,* 67–73.

36. Miller, "Guachama," 72–73; *Federal Manuscript Census Schedules,* San Bernardino County, 1880.

37. "Guachama," 30, 78, 82. See also Vickery, *Defending Eden,* 82.

38. *Federal Manuscript Census Schedules,* San Bernardino County, 1900; Caballeria, *History of San Bernardino Valley,* 121; Miller, "Guachama," 30, 78. See also John R. Brumgardt and William David Putney, "San Salvador: New Mexican Settlement in Alta California," *Southern California Quarterly,* 59 (winter 1977):353–364.

39. Dana, *Two Years before the Mast, with subsequent matter by the author* (Boston, 1868), 450.

40. *Federal Manuscript Census Schedules,* San Diego County, 1860; U.S. Department of Interior, Eighth Census, 1860, *Population of the United States,* 31. See also Mary E. Morse, "Recollections of the Early Times in San Diego" (San Diego, 1898), 400–404; Elizabeth C. MacPhail, ed., "Early Days in San Diego: The Memoirs of Augusta Barrett Sherman," *Journal of San Diego History,* 18 (fall 1972):29.

41. Carl H. Heilbron, ed., *History of San Diego County* (San Diego, 1936), 7–9, 16–17, 26, quote on 83; Elizabeth C. MacPhail, *The Story of New San Diego and of Its Founder Alonzo E. Horton* (San Diego, 1969), 10–11; García, "Merchants and Dons," 56–57; Hughes, "Decline of the Californios: San Diego," 11; Smythe, *History of San Diego,* 339–343.

42. *San Diego Union,* 22 March 1871, 20 June 1871, 19 July 1871,

1 November 1871, 21 April 1872, 8 May 1872, 8 and 12 July 1874; Smythe, *History of San Diego*, 366–375, 413–414, 433–442; Van Dyke, *City of San Diego*, 18–20.

43. 10 January 1875. For social, cultural, and patriotic events, see the following: *San Diego Union*, 17 September 1871, 7 and 13 February 1872, 2 April 1872, 25 May 1872, 12 June 1872, 10 and 23 December 1873, 12 April 1874, 28 June 1874, 17 September 1880; Winifred Davidson, *Old Town Talk* (San Diego, n.d.), vol. 1, 44.

44. MacPhail, *Early Days in San Diego*, 29.

45. John C. Moore, "Reminiscences of Old Town," *Silver Gate*, 1 (November 1899):6–7.

46. *San Diego Union*, 25 January 1874; Frank H. Mandeville, *Tourists' Guide to San Diego and Vicinity* (San Diego, 1888), 33; Susan D. Tiffany, "Memory Like the Ivy Clings," *Old Times in Old Town and San Diego, California* (San Diego, 1974), 7; U.S. Department of Interior, 1870, vol. 1, *Population*, 90, and 1890, pt. 1, *Population*, 73.

47. San Diego had a much larger percentage of ranchers and skilled workers and fewer unskilled workers in its occupational structure than did the other pueblos. The presence of a sizable Indian population nearby or the less productive local cattle economy may have accounted for the smaller percentage of unskilled workers. For an example of seasonal employment in the pastoral economy by pueblo residents and seasonal subsistence farming, see Davidson, *Old Town Talk*, vol. 1, 43; Douglas Gunn, *A Historical Sketch of San Diego, San Diego County, California* (n.p., 1884), 7–8; U.S. General Land Office, *Pueblo Lands of San Diego*, 5–7; Vickery, *Defending Eden*, 58, 72–73.

48. Griswold del Castillo, "La Raza Hispano Americana," 85. Even as the percentage of ranchers and farmers decreased and the percentage of skilled and unskilled workers increased, there was a large growth in the total number of Chicano workers in Los Angeles between 1850 and 1860 (from 298 to 863). The migration of many Mexican-born individuals may also partially account for the increase of skilled and unskilled workers. Griswold del Castillo's occupational classifications do not exactly correspond to those used in this study; however, they are generally consistent with mine. Slight variations of the Los Angeles case from the other towns may, therefore, be a result of the discrepancies in the two occupational classifications. At least one author has suggested that the economic trends typical of Los Angeles after 1850 were part of an urban-oriented economy that had been evolving since the 1830s; see Howard J. Nelson, "The Two Pueblos of Los Angeles: Agricultural Village and Embryo Town," *Southern California Quarterly*, 59 (spring 1977):1–11.

49. Griswold del Castillo, "La Raza Hispano Americana," 78–79, 81.

50. Ibid., 78, 96.

51. The comparison between the two occupational groups in the San Bernardino Valley is between Chicanos in San Salvador and Anglos in the nearby town of San Bernardino as well as in San Salvador; very few Anglos, however, lived in San Salvador.

52. The 1880 occupational structure clearly indicates that the pastoral economy had been replaced by an agrarian and urban commercial-oriented economy.

53. "La Raza Hispano Americana," 63–64, 91, quote on 112–113; see also Tables 11, 12, and 13; Vickery, *Defending Eden,* 82.

54. McWilliams, *Southern California Country,* 65–66; Cleland, *Cattle on a Thousand Hills,* 139–142; Pitt, *Decline of the Californios,* 254; Miller, "Guachama," 72.

55. *Federal Manuscript Census Schedules,* Santa Barbara and San Diego County, 1880. The pattern of resistance to employment in the new labor market was evident in Santa Barbara and San Salvador during the 1870s. It is logical to assume that this pattern occurred in Los Angeles and San Diego as well, judging by the presence of sizable numbers of other ethnic workers (Chinese and Indians) who filled most unskilled labor needs until the late 1870s.

56. For the use of Indian and Chinese labor, see the following: McWilliams, *Southern California Country,* 44–46, 84–95; *Federal Manuscript Census Schedules* for San Diego, Santa Barbara, and San Bernardino Counties, 1860–1880; Daughters of the American Revolution, *San Diego Yesterdays* (San Diego, 1921), 65; Nordoff, *California,* 133; Mary C. Miller, "The Anti-Chinese Movement in San Diego, 1870–1882" (unpublished paper, San Diego, 1972), 3–15; *San Diego Union,* 9 November 1871.

57. Miller, "Guachama," 67–68; Ratcliffe Hicks, *Southern California; or, The Land of the Afternoon* (Springfield, Massachusetts, 1898), 71; Patterson, *A Colony for California,* 350–351; Cleland, *Cattle on a Thousand Hills,* 150; Griswold del Castillo, "La Raza Hispano Americana," 89–90.

58. *Federal Manuscript Census Schedules,* Santa Barbara, San Diego, and San Bernardino, 1880 and 1900; Griswold del Castillo, "La Raza Hispano Americana," 128; Tiffany, *Old Times in Old Town,* 9. The small number of employed Chicana heads of household in San Bernardino did not increase between 1880 and 1900; no information on Chicana employment is available for Los Angeles in 1900. The Chicano family structure during this period provides an important and interesting area for future study.

59. Quoted in Griswold del Castillo, "La Raza Hispano Americana," 120 (note 29).

60. Caballeria, *History of San Bernardino Valley,* 212.

61. By 1900 San Salvador was no longer designated separately in the census manuscript schedules. Most likely the small population remaining in the original San Salvador area was incorporated into the

nearby Colton township of San Bernardino County and Riverside township of Riverside County. Thus, occupations for Spanish-surnamed persons are designated for Mexicans of San Bernardino city for the period beginning 1900.

6. Mexican Immigration and the Expansion of the Santa Barbara Chicano Community

1. *Morning Press*, 22 May 1900, 12 June 1900.
2. *Independent*, 24 May 1900. See also *Morning Press*, 26 August 1899, 2 May 1900, 20 June 1900.
3. Interview with Yldefonso ("Poncho") Osuna (23 August 1974). Osuna was in a most advantageous position to view the development of the Mexicano community. His father migrated to Santa Barbara from Sonora during the 1890s and subsequently established the first store to cater to the foreign-born Mexicano population. As a delivery boy, Osuna had contact with most Mexicanos residing in Santa Barbara during the early 1900s. See also *Morning Press*, 1 July 1894, 21 March 1899, 25 February 1903. For oral history interviews, see Appendix 1.
4. This process of familial immigration was common to Mexicanos as well as to most immigrant groups in the United States. For example, the father of the interviewee mentioned above, Mr. Osuna, was urged to come to Santa Barbara by a friend who had migrated there a few years earlier. Osuna's father brought his family and was followed by another family from the same pueblo near Guaymas, Sonora. The mother of another interviewee, Walter Cordero (19 September 1974), arrived in Santa Barbara during the 1890s. For references to other foreign-born Mexicans, see *Morning Press*, 26 February 1903, 17 December 1905, 9 February 1912, 19 March 1913, 4 January 1914, 1 January 1922.
5. *Independent*, 28 May 1906; *Morning Press*, 12 May 1911, 16 June 1912. For other political-religious exiles, see *Daily News*, 7 February 1916.
6. Interviews with Federico López (7 October 1974), Hortencia Castro de Cuellar (11 September 1974), Anita and Reyes Castro (25 September 1974), Leo Cordero (20 September 1974), Mary Ortega (14 September 1974), Yldefonso Osuna and Vereanda Sánchez (2 October 1974).
7. The number of Mexican-born residents in Santa Barbara by 1915 is difficult to ascertain. City directories do not differentiate among native-born and foreign-born Spanish-surnamed people, and census reports are grossly inaccurate in recording the "real" number of Mexicanos in any given period prior to 1930. The 1910 census enumerated only 123 Mexican-born individuals; see U.S. Department of Commerce, Thirteenth Census, 1910, *Abstract of the Census with Supple-*

ment for California (Washington, D.C., 1913), 612. However, the number of Spanish-surnamed male heads of household and adult employed residents listed in the city directories increased from 283 in 1896 to 422 in 1909–1910. Mexicanos must have constituted the majority of the increase at this time. Moreover, impressions from the various interviewees contradict the 1910 census figures. A rough estimate for the 1915 Mexican-born population would range from 175 to 225 households, or approximately 750 to 1,000 people.

8. 19 August 1916.

9. Interview with Federico López, translated from Spanish. A sizable percentage of Mexicans from the state of Durango migrated from the rural rancho areas south of the city of Durango, particularly from Santiago-Papasquiaro; interviews with José Martínez (25 September 1974), Angela Cordero (21 September 1974), and Hortencia Castro de Cuellar. Martínez and Cordero migrated from Santiago, Durango.

10. Camarillo, "Making of a Chicano Community," 202–204.

11. *Santa Barbara City Directory*, 1911–1912, 1920, and 1929–1930, "Street and Avenue Guide and Householder's Directory." Beginning with the 1911 directory, a street guide that listed the last name of each resident on all Santa Barbara city streets facilitated the plotting of Spanish-surnamed residents. The areas of the lower eastside barrio and Pueblo Viejo were then distinctly outlined. Also, the interviewees furnished a description of barrio boundaries and areas of dense Mexicano population that paralleled the areas mapped from the city directories. Interviews with Dolores and Daniel Vásquez (25 September 1974), Jesse and Luis Acosta (29 January 1975), José Martínez, Walter Cordero, Mary Ortega, Lydia and Albert Caballero (24 August 1974), Nellie Pérez (12 September 1974), and Angela Cordero.

12. The Chinese and Japanese inhabited the Chinatown area on Canon Perdido Street, next to the Pueblo Viejo barrio. A small number of Italian families clustered together on Canal Street above Ortega Street (see map).

13. Interviews with Jesse and Luis Acosta, José Martínez, Walter Cordero, and Mary Ortega; *Our Lady of Guadalupe Parish, Silver Jubilee, 1928–1953, Santa Barbara, California* (Santa Barbara, 1953), 7–8.

14. For Italian immigrant mutual-aid societies in Santa Barbara, see *Morning Press*, 2 September 1898, 18 August 1903, 25 September 1910, 20 April 1914. For other European and North American immigrant groups as well as the Asian-American societies, see *Daily Press*, 3 and 24 March 1877; *Morning Press*, 17 January 1909, 10 June 1914, 22 August 1914.

15. There have been few studies that have analyzed the internal dynamics of Mexicano mutualistas. The works of Manuel Gamio and Paul Taylor (listed in the Bibliography) still remain two of the best general surveys. Recent studies that have focused on Chicano organizational activity in the twentieth century have placed too little emphasis

on the mutualistas as important institutions in the socioeconomic and political history of the Chicano; see, for example, Miguel Tirado, "Mexican American Community Political Organization," *Aztlán*, 1 (spring 1970):53–78, and Armando Navarro, "The Evolution of Chicano Politics," *Aztlán*, 5 and 2 (spring and fall 1974):57–84.

16. *Club Mexicano Independencia, President's Notebook*, 1914–1917. The Spanish-language original was in the possession of Federico López, the last president of the CMI, who died in 1975. See also *Constitución del Club Mexicano Independencia y Artículos de Incorporación*. The CMI was incorporated under the laws of the county and state in 1924.

17. *CMI, President's Notebook*.

18. *Constitución del CMI*, chap. 2, 3, and 7.

19. Interview with Federico López. See also *Constitución del CMI*.

20. *Constitución del CMI*, chap. 6. Also interviews with Federico López, Dolores and Daniel Vásquez. Vásquez was secretary of the CMI during the 1920s.

21. *Ritual del Club Mexicano Independencia* (Santa Barbara, 1927), 10; *Constitución del CMI*, 17–36.

22. *Daily News*, 17 April 1917. Ventura County had experienced periodic strikes by Mexicano workers in Oxnard in 1903 and at the Limonera Ranch in 1917. There was a report in 1913 that Mexicanos, angered at the U.S. bombardment of Vera Cruz, were going to set fire to Oxnard. Strikes also occurred at various times in the city of Santa Barbara. The anti-Mexican hysteria created by the discovery of the Zimmerman note of March 1917, from the German ambassador to a Mexican official calling for Mexico to declare war on the United States, no doubt increased the paranoia of Anglos. See *Morning Press*, 24 April 1914; *Daily News*, 28 March 1917.

23. 19 April 1917.

24. Interviews with Federico López, Luis Acosta, Dolores and Daniel Vásquez. See also *Morning Press*, 23 April 1922, 6 January 1928.

25. *Constitución del CMI*, 36–37. See also *Daily News*, 12 October 1926, 22 January 1927, 27 May 1927, 9 February 1928.

26. 21 July 1919. Interview also with Reyes Castro, one of the few surviving cofounders. See also *Morning Press*, 16 September 1913; *Daily News*, 17 July 1919.

27. Interview with Reyes Castro.

28. 28 August 1919.

29. Interviews with Reyes Castro, Yldefonso Osuna, Lydia and Albert Caballero.

30. Ibid. For social activities, see *Morning Press*, 3 May 1922, 23 and 30 October 1928; *Daily News*, 27 February 1926, 26 June 1926, 10 September 1926, 6 January 1927, 4 November 1927.

31. Interviews with Lydia and Albert Caballero, Nellie Pérez, and

Yldefonso Osuna. Very little is known about La Liga Protectora; none of the interviewees were members. La Sociedad Internacional de Beneficios Mutuos in all likelihood had chapters in Mexico as well as in the southwestern United States. In California there were chapters in Carpinteria, Goleta, San Jose, Los Angeles, Oakland, and probably other cities too.

32. Interviews with Yldefonso Osuna, a cofounder of the Acacia Lodge; with Hortencia Castro de Cuellar and Jesse Acosta, both of whom were members of La Cruz Azul Mexicana; and with Lydia Caballero, a member of Club La Rosita. For the Mexican Ladies' Society, see *Morning Press,* 18 November 1921.

33. 16 and 17 September 1924. Interviews with Federico López and Yldefonso Osuna. For the post-1917 celebrations conducted by the Junta Patriótica, see *Morning Press,* 15 September 1917, 12 and 17 September 1921, 15 and 16 September 1922, 15 September 1923, 16 September 1925; *Daily News,* 15 September 1926, 29 January 1927, 4 May 1927.

34. Interview with Hortencia Castro de Cuellar; also with Yldefonso Osuna and Lydia and Albert Caballero.

35. O'Neill, *History of Santa Barbara County,* 305–306; Spaulding, *A Brief Story,* 71; F. R. Maulsby, *Santa Barbara, California* (Santa Barbara, circa 1914), 4. See also *Morning Press,* 17 and 18 July 1902, 4 March 1905, 2 February 1913, 30 October 1913; *Independent,* 16 April, 1906.

36. *Morning Press,* 31 July 1906; interview with Yldefonso Osuna. For reference to railroad workers, the vast majority of whom have Spanish surnames, see, for example, *Morning Press,* 15 April 1904, 16 July 1904, 14 April 1905, 13 March 1906. For reference to "cholo laborers," see *Morning Press,* 20 November 1907.

37. 16 July 1911. See also 12 September 1907, 21 September 1909.

38. Interview with Federico López. Interviews also with Angela and Walter Cordero, Jesse and Luis Acosta, and Miguel García.

39. Interviews with Jesse and Luis Acosta, Albert Caballero, José Martínez, Angela Cordero and Antonio ("Ike") Bonilla (21 August 1974). For the development of light industry in the lower east side, see *Daily News,* 27 February 1926; *Morning Press,* 1 August 1905, 31 July 1906. Because of the inflation of the 1920s, the prevailing wage paid to Mexican street workers increased between 35 and 50 cents per hour.

40. With the exception of its walnut, lemon, avocado, and livestock production, however, Santa Barbara County remained behind most other southern California counties in overall agricultural production. See, for example, *Monthly Bulletin, Fifth Report of the California Department of Agriculture* for the period ending 31 December 1924, vol. 13 (July–December 1924), 255–267, and vol. 17 (December 1928), 815–823, 833–834.

41. *Independent*, 6 November 1909; *Morning Press*, 26 December 1924.

42. Interviews with Anita and Reyes Castro, Federico López, Jesse and Luis Acosta, Dolores and Daniel Vásquez, Nellie Pérez, Walter Cordero, Alfred Domínguez, Mary Ortega, and Vereanda Sánchez.

43. Interviews with Dolores Vásquez, Anita and Reyes Castro, Jesse and Luis Acosta, and Vereanda Sánchez.

44. The Johnston Fruit Company consistently handled the processing and packing of lemons throughout the region until the late 1920s. Not until the early 1920s, however, did the lemon culture begin to flourish in and near the city of Santa Barbara. See *Morning Press*, 1 July 1910, 26 December 1924; *Monthly Bulletin of the California Department of Agriculture*, vol. 13, 258. Approximately 90 percent of the packing house work force was Mexican; a small number of Italians were employed as foremen and laborers.

45. Interviews with Jesse Acosta, Nellie Pérez, Dolores Vásquez, and José Martínez. Mrs. Acosta began working prior to 1920 and claimed that the packing house work force at that time, with a few exceptions, was all Mexicano. Martínez began working in 1925 and became the first and only Mexicano foreman at the packing house; between them, he and his wife worked a total of 73 years there. For 1916 minimum wages for women, see *Daily News*, 15 February 1916. See also Camarillo, "Making of a Chicano Community," 223–224.

46. Lloyd W. Fellows, "Economic Aspects of the Mexican Rural Population in California with Special Emphasis on the Need for Mexican Labor in Agriculture" (Master's thesis, University of Southern California, 1929), 22–23.

47. Ira V. Hiscock, *A Survey of Health and Welfare Activities in Santa Barbara County, California* (Santa Barbara, 1930), 86.

48. 7 October 1921.

49. Interview with Mary Ortega. The only area of substantial Spanish-surname home ownership from 1926 to 1930 was the area of Pueblo Viejo. See *Assessor's Block Book, City of Santa Barbara, 1926 to 1930* (Documents of Santa Barbara County Assessor, County Administration Building).

50. *Morning Press*, 18 January 1924.

51. *Public Health Appraisal, Santa Barbara County, California, 1935*, County Health Department and Chamber of Commerce Committee (Santa Barbara, 1935), tables 14B and 14D.

52. *Morning Press*, 23 October 1923.

53. *Daily News*, 6 April 1918.

54. *Morning Press*, 16 June 1922. See also 7 October 1921, 1 March 1922.

55. *Morning Press*, 25 June 1922.

56. Ibid.

57. *Naturalization Petition and Record,* vols. 1–5, nos. 51–900 (1910–1927), County of Santa Barbara, Office of the County Clerk, Santa Barbara County Court House. From 1932 to 1940, under 3.0 percent of the more than 1,000 immigrants who filed petitions were Mexican; see Santa Barbara City Schools Curriculum Laboratory, *Living: The Basis for Learning* (Santa Barbara, 1942), 56. For Americanization programs of various social welfare agencies, see *Morning Press,* 22 January 1928; Grace R. Southwick, "Schooling for Grown-Ups," *Western Woman—Santa Barbara California Souvenir Edition,* 7 (March 1931):36.

58. *Daily News,* 10 June 1926, 10 July 1926. See also 9 January 1926; Hiscock, *A Survey of Health and Welfare Activities,* 35, 85.

59. Hiscock, *A Survey of Health and Welfare Activities,* 75; *Daily News,* 25 March 1926.

60. Interview with Ida Cordero (19 September 1974). Mrs. Cordero began working for the Catholic Welfare Service (East Side Social Center) in 1934, when some Mexicanos were still being repatriated. Interview also with Mary Ortega, who was the interpreter at the East Side Social Center throughout the repatriation period.

61. Interview with Mary Ortega.

62. *Public Health Appraisal, Santa Barbara County,* 8A.

63. Interviews with Ida Cordero, Mary Ortega, José Martínez, Jesse Acosta, Dolores and Daniel Vásquez, Federico López, Yldefonso Osuna, and Nellie Pérez.

64. Ibid.

7. Chicanos and the Labor Market of the Early 1900s

1. The only pastoral-related occupation that persisted into the twentieth century was the seasonal sheepshearing carried on by a small group of local Chicanos. For Santa Barbara sheepshearing activities in the twentieth century, see *Morning Press,* 30 March 1900, 13 May 1900, 20 July 1904, 20 April 1915, and 27 April 1929. Also interviews with Miguel García, who participated in the sheepshearing circuit from 1906 until about 1920, and Leo Cordero, Walter Cordero, and Alfred Ruiz, all of whom had relatives who were sheepshearers. For the western states migration, see *Morning Press,* 2 March 1900, 19 March 1908, and interviews with Miguel García and Russell A. Ruiz.

2. Interview with Leo Cordero, who worked at Johnston's as a young man in 1914. See also *Morning Press,* 26 October 1905.

3. Interview with Alfred Domínguez; also interviews with Walter Cordero, Herman Cordero, and Miguel García. See also *Daily News,* 18 August 1919.

4. *Morning Press,* 2 November 1911. The practice of taking school-age children on the seasonal harvests began in the early 1880s.

5. Ibid., 26 September 1912; see also 20 October 1912.

6. *Morning Press*, 1 October 1921. Interview with Mary Ortega, who claimed that one of the major problems in educating Chicano children was keeping them in school, particularly during the seasonal harvests.

7. For mention of women as agricultural workers in local newspapers, see *Morning Press*, 20 September 1912; *Daily News*, 15 February 1916, 16 July 1917. Information on job functions and types of work performed by Chicanas was gathered from interviews with Angela Cordero, Nellie Pérez, Dolores Vásquez, Jesse Acosta, Vereanda Sánchez, Margarita Villa, Anita Castro, Hortencia Castro de Cuellar, Antonio Bonilla, and Herman Cordero.

8. For the listing of Spanish surnames on the local county road crews, see, for example, *Morning Press*, 12 June 1902, 7 December 1902, 11 January 1903, 19 January 1905. Information on native-born Chicanos as street laborers was gathered from interviews with Yldefonso Osuna, Herman Cordero, Walter Cordero, Alfred Ruiz, Leo Cordero, and Miguel García. For wages of teamsters and laborers, see *Morning Press*, 26 March 1907, 26 October 1913; also interviews with Walter Cordero, Yldefonso Osuna, and Federico López.

9. Interviews with Yldefonso Osuna, Miguel García, Federico López, Vereanda Sánchez, Herman Cordero, Dolores and Daniel Vásquez, Lydia and Albert Caballero.

10. *Index to Precinct Registers of Santa Barbara County, 1920*, Documents of Santa Barbara County Elections Office, County Administration Building; *Santa Barbara City Directory*, for 1909–1910, 1920, and 1929–1930. The 1920 *Index to Precinct Registers* listed Spanish-surnamed voters (almost exclusively native-born) and their respective occupations. The total number of Spanish-surnamed male registered voters was 242; the percentage breakdown of occupations is as follows: high white-collar: professional, 1.7, and proprietorial, 4.5; low white-collar: 10.7; high blue-collar: skilled, 14.0; low blue-collar: semiskilled, 22.3, and unskilled, 45.9; unknown: 0.8. Presumably this group of predominantly native-born Chicanos might have had a more even distribution of occupations than the foreign-born, yet their occupational percentages vary only slightly from the overall Spanish-surname occupational structure given in Table 15.

11. Interviews with Theodore Cota, Yldefonso Osuna, and Herman Cordero; *Santa Barbara City Directories* for 1909–1910, 1920, 1929–1930.

12. Interviews with Alfred Ruiz, Leo Cordero, Antonio Bonilla, Miguel García, Angela Cordero, Veronica Medina, and Theodore Cota. See also *Daily News*, 28 December 1910; *Morning Press*, 16 December 1920, 1 September 1921.

13. Interview with Anita Castro.

14. For the Oxnard strike, see Juan Gómez-Quiñones, "The First Steps: Chicano Labor Conflict and Organizing, 1900–1920," *Aztlán*, 3

(spring 1972):24–26; see also *Morning Press*, 28 February 1903. It is highly probable that local Chicanos participated in the union strike activities in the 1903 Oxnard conflict, since laborers were recruited annually out of Santa Barbara.

15. 14 July 1903.

16. *Independent*, 15 July 1903. See also *Morning Press*, 15 July 1903. The work force at Johnston's at this time was primarily native-born, with probably a few foreign-born Mexicanos and Italians (one Chinese worker was employed in 1903). Of the Spanish-surnamed workers listed in the 1903 *Santa Barbara City Directory*, twenty-one listed their occupation as either lemon packer or grader. Although women must have participated in the unified strike, they were not mentioned in the newspapers.

17. *Independent*, 9 November 1909. For the earlier threatened strikes by Anglo skilled worker labor unions, see *Morning Press*, 2 July 1902, 14 April 1903.

18. 9 November 1909.

19. *Morning Press*, 28 October 1913; see also 26 and 29 October 1913. The ethnicity of the striking workers was not mentioned per se. However, Spanish surnames predominate in newspaper references to street workers before and after this period. See, for example, the reference to the Spanish-surnamed worker who was later injured on this same street project, *Morning Press*, 8 November 1913, and individuals mentioned in the 28 March 1913 issue. Moreover, from the observations of interviewees one must conclude that the street-paving crews throughout the period were nearly all native-born or foreign-born Mexican.

20. *Morning Press*, 8 October 1908.

21. In the Ventura–Santa Barbara county area, in addition to the strikes previously cited, Chicanos engaged in the following labor conflicts; Santa Paula, lemon strike (Limonera Ranch) in 1917; actions of pipelayers and laborers taken against the Southern Counties Gas Company in 1923 (*Morning Press*, 15 December); agricultural strikes in Ventura County in 1933 and in 1936, and in Santa Barbara County in 1934 (two) and in 1935. See also Gómez-Quiñones, "The First Steps."

22. Interview with Albert Caballero. A similar experience was related by another interviewee (Herman Cordero), whose brother-in-law was rejected by the local plasterers' union in the 1920s.

23. *Morning Press*, 12 and 25 October 1922, 4 March 1928. For the development of Anglo labor unions see, for example, *Morning Press*, 3 June 1903, 22 March 1905, 31 August 1912.

24. A majority of the nondescriptive occupations listed in the 1909–1910, 1920, and 1929–1930 city directories stated the name of the employee's company. In the case of Spanish-surnamed persons, the companies frequently listed were those that were labor intensive (construction companies and building supply companies, for example). It is

logical to assume that a great majority of the Spanish-surnamed individuals in the "unknown or unlisted" category are low blue-collar workers. In addition, the larger percentages of unknown occupations beginning in 1910 may reflect increasing unemployment among Spanish-surnamed workers.

25. The 1926 Santa Barbara City Directory listed the greatest number of Spanish surnames (1,839) for any year during the 1920s. The number of Chicano individuals listed in the directory decreased by 236 in 1929–1930, partly because of the drive a few years earlier to deport Mexicanos. The 1929–1930 directory enumeration was evidently taken before the concerted repatriation movement that began in mid-1930.

26. The only variation within the small percentages of upwardly and downwardly mobile Mexican workers occurred within the percentage of workers who experienced upward job mobility· between 1920 and 1930 (7.3 percent). The mobility of several low blue-collar workers to low white-collar jobs may be attributable to the small but growing group of Mexican store clerks and salespeople who serviced the Spanish-speaking community (from both Anglo and Mexican-owned retail stores). Women, not men, predominated in these occupations.

27. The high percentages of persons for whom the directories did not list an occupation in one or more of the decades may have distorted the other findings. However, since the great majority of the unknown persistent workers were listed in at least one directory period as either semiskilled or unskilled workers, it is highly doubtful that this group would have deviated from the norm had occupations been listed for them in the other directory periods. They would most likely have followed the floating mobility and static occupational patterns of the majority of workers.

28. Interviews with Nellie Pérez, Angela Cordero, Jesse Acosta, Dolores Vásquez, Vereanda Sánchez, Hortencia Castro de Cuellar, and Anita Castro; *Federal Manuscript Census Schedules,* 1900.

29. Notably, of the Spanish-surnamed women listed in the 1909–1910 city directory over one-fourth (26.5 percent) listed an occupation. The percentage increase of skilled workers (6 of the 54 female workers) in 1910 and the subsequent decrease in 1920 cannot be explicitly explained. Perhaps the difference between the manuscript census and the city directory in the reporting of women's occupations helps explain this deviation.

30. *Federal Manuscript Census Schedules,* 1900.

31. From the analysis of the 1929–1930 city directory, Spanish-surnamed workers constituted 35.6 percent of all unskilled workers. But their percentage in the building-construction industry and agriculture was much higher, since the bulk of the Chicano work force was in these two general work areas. For a breakdown of all gainfully employed people in Santa Barbara, see United States, Fifteenth Census of the United States: 1930, *Population,* vol. 3, pt. 1, 278.

8. Race Relations in Twentieth-Century Santa Barbara

1. George W. James, *Travelers' Handbook to Southern California* (Pasadena, 1904), 341; see also Santa Barbara Chamber of Commerce, *The City and Valley of Santa Barbara* (Santa Barbara, 1904?), 9. For other accounts from 1901 to 1904, see Charles A. Moody, "Santa Barbara," *The Land of Sunshine: The Magazine of California and the West* (Los Angeles, 1901), 401–415; J. Torrey Connor, *Saunterings in Summerland* (Los Angeles, 1902), 64; E. M. Heath, *A Guide to Rides and Drives in Santa Barbara and Vicinity* (Santa Barbara, 1904), 17.

2. Heath, *A Guide to Rides*, 17–18.

3. *Assessor's Block Book, City of Santa Barbara, 1906*, Documents of Santa Barbara County Assessor's Office, County Administration Building, and *Block Book, 1926–1930*. The only other small pocket of Spanish-surname property ownership was located on Canal Street near De la Guerra Street; a cluster of foreign-born Mexican residents inhabited this area. There was also an increase of several Spanish-surnamed owners in the lower eastside area peripheral to Pueblo Viejo. By 1926, Spanish-surnamed owners of individual lots in the Pueblo Viejo area had been reduced to approximately 30 percent of the total property owners. This trend occurred in response to the expansion of residential development in the area, and the relocation of several native-born Mexican families seeking less expensive property in undeveloped sections of the city. See also "Street and Avenue Guide and Householders' Directory," *Santa Barbara City Directory*, 1920 and 1929–1930; the area of Pueblo Viejo contained most of the same families listed in the earlier directories—many as renters, but also many as homeowners.

4. Interviews with Alfred Domínguez, Leo Cordero, Miguel García, Antonio Bonilla, Herman Cordero, and Alfred Ruiz. See also Edward S. Spaulding, *Santa Barbara, 1898–1925, as seen by a boy* (MS, Santa Barbara Historical Society, 1966?), 38–39. For references to the Tenderloin area, see *Morning Press*, 25 March 1904, 8 July 1905, 12 June 1906, 24 March 1910. For references to the out-migration of native-born Chicanos, see *Morning Press*, 14 August 1903, 22 October 1903, 9 September 1905, 17 December 1905, 25 February 1906, 7 September 1907. For the in-migration of Montecito residents, see *Morning Press*, 27 January 1914 and *Daily Press*, 18 January 1926; also interviews with Veronica Medina and Margarita Villa.

5. Interview with Miguel García.

6. Interview with Alfred Domínguez. Also interviews with Herman Cordero and Walter Cordero. See also O'Neill, *History of Santa Barbara County*, 301–302, for a case of assistance of an elderly Chicana by Caesar Lataillade.

7. *Indigent List of Santa Barbara County, 1901–1909*, Documents

of Santa Barbara County Tax Collector, County Administration Building; see also *Morning Press*, 9 July 1913. For Associated Charities' work in Pueblo Viejo, see *Daily News*, 25 March 1926.

8. Camarillo, "Making of a Chicano Community," see table 34, 289.

9. *Morning Press*, 5 June 1900; interviews with Alfred Domínguez, Theodore Cota, and Yldefonso Osuna. The Corte Serra chapter may have originated in the late 1890s, but the earliest mention of the organization is 1900. For the listing of officers of both chapters of the Foresters during the early twentieth century, see *Morning Press*, 3 and 5 December 1901, 15 January 1902; see also *Santa Barbara City Directory, 1920*, 17.

10. Interviews with Theodore Cota, Yldefonso Osuna, and Alfred Ruiz.

11. Interviews with Miguel García, Alfred Ruiz, Theodore Cota, Leo Cordero, Herman Cordero, and Walter Cordero.

12. *Morning Press*, 10 July 1906, 18 July 1907, 28 June 1914, 9 and 26 July 1914.

13. 10 November 1907. See also *Index to the Great Register of Santa Barbara County, 1904*, Document of Santa Barbara County Elections Office (Santa Barbara, 1904); *Index to Precinct Registers of Santa Barbara County, 1920; Daily Press*, 25 September 1884; *Morning Press*, 13 and 16 September 1896, 31 October 1896, 2 November 1898, 28 October 1900, 4 November 1900.

14. For nineteenth-century racial attitudes against Mexicans see, for example, the following: Ellison, *Diary of Charles Huse; Weekly Press*, 19 January 1878; *Daily Press*, 18 November 1874, 12 March 1883; *San Luis Obispo Tribune*, 20 May 1876; Dall, *My First Holiday*, 5, 7, 273. For the use of the derogatory term *cholo* to refer to Mexicans see, for example, *Morning Press*, 29 July 1894, 12 June 1900, 21 November 1906, 20 November 1907, 4 June 1910, 27 July 1910.

15. This particular conclusion is based on the opinions of a large majority of the Mexicans interviewed for this study, both foreign-born and native-born.

16. Interview with Margarita and LeRoy Villa.

17. Interview with Antonio Bonilla.

18. *North from Mexico*, 213.

19. Interviews with Yldefonso Osuna, Nellie Pérez, Hortencia Castro de Cuellar, Herman Cordero, Anita and Reyes Castro, Lydia and Albert Caballero.

20. Interview with Yldefonso Osuna. Carey McWilliams also refers to a schism in the early twentieth-century Chicano communities between the native-born and Mexicano immigrants; see *North from Mexico*, 209–210, and *Brothers under the Skin* (Boston, 1964), 118–119.

21. Interview with Walter Cordero.

22. Interview with Federico López. Also interviews with Jesse and Luis Acosta, Dolores Vásquez, Lydia and Albert Caballero.

23. Interview with Federico López.

24. Most of those interviewed related experiences where minor differences in word usage existed between the two groups.

25. Interview with Margarita Villa.

26. Historically, foreign-born Mexicanos had been readily integrated into local society. Throughout the period 1893–1916, the number of foreign-born in relation to the native-born Chicano population in Santa Barbara remained a minority. However, between 1916 and 1927 the in-migration of foreign-born reversed the previous proportion; this no doubt upset the earlier conditions, which had fostered the complete integration of foreign-born into the community. Importantly, Mexicans after 1870 were entering an Anglo, not a Mexican, society.

27. McWilliams makes reference to this characteristic of Anglo society and the perception of all Spanish-speaking people as "Mexicans"; see *North from Mexico,* 209. This quality of Anglo society was also noted by members of the native-born Chicano community, as indicated in interviews with Margarita and LeRoy Villa, Miguel García, and Herman Cordero. At least one individual, however, believed that Anglos did make distinctions between native-born and foreign-born (interview with Antonio Bonilla).

28. Interview with Margarita Villa. Also interviews with Luis Lugo, Alfred Ruiz, Miguel García, Walter Cordero, Alfred Domínguez, and Veronica Medina. A similar story concerning bitterness over lost land grants was recounted by Alfred Domínguez.

29. Interview with Walter Cordero. Also interviews with Leo Cordero and Antonio Bonilla. Two interviewees (LeRoy Villa and José Martínez) claimed that Chicanos and Anglos got along well in their infrequent interaction, but none denied that discrimination existed.

30. Interview with Miguel García.

31. Interview with Hortencia Castro de Cuellar. Similar feelings of bitterness against Anglos were articulated in the interviews with Jesse and Luis Acosta, Dolores Vásquez, Vereanda Sánchez, Lydia and Albert Caballero, Federico López, Anita and Reyes Castro, and Nellie Pérez.

32. Interview with Federico López.

33. Interview with Walter Cordero. Several other individuals were cognizant of this color-line discrimination (interviews with Alfred Ruiz, Luis Lugo, Jesse and Luis Acosta, Miguel García, and Antonio Bonilla). To judge from the interviewees' experiences with individual and institutional racism, the hueros were generally less bitter toward Anglos than the prietos and had encountered fewer overt acts of discrimination. In addition, skin color often affected status achieved

within and outside the Chicano community; hueros had more opportunities to move into the dominant society.

34. Interview with Yldefonso Osuna. Other interviewees (Jesse and Luis Acosta, Federico López, Dolores and Daniel Vásquez) conveyed the same impression.

35. Interviews with Walter Cordero, Yldefonso Osuna, Luis Lugo, Miguel García, Mary Ortega, Herman Cordero, Federico López, Jesse and Luis Acosta, Dolores and Daniel Vásquez, and Alfred Domínguez. One interviewee who attempted to use the pool was regularly admitted; he is a light-complected native Barbareño. However, this individual's brother, who is much darker skinned, was not admitted (interviews with Leo and Herman Cordero).

36. Interview with Jesse Acosta.

37. *Morning Press,* 27 May 1923; see also 18 and 19 May 1923, 29 July 1923. For the nineteenth-century origin of the local chapter, see *Morning Press,* 20 May 1897.

38. *Morning Press,* 29 July 1923.

39. Tompkins and Ruiz, *Historical High Lights,* 120–121.

40. Ibid. According to the 1920 U.S. census, there were only 186 blacks and 399 other nonwhites ("Indians, Chinese, Japanese, and others") in the city of Santa Barbara; see U.S. Department of Commerce, Fourteenth Census of the United States, 1920, *Population,* vol. 3, 130. The total Chicano population in 1923, which was expanding rapidly as a result of Mexicano migration, probably ranged between 2,700 and 3,300 persons.

41. *Morning Press,* 15, 16, 18, and 19 September 1923, 11 December 1923, 16 March 1924, 4 October 1926; Tompkins and Ruiz, *Historical High Lights,* 121–122.

42. Interview with Hortencia Castro de Cuellar.

43. Interview with Walter Cordero.

44. *Morning Press,* 27 and 28 November 1897, 21 March 1899. For the historical development of Protestant missions, see also *Daily News,* 1883 (date not recorded), *Morning Press,* 23 September 1898, 19 March 1901.

45. For references to the development of the Spanish Baptist Mission until its reassigned status in 1919, see *Morning Press,* 27 May 1902, 28 June 1916, 27 January 1917; *Daily News,* 25 April 1918, 10 May 1918, 7 April 1919. After 1915 and throughout the 1920s the mission's services were regularly attended by many of the younger members of the Pueblo Viejo and the lower eastside barrio communities (interviews with Antonio Bonilla and Federico López). An analysis of the *Directory of Membership 1874–1924, First Baptist Church* (Santa Barbara, 1924) revealed that of the approximately 350 members of the Anglo congregation in 1924 none had a Spanish surname. For the expansion of the Chicano congregation, see *Morning Press,* 8 October 1921. Significantly, the Catholic church, apparently concerned about

the ongoing conversion of Chicanos by Protestants, began its own missionary attempts; see, for example, *Morning Press*, 24 April 1904, 22 November 1908; *Daily News*, 18 January 1917, 4 April 1927. In addition, the Catholic parish created another mission in the lower eastside barrio at approximately the same time that the Spanish Baptist Mission became an official church; see *Our Lady of Guadalupe Parish*, 42–43.

46. The 1930 census recorded 3,279 "Mexicans" in the city of Santa Barbara; see U.S. Department of Commerce, Fifteenth Census of the United States: 1930, *Population* (Washington, D.C., 1931), vol. 1, 145, and vol. 3, 266. The figure of 4,262 (or 12.3 percent) was calculated by adding 30 percent to the 1930 census "recorded" figure in order to adjust for the "real or actual" figure, and by adjusting the total population figure upward to 34,596. A noted student of Mexican immigration, Emory S. Bogardus, used this formula to arrive at more realistic estimates of foreign-born Mexicano populations during the 1920s; see Bogardus, *The Mexican in the United States* (Los Angeles, 1934), 15.

47. Approximately 150 Spanish-surnamed households were listed in the 1929–1930 city directory for the immediate area of the Pueblo Viejo barrio. The population estimate of 750 to 900 is based upon these 150 households, each containing an average of five family members. An unknown number of native-born, however, lived outside Pueblo Viejo by 1929–1930. See also *Public Health Appraisal, Santa Barbara County*, 8A.

48. The 1930 census for "Mexicans" in California ranked Santa Barbara as having the fifth largest ratio of Mexicanos to the total population of cities of 25,000 or more people; see U.S. Department of Commerce, Fifteenth Census: 1930, *Population*, vol. 1, 22, and vol. 3, pt. 1, 266. Mexicans accounted for 6.5 percent (368,013) of the total population of California as listed in the 1930 census. Together the native-born and foreign-born Mexicans of Santa Barbara in 1930 probably ranked as the third or fourth highest proportion of Chicanos in California cities of 25,000 or more people.

9. Urban Chicanos in Predepression Southern California

1. Other writers have offered descriptive typologies of Mexican community settlement in southern California, but most do not mention the multiplicity of factors involved nor is the Chicano barrio development fully explored as a historical process. See the following: McWilliams (perhaps the best description), *North from Mexico*, 217–226; Bogardus, *The Mexican in the United States*, 18–23; Robin F. Scott, "The Mexican-American in the Los Angeles Area, 1910–1950: From Acquiescence to Activity" (Ph.D. dissertation, University of Southern California, 1971), 66–68, 70–72.

2. Pedro Castillo, "Urbanization, Migration, and the Chicanos in

Los Angeles, 1900–1920" (paper presented at the 88th annual meeting of the American Historical Association, San Francisco, 30 December 1973), 5–7, 13–15; Romo, "Mexican Workers in the City," 81–82.

3. Two 1908 studies made distinctions between the newly arrived immigrants and the native-born residents in Los Angeles; see Clark, *Mexican Labor in the United States,* 507; *Report of the Housing Commission of the City of Los Angeles* (30 June 1908 to 30 June 1909), 4, and (30 June 1909 to 30 June 1910), 4.

4. Romo, "Mexican Workers in the City," 82–83.

5. *Report of the Housing Commission* (20 February 1906 to 30 June 1908), 3–4, 6.

6. Castillo, "Chicanos in Los Angeles," 9.

7. *Report of the Housing Commission* (20 February 1906 to 30 June 1908), 4, 7–8, 28–31; quote on 7.

8. Ibid. (1 July 1910 to 31 March 1913), 41–42, and ibid. (20 February 1906 to 30 June 1908), 12–14, 18–19.

9. Romo, "Mexican Workers in the City," 78, 84–87; *Report of the Housing Commission* (1 July 1910 to 31 March 1913), 22–33; G. Bromley Oxnam, *The Mexican in Los Angeles, Los Angeles City Survey, 1920,* 23; Bogardus, *The Mexican in the United States,* 18.

10. Castillo, "Chicanos in Los Angeles," 6–7; Romo, "Mexican Workers in the City," 78, 84–85; *Report of the Housing Commission* (1 July 1910 to 31 March 1913), 22.

11. Romo, "Mexican Workers in the City," 8, 87–96, 136, 151–153, 171–181; Castillo, "Chicanos in Los Angeles," 16. See also Alberto M. Camarillo, "Chicano Urban History: A Study of Compton's Barrio, 1936–1970," *Aztlán,* 2 (fall 1971):79–106; and Gilbert G. González, "Factors Relating to Property Ownership of Chicanos in Lincoln Heights, Los Angeles," *Aztlán,* 2 (fall 1971):107–143.

12. Romo, "Mexican Workers in the City," 97.

13. *Federal Manuscript Census Schedules,* San Bernardino County, 1880.

14. Ibid., 1900. An additional 25 percent of the Mexican population lived in Ward 1 of the city, but it is not known whether this ward was near the railroad company barrio or whether the Mexican population in this ward constituted a colony. The low census enumeration for the total Mexican population is suspect.

15. *San Bernardino Daily Sun,* 5 June 1909.

16. Ibid., 6 and 11 June 1909.

17. Ibid., 26 December 1909.

18. *San Bernardino City Directory, 1910–1911* (Los Angeles, 1910). The 1910 United States census reports (*Population,* vol. 2, 174) enumerated 888 foreign-born Mexicans. The 1910–1911 city directory listed 240 Spanish-surnamed heads of household. Allowing for the population of California-born and other native-born Mexicans as well as for census underenumeration of foreign-born, the total Mexican population

probably ranged between 1,300 and 1,600—10 to 12.5 percent of the city's total population in 1910 (12,779).

19. *San Bernardino City Directory*, "Street and Householders' Guide," 1920 and 1928; U.S. Department of Commerce, Fifteenth Census: 1930, *Population*, vol. 3, pt. 1 (Washington, D.C., 1932), 266. See also Raup, *San Bernardino*, 43. For examples of residential and school segregation and municipal neglect, see *San Bernardino Daily Sun*, 20 October 1918, 8 October 1927, 18, 19, and 29 October 1929, 5 November 1929, 25 January 1930. For social, patriotic, and organizational activities see, for example, 17 September 1908, 14 October 1909, 17 September 1910, 16 September 1913, 17 September 1927.

20. U.S. Bureau of the Census, *Population*, vol. 2, 148–153; Cynthia J. Shelton, "The Neighborhood House of San Diego: Settlement Work in the Mexican Community, 1914–1940" (Master's thesis, San Diego State University, 1975), 28; LeRoy E. Harris, "The Other Side of the Freeway: A Study of Settlement Patterns of Negroes and Mexican Americans in San Diego, California" (Ph.D. dissertation, Carnegie-Mellon University, 1974), 112. The 1900 Federal Manuscript Census enumerated only 638 Spanish-surnamed persons, or 3.6 percent of the total population of the city.

21. College Women's Club, *Pathfinder Social Survey of San Diego* (San Diego, 1914), 12, 34.

22. Ibid.

23. Shelton, "Neighborhood House of San Diego," 35–36, 62–63. See also Harris, "Other Side of the Freeway," 26, 111–113, 145–146, 176–182; George B. Mangold, *Community Welfare in San Diego* (San Diego, 1929), 20; Federal Writers' Project, *San Diego*, 16; *San Diego Union*, 1 January 1931.

24. Shelton, "Neighborhood House of San Diego," 71. See also Mangold, *Community Welfare in San Diego*, 176, 178; Miguel González, "San Diego's Neighborhood House Association, 1928 to 1938" (unpublished paper, 1969), 2–3; Clare Crane, *Logan Heights: An Historical Survey* (San Diego, 1971), 8.

25. *Mexicans in California*, Report of Governor C. C. Young's Mexican Fact-Finding Committee (San Francisco, 1930), 79, 82–84, 87–91. For an excellent reference source on Mexican agricultural labor in southern California, and for agricultural and urban employment elsewhere in selected areas of the United States, see Taylor, *Mexican Labor in the United States*.

26. Castillo, "Chicanos in Los Angeles," 5–6, 10–12; Romo, "Mexican Workers in the City," 5–7, 81–82, 134, 140–142; *Report of the Housing Commission* (1906 to 1908), 4, 8, 24, 41–42; *Mexicans in California*, 82–83; U.S. Census Reports, *Population* (1910), 166, 182 (1920, vol. 3), 118–119, 124 (1930, vol. 3, pt. 1), 266.

27. Quoted in Romo, "Mexican Workers in the City," 137.

28. Ibid., 156–157.

29. College Women's Club, *Social Survey of San Diego*, 31, 34; Shelton, "Neighborhood House of San Diego," 35–36, 67; Federal Writers' Project, *San Diego*, 56; *San Diego Union*, 1 January 1931; Heilbron, *History of San Diego County*, 202–205, 299–303; Nellie Greene and Isaac Aceves, "Spanish and American Pioneers, Part II: History, The Spanish Influence in San Diego" (San Diego, n.d.), 2; *San Diego Labor Leader*, 18 April 1924, 20 July 1928.

30. *Labor Leader*, 18 April 1924; Shelton, "Neighborhood House of San Diego," 67; Mangold, *Community Welfare in San Diego*, 24; Constantine Panunzio and the Heller Committee, *How Mexicans Earn and Live: A Study of the Incomes and Expenditures of One Hundred Mexican Families in San Diego, California* (Berkeley, 1933), 14–15, 68–69.

31. The 1910–1911 *San Bernardino City Directory*, which frequently named the employers of male heads of household, listed 93 percent of the Spanish-surnamed males who indicated an employer as working for the Santa Fe Railroad. Approximately 44 percent of all Spanish-surnamed workers listed the railroad as employer. See also *San Bernardino Daily Sun*, 3 February 1906, 30 January 1908; Raup, *San Bernardino*, 38–39; Brown, *History of San Bernardino*, 638.

32. *Report of the Housing Commission*, (1908 to 1909), 12–14, 16. For other references to the contract system of Mexican labor in Los Angeles, see Romo, "Mexican Workers in the City," 51–53, 56; Charles Wollenberg, "Working on El Traque: The Pacific Electric Strike of 1903," *Pacific Historical Review*, 42 (August 1973):363–364. For contract labor in California and the Southwest, see Bogardus, *The Mexican in the United States*, 39–40; Clark, *Mexican Labor in the United States*, 470–471, 475–478; *Mexicans in California*, 108–109.

33. See, for example, *San Bernardino Daily Sun*, 27 January 1907, 5 June 1909, 26 December 1909, 17 September 1919; *San Diego Labor Leader*, 18 April 1924.

34. *La Crónica*, 28 April 1883, cited in Griswold del Castillo, "La Raza Hispano Americana," 82; *Report of the Housing Commission* (1908 to 1909), 12; *San Diego Labor Leader*, 20 July 1928; Clark, *Mexican Labor in the United States*, 479; Castillo, "Chicanos in Los Angeles," 11–12; Taylor, *Mexican Labor in the United States*, vol. 1, 37.

35. See, for example, the following: Gómez-Quiñones, "The First Steps," 24–27; Wollenberg, "Working on El Traque;" Camarillo, "Making of a Chicano Community," 251–255; *San Bernardino Daily Sun*, 16 and 18 August 1922. For a general treatment of Chicano labor activity throughout the Southwest, see Acuña, *Occupied America*, chap. 7; Sam Kushner, *Long Road to Delano* (New York, 1974); Gómez-Quiñones, "The First Steps."

36. Mary Miller, "Attitudes of the San Diego Labor Movement

toward Mexicans, 1917–1936" (Master's thesis, San Diego State University, 1974), 33–36, 58–59. See also *San Diego Labor Leader*, 13 June 1919, 26 February 1926, 27 August 1926.

37. The higher percentages of unknown occupations for the period 1910 to 1930 result from the more nondescriptive nature of occupations listed in the city directories and their greater frequency of omission as compared to the federal manuscript census schedules.

38. Other survey studies that have analyzed the occupational distribution of Mexican workers for San Diego in 1930, for Santa Barbara in 1929–1930, and for Los Angeles in 1918 and in 1920 confirm the occupational distribution of Mexicans presented in this study. See the following: Ricardo Romo, "Work and Restlessness: Occupational and Spatial Mobility among Mexicans in Los Angeles, 1918–1928," *Pacific Historical Review*, 46 (May 1977):165; Oxnam, *The Mexican in Los Angeles*, 14; Panunzio, *How Mexicans Earn and Live*, 11–12; Hiscock, *A Survey of Health and Welfare Activities*, 86.

39. Romo, "Mexican Workers in the City," 147, 149, and "Work and Restlessness," 172. The Thernstrom studies are discussed in Appendix 1.

40. Romo, "Mexican Workers in the City," 143–146.

41. Lori Helmbold, "The Work of Chicanas in the United States: Wage Labor and Work in the Home, 1930 to the Present" (unpublished paper, Stanford University, 1977); Panunzio, *How Mexicans Earn and Live*, 11–13. The 1900 federal manuscript census for San Diego and Santa Barbara reflected the total number of female Spanish-surnamed employees more accurately than did the city directories, since it included part-time and full-time workers. San Bernardino, however, apparently never had a significant number of Mexican women workers—most probably because Mexicans predominantly worked in the railroad industry, which employed few females. Only after the diversification of the local economy by 1930 does a sizable Chicana working population manifest itself.

42. The percentage of low blue-collar workers in San Diego by 1930 includes a sizable population of blacks whose surnames are indistinguishable from other non-Spanish surnames. Between 1920 and 1930 the black population increased considerably, from 997 to 2,723. Only San Diego and Los Angeles had relatively large black populations prior to the Great Depression (Los Angeles blacks numbered 15,579 in 1920 and 38,894 in 1930).

43. The significant decrease in the percentages of the proprietorial group in San Bernardino from 1900 to 1910–1930 and the increase in low white-collar occupations was not the result of a downward mobility of the former group. What occurred by 1910 in San Bernardino was a sizable decrease in the number of farmers who had lived in the city in 1900 but had relocated by 1910. San Bernardino was the only city of those selected for this study that still retained its agricultural economic

importance by 1900. The activity involved was carried on in the hinterlands after 1900, however. The increase in low white-collar jobs followed the pattern established in cities throughout southern California for the period.

44. *Mexicans in California,* 46, 49; U.S. Department of Commerce, Fifteenth Census of the United States: 1930, *Population,* vol. 3, pt. 1, 266.

45. During World War I, however, attention was drawn to the Mexican people in the United States after it was discovered that Germany had hoped to ally itself with Mexico. In addition, earlier incidents between the United States and Mexico along the border, resulting from Mexican revolutionary activity, created tension between the two countries. See, for example, Romo, "Mexican Workers in the City," 104-126; *San Bernardino Daily Sun,* 28 June 1916, 11 July 1916, 1 March 1917.

46. Shelton, "Neighborhood House of San Diego," 123-125.

47. College Women's Club, *Social Survey of San Diego,* 47; Shelton, "Neighborhood House of San Diego," 51, 55-56, 62, 122; *San Bernardino Daily Sun,* 20 March 1915, 26 January 1926; Romo, "Mexican Workers in the City," 188-197.

48. See, for example, the following: Miller, "Attitudes of the Labor Movement," 26-27, 37-39, 42, 46-47; Shelton, "Neighborhood House of San Diego," 77; *San Diego Labor Leader,* 12 February 1926, 3 and 10 February 1928, 10 May 1929; *San Bernardino Daily Sun,* 18 December 1925, 10 and 11 January 1926, 10 March 1928, 18 and 27 September 1929, 7 October 1930. See also Ricardo Romo, "Responses to Mexican Immigration, 1910-1930," *Aztlán,* 6 (summer 1975):173-194.

49. For a general treatment of Mexican repatriation for the period, which focuses on Los Angeles developments, see Abraham Hoffman, *Unwanted Mexican Americans in the Great Depression: Repatriation Pressures, 1929-1939* (Tucson, 1974). See also *San Bernardino Daily Sun,* 7 August 1924, 10 September 1924; *San Diego Union,* 30 January 1930; Mauricio Mazón, "Illegal Alien Surrogates: A Psychohistorical Interpretation of Group Stereotyping in Time of Economic Stress," *Aztlán,* 6 (summer 1975):305-311.

50. For historical surveys that have identified similar nineteenth-century and twentieth-century developments in different areas of the United States, see for example: Acuña, *Occupied America;* McWilliams, *North from Mexico;* Weber, *Foreigners in Their Native Land;* Paul, "The Spanish-Americans in the Southwest"; Gómez-Quiñones, "Perspective on Chicano History" and "The First Steps."

51. For a good discussion on the status of Chicano research, see Gómez-Quiñones and Arroyo, "On the State of Chicano History." For several notable studies either completed or in progress, see for example: Tomás Almaguer, "Interpreting Chicano History: The 'World

System' Approach to Nineteenth-Century California" (Berkeley, 1977); Mario Barrera, *Race and Class in the Southwest* (Notre Dame, Indiana, forthcoming); Mario T. García, "Modernization and Labor in the Southwest: A Case Study of the Mexican Population of El Paso, Texas, 1880–1920" (Ph.D. dissertation, University of California, San Diego, 1975); David Montejano, "Race, Labor Repression, and Capitalist Agriculture: Notes from South Texas, 1920–1930" (Berkeley, 1977); Ricardo Romo, "The Urbanization of Southwestern Chicanos in the Early Twentieth Century," *New Scholar*, 6 (1977):183–207.

52. I am currently conducting my own comparative urban historical research for a book to be entitled *The Urban Chicanos: Mexican Americans in the Cities of the Southwest and Midwest*. The study will focus on the late nineteenth and the twentieth centuries in several of the main cities in which Chicanos have historically resided in the Southwest: San Antonio, Houston, and El Paso, Texas; Los Angeles and the other cities of southern California examined in *Chicanos in a Changing Society;* Santa Fe and Albuquerque, New Mexico; and Tucson, Arizona. Chicanos in two midwestern cities—Chicago, Illinois, and Omaha, Nebraska—will be studied for comparative purposes and to illustrate that Chicanos have been residents also of cities outside the Southwest throughout most of the twentieth century. Research for the book is supported by grants from the National Endowment for the Humanities, the National Chicano Council on Higher Education, and the Andrew Mellon Foundation (through Stanford University). A bibliographic research guide to Chicano urban history, which constituted the first stage of research on the project, will be published in 1980 (*Chicano Urban Studies Research Bibliography*, c/o Office of the Assistant to the President for Chicano Affairs, Stanford University, Stanford, California 94305).

Appendix 1. A Note on Sources and Methodologies

1. It is very probable that an underenumeration of Spanish-surnamed people occurred in 1880. A sharp decline in the total number of heads of household and the total Spanish-surname population from 1870 to 1880 may have been attributable to the emerging patterns of migratory work carried on by Chicanos; this is especially true for migratory agricultural and sheepshearing occupations, which coincide with the summer months of the census enumeration. For a discussion of underenumeration in census schedules caused by migration and omission, see Peter R. Knights, "A Method of Estimating Census Under-Enumeration," *Historical Methods Newsletter*, 3 (December 1969):5–8, and Oscar Martínez, "On the Size of the Chicano Population: New Estimates, 1850–1900," *Aztlán*, 6 (spring 1975):43–67. Without other sources to gauge the extent of Chicano summer migration, a calculated estimate of underenumeration is not feasible. A rough

estimate for omission of Chicanos in the 1880 census, as well as for subsequent nineteenth-century enumerations, would be in the range of 20 to 40 percent.

2. Thernstrom provides the most thorough discussion of city directories and problems related to their use; see *The Other Bostonians*, 279–288. See also Peter R. Knights, "City Directories as Aids to Ante-Bellum Urban Studies: A Research Note," *Historical Methods Newsletter*, 2 (September 1969):1–10; Stephan Thernstrom, *Poverty and Progress: Social Mobility in a Nineteenth Century City* (New York, 1971), 31–32.

3. Thernstrom provides a good discussion on the differences between comparison of individual and total population coverage in city directories; see *The Other Bostonians*, 283–284.

4. "Occupational Mobility in Nineteenth Century America: Problems and Possibilities," *Journal of Social History*, 5 (spring 1972):318. Other discussions of occupational classification agree with Griffen's conclusion that two occupational schemes, one for mobility and one for structure, are necessary. See Michael Katz, "Occupational Classification in History," *Journal of Interdisciplinary History*, 3 (summer 1972):65–66.

5. Griffen, "Occupational Mobility," 310. For examples of sociological classifications of occupation for mobility studies, see Peter M. Blau and Otis D. Duncan, *The American Occupational Structure* (New York, 1967).

6. Griffen, "Occupational Mobility," 312–313, 316; Katz, "Occupational Classification," 67–70.

7. For the application of mean wealth or mean annual wages in the ranking of occupations, see, for example, Stuart Blumin, "Mobility and Change in Ante-Bellum Philadelphia," in *Nineteenth Century Cities: Essays in the New Urban History*, ed. Stephan Thernstrom and Richard Sennett (New Haven, 1969), and Thernstrom, *Poverty and Progress*, 80–96.

8. Griffen, "Occupational Mobility," 318; Katz, "Occupational Classification," 86.

9. *Poverty and Progress*, 94.

10. Gómez-Quiñones, "Perspective on Chicano History," 38; Carlos E. Cortés, "CHICOP: A Response to the Challenge of Local Chicano History," *Aztlán*, 1 (fall 1970):10; Charles W. Crawford, "Oral History: The State of the Profession," *Oral History Review* (1974):3. For examples of the use of Chicano oral history research see Devra A. Weber, "The Organization of Mexicano Agricultural Workers, the Imperial Valley, and Los Angeles, 1928–1934, an Oral History Approach," *Aztlán*, 3 (fall 1972):307–347, and Albert M. Camarillo, "Research Note on Chicano Community Leaders: The G.I. Generation," *Aztlán*, 2 (fall 1971):145–150. I personally have been active as a historian-interviewer for over nine years.

11. Saul Benison, "Reflections on Oral History," *American Archivist*, 28 (January 1965):73, 75.

12. For examples of commonly discussed procedural techniques in oral history, see Corinne L. Gilb, "Tape-Recorded Interviewing: Some Thoughts from California," *American Archivist*, 20 (October 1957):335–344; Helen M. White, "Thoughts on Oral History," *American Archivist*, 20 (January 1957):19–30; Vaughn D. Bornet, "Oral History Can Be Worthwhile," *American Archivist*, 18 (July 1955):241–253. For further discussion of the need for more consistent procedures and accuracy in interviewing, see Donald C. Swain, "Problems for Practitioners of Oral History," *American Archivist*, 28 (January 1965):63–69; and Gould P. Colman, "Oral History: An Appeal for More Systematic Procedures," *American Archivist*, 28 (January 1965):79–83.

13. Gilb, "Tape-Recorded Interviewing," 338; Gould P. Colman, "Taped Interviews and Community Studies," *Social Education*, 27 (December 1965):537. See also Swain, "Problems for Practitioners of Oral History," 69.

14. Two of the native-born Chicanos, however, had limited command of the Spanish language. These two were the only interviewees who were products of intermarriage.

15. The tape-recorded oral interviews will be placed in the Chicano reference library of the University of California, Santa Barbara, for future research use.

Bibliography

I. Articles, Books, Theses, and Unpublished Papers

Acuña, Rodolfo. *Occupied America: The Chicano's Struggle toward Liberation.* San Francisco: Canfield Press, 1972.

All about Santa Barbara, California, The Sanitarium of the Pacific Coast. Santa Barbara: Daily Advertizer Printing House, 1878.

Almaguer, Tomás. "Historical Notes on Chicano Oppression: The Dialectics of Racial and Class Domination in North America." *Aztlán—Chicano Journal of the Social Sciences and the Arts,* 5 (spring and fall 1974):27–56.

———. "Interpreting Chicano History: The 'World-System' Approach to Nineteenth-Century California." Institute for the Study of Social Change, Working Papers Series no. 101, Berkeley, California, 1977.

Bancroft, Hubert H. *California Pastoral, 1769–1848,* vol. 34. San Francisco: History Co., 1888.

———. *History of California,* vols. 1–3. San Francisco: A. L. Bancroft and Co., 1884, 1885.

———. *Popular Tribunals,* vol. I. San Francisco: History Co., 1890.

Barrera, Mario. *Race and Class in the Southwest.* Notre Dame, Indiana: Notre Dame University Press, forthcoming.

Baur, John E. *The Health Seekers of Southern California, 1870–1900.* San Marino, California: Huntington Library, 1959.

Beattie, George William, and Helen Pruitt Beattie. *Heritage of the Valley: San Bernardino's First Century.* Pasadena, California: San Pasqual Press, 1939.

Bell, Horace, *Reminiscences of a Ranger; or, Early Times in Southern California.* Los Angeles: Yarnell, Caystile, and Mathes, 1881.

Bell, Katherine M. *Swinging the Censer: Reminiscences of Old Santa Barbara.* Santa Barbara: compiled by Katherine Bell Cheney, 1931.

Benison, Saul. "Reflections on Oral History." *American Archivist,* 28 (January 1965):71–77.

Berman, Art, and Elaine Berman. "This Land Was Their Land." *West Magazine, Los Angeles Times,* 2 April 1972.

Blau, Peter M., and Otis D. Duncan. *The American Occupational Structure.* New York: John Wiley and Sons, 1967.

Blumin, Stuart. "Mobility and Change in Ante-Bellum Philadelphia." In Stephan Thernstrom and Richard Sennet, eds., *Nineteenth Century Cities: Essays in the New Urban History.* New Haven: Yale University Press, 1969.

Bogardus, Emory S. *The Mexican in the United States.* Los Angeles: University of Southern California Press, 1934. (Reprinted by Arno Press, New York, 1970.)

Bornet, Vaughn Davis. "Oral History Can Be Worthwhile." *American Archivist,* 18 (July 1965):241–253.

Brackett, R. W. *The History of San Diego County Ranchos,* 5th ed. San Diego: Union Title Insurance Co., 1960.

Brown, John, Jr., and James Boyd. *History of San Bernardino and Riverside Counties.* vol. 1. Chicago: Lewis Publishing Co., 1922.

Brumgardt, John R., and William David Putney. "San Salvador: New Mexican Settlement in Alta California." *Southern California Quarterly,* 59 (winter 1977):353–364.

Caballeria, Father Juan. *History of San Bernardino Valley: From the Padres to the Pioneers, 1810–1851.* San Bernardino: Times-Index Press, 1902.

Camarillo, Albert M. "Chicano Urban History: A Study of Compton's Barrio, 1936–1970." *Aztlán—Chicano Journal of the Social Sciences and the Arts,* 2 (fall 1971):79–106.

———. "The Making of a Chicano Community: A History of the Chicanos in Santa Bárbara, California, 1850–1930." Ph.D. dissertation, University of California, Los Angeles, 1975.

———. "Research Note on Chicano Community Leaders: The G.I. Generation." *Aztlán—Chicano Journal of the Social Sciences and the Arts,* 2 (fall 1971):145–150.

Carrillo, Leo. *The California I Love.* Englewood Cliffs, New Jersey: Prentice-Hall, 1961.

Cassidy, Joseph E. "Life and Times of Pablo de la Guerra, 1819–1874." Ph.D. dissertation, University of California, Santa Barbara, 1977.

Castillo, Pedro. "Mexicans in Los Angeles, 1890–1920." Ph.D. dissertation, University of California, Santa Barbara, 1978.

———. "Urbanization, Migration, and the Chicanos in Los Angeles, 1900–1920." Paper presented at the 88th annual meeting of the American Historical Association, San Francisco, 30 December 1973. Translated into Spanish and published in David Maciel and Patricia Bueno, eds., *Aztlán: historia contemporanea del pueblo Chicano.* Mexico City: Sep Sententas, 1976.

——— and Albert Camarillo, eds. *Furia y Muerte: Los Bandidos Chi-*

canos. Los Angeles: Aztlán Publications, Monograph no. 4, Chicano Studies Center, University of California, Los Angeles, 1973.

Caughey, John W. *California,* 2nd ed. Englewood Cliffs, New Jersey: Prentice Hall, 1953.

Christian, Robert N. "A Study of the Historical Development of the Santa Barbara School District." Master's thesis, University of Southern California, 1963.

Clark, Victor S. *Mexican Labor in the United States.* U.S. Bureau of Labor, Department of Commerce and Labor, Bulletin no. 78, 466–522 (September 1908). Washington, D.C.: Government Printing Office, 1908.

Cleland, Robert Glass. *The Cattle on a Thousand Hills.* San Marino, California: Huntington Library, 1951.

The College Women's Club. *Pathfinder Social Survey of San Diego.* San Diego: Labor Temple Press, March 1914.

Colman, Gould P. "Oral History: An Appeal for More Systematic Procedures." *American Archivist,* 28 (January 1965):79–83.

————. "Taped Interviews and Community Studies." *Social Education,* 27 (December 1965):537–538.

Cone, Mary. *Two Years in California.* Chicago: S. C. Griggs, 1876.

Connor, J. Torrey. *Saunterings in Summerland.* Los Angeles: Ernest K. Foster, 1902.

Cook, Sherburne F. *The Conflict between the California Indian and White Civilization.* Berkeley and Los Angeles: University of California Press, 1976.

————. *The Populations of California Indians, 1769–1970.* Berkeley and Los Angeles: University of California Press, 1976.

Cortés, Carlos E. "CHICOP: A Response to the Challenge of Local Chicano History." *Aztlán—Chicano Journal of the Social Sciences and the Arts,* 1 (fall 1970):1–14.

————, ed. "The Bent Cross: A History of the Mexican American in the San Bernardino Valley." Manuscript of the Inland Empire Chicano Cooperative History Project, University of California, Riverside.

Corwin, Arthur F. "Mexican-American History: An Assessment." *Pacific Historical Review,* 42 (August 1973):269–308.

Crawford, Charles W. "Oral History: The State of the Profession." *History Review* (1974):1–9.

Cunningham, Edith Perkins, ed. *Letters and Journal of Edith Forbes Perkins, 1908–1925,* vol. 4. Riverside Press, 1931.

Dall, Caroline H. *My First Holiday; or, Letters Home from Colorado, Utah, and California.* Boston: Roberts Brothers, 1881.

Dana, Richard Henry. *Two Years before the Mast.* New York: Bantam Pathfinder edition, 1959.

————. *Two Years before the Mast, with subsequent matter by the author.* Boston: Houghton Mifflin and Co., 1868.

Daughters of the American Revolution, San Diego Chapter. *San Diego Yesterdays.* San Diego: Book Committee, D.A.R., 1921.

Dawson, Muir. "Southern California Newspapers, 1851–1876." *Historical Society of Southern California Quarterly,* 32 (March and June 1950):5–44, 139–174.

de la Rocha, Ismael. "A Study of Social Mobility Patterns of Mexicans and Irish in Santa Barbara, 1870–1890." Unpublished paper, Department of History, University of California, Santa Barbara, 1973.

Dumke, Glenn S. *The Boom of the Eighties in Southern California,* 4th ed. San Marino, California: Huntington Library, 1955.

Ellison, William H., ed. " 'Recollections of Historical Events in California, 1843–1878' of William A. Streeter." *California Historical Society Quarterly,* 18 (March, June, and September 1939).

Englehardt, Fr. Zephyrin, O.F.M. *Santa Barbara Mission.* San Francisco: James H. Barry Co., 1923.

Farquhar, Francis P., ed. *Up and down California in 1860–1864: The Journal of William H. Brewer.* New Haven: Yale University Press, 1930.

Federal Writers' Project, Work Projects Administration. *San Diego: A California City.* San Diego: San Diego Historical Society, 1937.

Fellows, Lloyd W. "Economic Aspects of the Mexican Rural Population in California with Special Emphasis on the Need for Mexican Labor in Agriculture." Master's thesis, University of Southern California, 1929.

Francis, Jesse. "An Economic and Social History of Mexican California, 1822–1846." Ph.D. dissertation, University of California, Berkeley, 1936.

Gamio, Manuel. *The Life Story of the Mexican Immigrant.* New York: Dover Publications, 1971. (First published by the University of Chicago Press as *The Mexican Immigrant: His Life Story,* 1931.)

————. *Mexican Immigration to the United States: A Study of Human Migration and Adjustment.* New York: Dover Publications, 1971. (First published by the University of Chicago Press, 1930.)

García, Mario T. "The Californios of San Diego and the Politics of Accommodation." *Aztlán—International Journal of Chicano Studies Research,* 6 (spring 1975):69–85.

————. "Merchants and Dons: San Diego's Attempt at Modernization, 1850–1860." *Journal of San Diego History,* 21 (winter 1975):52–80.

————. "Modernization and Labor in the Southwest: A Case Study of the Mexican Population of El Paso, Texas, 1880–1920." Ph.D. dissertation, University of California, San Diego, 1975.

Geiger, Maynard, O.F.M. *The Indians of Mission Santa Barbara in Paganism and Christianity.* Santa Barbara: Franciscan Fathers of Mission Santa Barbara, 1960.

————. *Mission Santa Barbara, 1782–1965.* Santa Barbara: Heritage Printers, 1965.

Gidney, C. M., Benjamin Brooks, and Edwin M. Sheridan. *History of Santa Barbara, San Luis Obispo, and Ventura Counties, California,* vol. 1. Chicago: Lewis Publishing Co., 1917.

Gilb, Corinne Lathrop. "Tape-Recorded Interviewing: Some Thoughts from California." *American Archivist,* 20 (October 1957):335–344.

Gómez-Quiñones, Juan. "The First Steps: Chicano Labor Conflict and Organizing, 1900–1920." *Aztlán—Chicano Journal of the Social Sciences and the Arts,* 3 (spring 1972):13–49.

————. "Toward a Perspective on Chicano History." *Aztlán—Chicano Journal of the Social Sciences and the Arts,* 2 (fall 1971):1–49.

———— and Luis Leobardo Arroyo. "On the State of Chicano History: Observations on Its Development, Interpretations, and Theory, 1970–1974." *Western Historical Quarterly,* 7 (April 1976):155–185.

González, Gilbert G. "Factors Relating to Property Ownership of Chicanos in Lincoln Heights, Los Angeles." *Aztlán—Chicano Journal of the Social Sciences and the Arts,* 2 (fall 1971):107–143.

Goodman, W. Taylor, compiler. *Pacific Directory Company's Business Directory and Pocket Guide to Santa Barbara.* Santa Barbara: Pacific Directory Co., 1894.

Griffen, Clyde. "Occupational Mobility in Nineteenth Century America: Problems and Possibilities," *Journal of Social History,* 5 (spring 1972):310–330.

Griswold del Castillo, Richard A. "La Raza Hispano Americana: The Emergence of an Urban Culture among the Spanish Speaking of Los Angeles, 1850–1880." Ph.D. dissertation, University of California, Los Angeles, 1974.

Guinn, James M. *Historical and Biographical Record of Southern California.* Chicago: Chapman Publishing Co., 1902.

————. "The Passing of the Cattle Barons of California." *Historical Society of Southern California,* Annual Publications, 8 (1909–1911):51–60.

Gunn, Douglas. *A Historical Sketch of San Diego, San Diego County, California.* N.p., 4 July 1884.

————. *San Diego: Climate, Resources, Topography, Productions, etc.,* etc., rev. 4th ed. San Diego: n.p., 1 January 1886.

Hall-Wood, Mary C. F. *Santa Barbara As It Is.* Santa Barbara: Independent Publishing Co., 1884.

Harris, LeRoy E. "The Other Side of the Freeway: A Study of Settlement Patterns of Negroes and Mexican Americans in San Diego, California." Ph.D. dissertation, Carnegie-Mellon University, 1974.

Hawley, Walter A. *The Early Days of Santa Barbara, California.* Santa Barbara: Schauer Printing Studio, 1920.

Hayes, Benjamin. *Pioneer Notes: From the Diaries of Judge Benjamin*

Hayes, 1849–1875. Los Angeles: McBride Printing Co., 1929.

Heath, E. M. *A Guide to Rides and Drives in Santa Barbara and Vicinity*. Santa Barbara: W. W. Osborne, 1904.

Heilbron, Carl H., ed. *History of San Diego County*. San Diego: San Diego Press Club, 1936.

Helmbold, Lori. "The Work of Chicanas in the United States: Wage Labor and Work in the Home, 1930 to the Present." Unpublished paper, Department of History, Stanford University, 1977.

Hicks, Ratcliffe. *Southern California; or, The Land of The Afternoon*. Springfield, Massachusetts: Press of Springfield Printing and Binding Co., 1898.

Higgins, S. E. A. *La Casa de Aguirre of Santa Barbara, 1841–1884*. Santa Barbara: Press of El Barbareño, 1896.

Hill, Laurence L., and Marion Parks. *Santa Barbara—Tierra Adorada: A Community History*. Santa Barbara: Security–First National Bank of Los Angeles, 1930.

Hiscock, Ira V. *A Survey of Health and Welfare Activities in Santa Barbara County, California*. Santa Barbara: Committee on Administrative Practice, American Public Health Association, 1930.

Hoffman, Abraham. *Unwanted Mexican Americans in the Great Depression: Repatriation Pressures, 1929–1939*. Tucson: University of Arizona Press, 1974.

Hoffman, W. H. *Catalogue of Natural History Goods*. Santa Barbara: Independent Book and Job Printing House, 1886.

Hopkins, H. C. *History of San Diego: Its Pueblo Land and Water*. San Diego: City Printing Co., 1929.

Hughes, Charles. "The Decline of the Californios: The Case of San Diego, 1846–1856." *Journal of San Diego History*, 21 (summer 1975):1–31.

Huse, Charles E. *Sketch of the History and Resources of Santa Barbara City and County*. Santa Barbara: Daily Press, 1876.

Jackson, Reverend A. W. *Barbariana; or, Scenery, Climate, Soils, and Social Conditions of Santa Barbara City and County, California*. San Francisco: C. A. Murdock and Co., 1888.

James, George Wharton. *Travelers' Handbook to Southern California*. Pasadena: n.p., 1904.

Katz, Michael B. "Occupational Classification in History." *Journal of Interdisciplinary History*, 3 (summer 1972):63–88.

Knight, Emily M., Arda M. Hoenszel, and Gerald A. Smith. "Historic Chronology of San Bernardino County." *Quarterly of San Bernardino County Museum*, 9 (summer 1962):1–36.

Knights, Peter R. "City Directories as Aids to Ante-Bellum Urban Studies: A Research Note." *Historical Methods Newsletter*, 2 (September 1969):1–10.

———. "A Method for Estimating Census Under-Enumeration." *Historical Methods Newsletter*, 3 (December 1969):5–8.

Kushner, Sam. *Long Road to Delano.* New York: International Publishers, 1974.

Lloyd, Clio L. *Santa Barbara.* Santa Barbara: Daily Press Print, 1892(?).

McChesney, L. Studdiford. *Under the Shadow of the Mission, A Memory of Santa Barbara.* London: Methuen and Co., 1897.

McGrew, Clarence A. *City of San Diego and San Diego County.* 2 vols. Chicago: American Historical Society, 1922.

McGroarty, John Steven. *California of the South—A History.* Los Angeles: S. J. Clarke Publishing Co., 1933.

————. *Santa Barbara, California.* Southern Pacific Lines, 1926.

McKain, Walter C., Jr., and Sara Miles. "Santa Barbara County between Two Social Orders." *California Historical Society Quarterly,* 25 (December 1946):311–318.

MacPhail, Elizabeth C. *The Story of New San Diego and of Its Founder Alonzo E. Horton.* San Diego: Pioneer Printers, 1969.

————, ed. "Early Days in San Diego: The Memoirs of Augusta Barrett Sherman." *Journal of San Diego History,* 18 (fall 1972):29–34.

McWilliams, Carey. *Brothers under the Skin.* Boston: Little, Brown and Co., 1964. (First published in 1942.)

————. *North from Mexico: The Spanish-Speaking People of the United States,* reprint ed. New York: Greenwood Press, 1968.

————. *Southern California Country: An Island on the Land.* New York: Duell, Sloan and Pearce, 1946.

Maltsburger, Emma. *The Story of Colton, California.* Colton: n.p., 1974.

Mandeville, Frank H. *Tourists' Guide to San Diego and Vicinity.* San Diego: Gould and Hutton, 1888.

Mangold, George B. *Community Welfare in San Diego.* A survey conducted under the joint auspices of the Community Welfare Council of San Diego, the San Diego County Welfare Commission, and the City of San Diego, 1929.

Martínez, Oscar. "On the Size of the Chicano Population: New Estimates, 1850–1900." *Aztlán*—International Journal of Chicano Studies Research, 6 (spring 1975):43–67.

Mason, Jesse D. *History of Santa Barbara and Ventura Counties, California.* Oakland: Thompson and West, 1883. (New edition by Howell-North, Berkeley, 1961.)

Maulsby, F. R. *Santa Barbara, California.* Santa Barbara Chamber of Commerce booklet. Santa Barbara: Sunset Magazine Homeseekers' Bureau, circa 1914.

Mazón, Mauricio. "Illegal Alien Surrogates: A Psychohistorical Interpretation of Group Stereotyping in Time of Economic Stress." *Aztlán*—International Journal of Chicano Studies Research, 6 (summer 1975):305–324.

Mexicans in California. Report of Governor C. C. Young's Mexican

Fact-Finding Committee. San Francisco: California State Printing Office, 1930. (Reprinted by R and E Research Associates, San Francisco, 1970.)

Miller, Donald S. "Guachama: A Place to Eat." In Carlos E. Cortés, ed., "The Bent Cross: A History of the Mexican American in the San Bernardino Valley." Unpublished manuscript.

Miller, Mary Catherine. "Attitudes of the San Diego Labor Movement toward Mexicans, 1917–1936." Master's thesis, San Diego State University, 1974.

Montejano, David. "Race, Labor Repression, and Capitalist Agriculture: Notes from South Texas, 1920–1930." Institute for the Study of Social Change, Working Papers Series no. 102, Berkeley, California, 1977.

Monthly Bulletin, Fifth Report of the California Department of Agriculture, vols. 13 (July–December 1924) and 17 (December 1928). Sacramento: California State Printing Office.

Moody, Charles A. "Santa Barbara." Reprinted from *Land of Sunshine: The Magazine of California and the West*. Los Angeles: November 1901.

Moore, John Collins. "Reminiscences of Old Town." *Silver Gate*, 1 (November 1899):6–9.

Moquín, Wayne, and Charles Van Doren, eds. *A Documentary History of the Mexican Americans*. New York: Praeger Publishers, 1971.

Morefield, Richard. "The Mexican Adaptation in American California, 1846–1875." Master's thesis, University of California, Berkeley, 1955. (Reprinted by R and E Research Associates, San Francisco, 1971.)

Navarro, Armando. "The Evolution of Chicano Politics." *Aztlán—Chicano Journal of the Social Sciences and the Arts*, 5 (spring and fall 1974):57–84.

Nelson, Howard J. "The Two Pueblos of Los Angeles: Agricultural Village and Embryo Town." *Southern California Quarterly*, 59 (spring 1977):1–11.

Neri, Michael C. "A Journalistic Portrait of the Spanish-Speaking People of California, 1868–1925." *Historical Society of Southern California*, 65 (summer 1973):193–208.

Newmark, Harris. *Sixty Years in Southern California, 1853–1913*. New York: Knickerbocker Press, 1916.

Nordhoff, Charles. *California for Health, Pleasure, and Residence: A Book for Travelers and Settlers*. New York: Harper and Brothers, 1873.

O'Flaherty, Joseph S. *An End and a Beginning: The South Coast and Los Angeles, 1850–1887*. New York: Exposition Press, 1972.

O'Neill, Owen H., ed. *History of Santa Barbara County, State of California*. Santa Barbara: Union Printing Co., 1939.

Ord, Angustias de la Guerra. *Occurrences in Hispanic California*.

Translated and edited by Francis Price and William H. Ellison. Washington, D.C.: Academy of American Franciscan History, 1956.

Oxnam, G. Bromley. *The Mexican in Los Angeles, Los Angeles City Survey, 1920.* Interchurch World Movement of North America, 1920. (Reprinted by R and E Research Associates, San Francisco, 1970.)

Panunzio, Constantine, and the Heller Committee for Research in Social Economics of the University of California. *How Mexicans Earn and Live: A Study of the Incomes and Expenditures of One Hundred Mexican Families in San Diego, California.* Berkeley: University of California Press, 1933.

Patterson, Tom. *A Colony for California: Riverside's First Hundred Years.* Riverside, California: Press-Enterprise Co., 1971.

Paul, Rodman W. "The Spanish-Americans in the Southwest, 1848–1900." In *The Frontier Challenge: Responses to the Trans-Mississippi West,* ed. John G. Clark. Lawrence: University of Kansas Press, 1971.

Perkins, Joseph J. *A Business Man's Estimate of Santa Barbara County, California.* Santa Barbara: Daily Press Steam Printing Press, 1881.

Phillips, Michael James. *History of Santa Barbara County, California, from Its Earliest Settlement to the Present Time,* vols. 1 and 2. Los Angeles: S. J. Clarke Publishing Co., 1927.

Pitt, Leonard. *The Decline of the Californios: A Social History of the Spanish-Speaking Californians, 1846–1890.* Berkeley and Los Angeles: University of California Press, 1966.

Purslow, Ernest J. S. *Water Supply for Santa Barbara and Vicinity.* Santa Barbara: Report on Water Supply Project, 1896.

Ramsey, Edith F. *Santa Barbara from the Days of the Indian.* Santa Barbara: Santa Barbara Natural History Society, n.d.

Raup, H. F. *San Bernardino, California: Settlement and Growth of a Pass-Site City.* Berkeley: University of California Press, 1940.

Report of the Housing Commission of the City of Los Angeles. 4 vols. 1906–1913.

Richman, Irving B. *California under Spain and Mexico, 1535–1847.* Boston: Houghton Mifflin Co., 1911.

Rischin, Moses. "Continuities and Discontinuities in Spanish-Speaking California." In *Ethnic Conflict in California History,* ed. Charles Wollenberg. Los Angeles: Tinnon-Brown, 1970.

Roberts, Edwards. *Santa Barbara and around There.* Boston: Robert Brothers, 1886.

———. "A Santa Barbara Holiday." *Harper's Monthly Magazine,* 75 (November 1887):814–835.

Robinson, Alfred. *Life in California.* Santa Barbara: Peregrine Publishers, 1970.

Robinson, W. W. *Land in California.* Berkeley and Los Angeles: University of California Press, 1948.

Rodman, Willoughby. *History of the Bench and Bar of Southern California.* Los Angeles: William J. Porter, 1906.

Rogers, Cameron. *A County Judge in Arcady. Selected Private Papers of Charles Fernald.* Glendale, California: Arthur H. Clark C., 1954.

Romo, Ricardo. "Mexican Workers in the City: Los Angeles, 1915–1930." Ph.D. dissertation, University of California, Los Angeles, 1975.

————. "Responses to Mexican Immigration, 1910–1930." *Aztlán—International Journal of Chicano Studies Research,* 6 (summer 1975):173–194.

————. "The Urbanization of the Southwestern Chicanos in the Early Twentieth Century." *New Scholar,* 6 (1977):183–207.

————. "Work and Restlessness: Occupational and Spatial Mobility among Mexicans in Los Angeles, 1918–1928." *Pacific Historical Review,* 46 (May 1977):157–180.

Rouse, Stella Haverland. *Santa Barbara's Spanish Renaissance and the Old Spanish Days Fiesta.* Santa Barbara: Schauer Printing Studio, 1974.

Sánchez, George I. *The Forgotten People.* Albuquerque: University of New Mexico Press, 1940.

Sánchez, Nellie Van de Grift. *Spanish Arcadia.* Los Angeles: Powell Publishing Co., 1929.

Sands, Frank. *A Pastoral Prince: The History and Reminiscences of J. W. Cooper.* Santa Barbara: n.p., 1893.

————. *Santa Barbara at A glance.* Santa Barbara: Press of Kingsley-Barnes and Neuner Co., 1895.

Santa Barbara Chamber of Commerce. *The City and Valley of Santa Barbara, California.* Santa Barbara: W. H. Arne, 1904(?).

————. *Resources of Santa Barbara County, California.* Santa Barbara: Binder and Blank Book Manufacturing, 1901.

Santa Barbara City Schools Curriculum Laboratory. *Living: The Basis for Learning.* Santa Barbara: Educational Factors, 1942.

Saxton, Alexander. *The Indispensable Enemy: Labor and the Anti-Chinese Movement in California.* Berkeley and Los Angeles: University of California Press, 1971.

Scott, Robin F. "The Mexican American in the Los Angeles Area, 1910–1950: From Acquiescence to Activity." Ph.D. dissertation, University of Southern California, 1971.

Shaw, William. *Golden Dreams and Waking Realities: Being the Adventures of a Gold-Seeker in California and the Pacific Islands.* London: Smith, Elder and Co., 1851.

Shelton, Cynthia Jane. "The Neighborhood House of San Diego: Settlement Work in the Mexican Community, 1914–1940." Master's thesis, San Diego State University, 1975.

Smythe, William E. *History of San Diego, 1542–1908.* 2 vols. San Diego: History Co., 1908.

Southern California Writers' Project of the Work Projects Administration. *Santa Barbara: A Guide to the Channel City and Its Environs.* New York: Hastings House Publishers, 1941.

Southwick, Grace Ruth. "Schooling for Grown-Ups." *Western Woman—Santa Barbara California Souvenir Edition,* 7 (March 1931):36.

Southworth, John R. *Santa Barbara and Montecito: Past and Present.* Santa Barbara: Oreña Studios, 1920.

Spaulding, Edward Selden. *Adobe Days along the Channel.* Santa Barbara: Schaurer Printing Studio, 1957.

————. *A Brief Story of Santa Barbara.* Santa Barbara: Historical Society, Pacific Coast Publishing Co., 1964.

Standart, Sister M. Collette, O.P. "The Sonoran Migration to California, 1848–1856: A Study in Prejudice." *Southern California Quarterly,* 58 (fall 1976):333–358.

Stillman, Donald Lee. "A Historical Survey of the Santa Barbara, California, Area during the Early Years of the American Period, 1846–1864." Master's thesis, University of Southern California, 1948.

Storke, Thomas M. *California Editor.* Los Angeles: Westernlore Press, 1958.

Storke, Yda Addis. *A Memorial and Biographical History of the Counties of Santa Barbara, San Luis Obispo, and Ventura, California.* Chicago: Lewis Publishing Co., 1891.

Swain, Donald C. "Problems for Practitioners of Oral History." *American Archivist,* 28 (January 1965):63–69.

Taylor, Paul S. *An American-Mexican Frontier: Nueces County, Texas.* Chapel Hill: University of North Carolina Press, 1934.

————. *Mexican Labor in the United States.* Berkeley: University of California Press, 1928–1932.

Tays, George. *Plaza in Old San Diego.* California Historical Landmark Series, Work Projects Administration. Berkeley: n.p., 1937.

Thernstrom, Stephan. *The Other Bostonians: Poverty and Progress in the American Metropolis, 1880–1970.* Cambridge, Massachusetts: Harvard University Press, 1973.

————. *Poverty and Progress: Social Mobility in a Nineteenth Century City.* New York: Atheneum, 1971. (First published by Harvard University Press, Cambridge, Massachusetts, 1964.)

Thompson, Fr. Joseph A., O.F.M. *El Gran Capitán: José de la Guerra.* Los Angeles: Cabrera and Sons, 1961.

Tiffany, Susan Davis. *"Memory Like the Ivy Clings"—Old Times in Old*

Town and San Diego, California; Reminiscences of One Who Lived in the Bandini House, 1898–1911. San Diego: National Society of Colonial Dames of America, 1974.

Tirado, Miguel. "Mexican American Community Political Organization." *Aztlán—Chicano Journal of the Social Sciences and the Arts,* 1 (spring 1970):53–78.

Tompkins, Walter A. *California's Wonderful Corner, True Stories for Children from the History of the Santa Barbara Region.* Santa Barbara: McNally and Loftin, 1962.

———. "Santa Barbara Journalists, 1855–1973." *Noticias—Quarterly Bulletin of the Santa Barbara Historical Society,* 19 (winter 1973).

———. *Santa Barbara's Royal Rancho: The Fabulous History of Los Dos Pueblos.* Berkeley: Howell-North, 1960.

———. *Santa Barbara Yesterdays.* Santa Barbara: McNally and Loftin, 1962.

——— and Russell A. Ruiz. *Historical High Lights of Santa Barbara.* Santa Barbara National Bank, 1970.

United States General Land Office. *Pueblo Lands of San Diego: Exceptions to Survey Made by John C. Hays, July, 1858.* San Francisco: Mullin, Mahon and Co., 1869.

Van Dyke, T. S. *The City and County of San Diego.* San Diego: Leberton and Taylor, 1888.

Vickery, Joyce Carter. *Defending Eden: New Mexican Pioneers in Southern California.* Riverside, California: Department of History, University of California, and Riverside Museum Press, 1977.

Weber, David J., ed. *Foreigners in Their Native Land: Historical Roots of the Mexican Americans.* Albuquerque: University of New Mexico Press, 1973.

Weber, Devra Anne. "The Organization of Mexicano Agricultural Workers, the Imperial Valley, and Los Angeles, 1928–1934, an Oral History Approach." *Aztlán—Chicano Journal of the Social Sciences and the Arts,* 3 (fall 1972):307–347.

Webster, Albert F. *A Sketch of Santa Barbara.* Santa Barbara: Office of the *Santa Barbara Press,* 1876. Reprinted from *Appleton's Journal* for July 1876. (Republished in the *Santa Barbara Weekly Press,* 14 October 1876, with editorial comments.)

White, Helen McCann. "Thoughts on Oral History." *American Archivist,* 20 (January 1957):19–30.

Wills, Mary H. *A Winter in California.* Norristown, Pennsylvania: Morgan R. Wills, 1889.

Wilson, Leila Weekes, ed. *Santa Barbara, California.* Santa Barbara: Pacific Coast Publishing Co., 1913 (rev. 2nd ed., 1919).

Wollenberg, Charles. "Working on El Traque: The Pacific Electric Strike of 1903." *Pacific Historical Review,* 42 (August 1973):358–369.

II. Documents and Archival Sources (see Appendix 1 for discussion of the federal manuscript censuses and city directories as sources)

Assessment Roll for 1853. Santa Barbara County Tax Assessment, Document of Santa Barbara Courthouse.

Assessor's Block Book, Santa Barbara City, 1888. Document of Santa Barbara County Assessor's Office, County Administration Building.

Assessor's Block Book, City of Santa Barbara, 1906. Documents of Santa Barbara County Assessor's Office, County Administration Building.

Assessor's Block Book, City of Santa Barbara, 1926–1930. Documents of Santa Barbara County Assessor's Office, County Administration Building.

Bancroft Scrapbooks—California Counties, vol. 4. Manuscript, Bancroft Library, University of California, Berkeley.

Club Mexicano Independencia, President's Notebook, 1914–1917 (in Spanish). Original in possession of Federico López, Santa Barbara.

Constitución del Club Mexicano Independencia y Artículos de Incorporación. Incorporated 21 March 1924, Santa Barbara.

Crane, Clare. "Logan Heights: An Historical Survey." Manuscript, Library and Manuscripts Collection, Serra Museum Library, San Diego Historical Society, September 1971.

Davidson, Winifred. *Old Town Talk.* 3 vols. Manuscript, Library and Manuscripts Collection, Serra Museum Library, San Diego Historical Society.

Directory of Membership, 1874–1924, First Baptist Church. Santa Barbara Public Library, June 1924.

Ellison, William H., ed. *Diary of "Judge" Charles E. Huse.* Translated by Francis Price. University of California, Santa Barbara, 1953.

Gonzáles, Miguel. "San Diego's Neighborhood House Association, 1928 to 1938." Unpublished paper, Library and Manuscripts Collection, Serra Museum Library, San Diego Historical Society, 1969.

Great Register—General List of Citizens of the United States Resident in the County of San Diego, July 1867. San Diego: William B. Cooke and Co., 1867.

Great Register of San Bernardino County, General List of all Names now Registered, July 20th, A.D. 1867, with a Supplementary List up to August 10th, 1868. N.p.

Great Register of the County of San Bernardino, State of California, August 1, 1873. San Bernardino: San Bernardino Guardian Print, 1873.

Great Register of the County of San Bernardino, State of California, October 4, 1880. San Bernardino: Times Printing Office, 1880.

Great Register of San Diego County, California, October 5, 1872. San Diego: Bushyhead and Gunn, 1872.

Great Register, San Diego County, California, August, 1879. N.p.

Great Register of the County of Santa Barbara, 1866–1872. Santa Barbara: Times Company, 1873. (Bancroft Library, University of California, Berkeley.)

Great Register of the County of Santa Barbara, 1873. Santa Barbara: Times Company, 1873 (Bancroft Library, University of California, Berkeley.)

Great Register of the County of Santa Barbara, California, 1879. Documents of Santa Barbara County Elections Office. Santa Barbara: Daily Press Steam Printing House, 1879.

Great Register of the County of Santa Barbara, 1890. Documents of Santa Barbara County Elections Office. Santa Barbara: Independent Job Printing House, 1890.

Greene, Nellie, and Isaac Aceves. Research Notes of the American Guide to San Diego Project, Federal Writers' Project. "Spanish and American Pioneers, Part II: History. The Spanish Influence in San Diego." Library and Manuscripts Collection, Serra Museum Library, San Diego Historical Society.

Index to Great Register of Santa Barbara County, 1904. Document of Santa Barbara County Elections Office. Santa Barbara: Independent Print, 1904.

Index to Precinct Registers of Santa Barbara County, 1910. Documents of Santa Barbara County Elections Office, County Administration Building. Santa Barbara: Morning Press Print, 1910.

Index to Precinct Registers of Santa Barbara County, 1920. Documents of Santa Barbara County Elections Office, County Administration Building.

Indigent List of Santa Barbara County, 1901–1909. Documents of Santa Barbara County Tax Collector, County Administration Building.

Kroll, Francis Cooper. *Memories of Rancho Santa Rosa and Santa Barbara.* Manuscript, Santa Barbara Historical Society, 1964.

List of Registered Names for the County of Santa Barbara, July 30, 1867, as they appear on the Great Register of the County for the year 1867. San Francisco: John G. Hodge and Co. (Archives of Santa Barbara Historical Society, 1867.)

Lucy Wentworth's Notes, circa 1930. Manuscript, Library and Manuscripts Collection, Serra Museum Library, San Diego Historical Society.

Miller, Mary Catherine. "The Anti-Chinese Movement in San Diego, 1870–1882." Manuscript, Library and Manuscripts Collection, Serra Museum Library, San Diego Historical Society, 1972.

Morse, Mrs. Mary E. "Recollections of the Early Times in San Diego." Pioneer Society of San Diego, August 1898. Manuscript, Library and Manuscripts Collection, Serra Museum Library, San Diego Historical Society.

"Narración de Doña Teresa de la Guerra de Hartnell," *Pioneer Sketches*, no. 2, 1875. Manuscript, Bancroft Library, University of California, Berkeley.

Naturalization Petition and Record, vols. 1–5, no. 51–900 (1910–1927). County of Santa Barbara, Office of the County Clerk, Santa Barbara County Court House.

Old City and Election Information. Office of City Clerk, Santa Barbara City Hall.

Oreña, Dario. *Reminiscences of Early California.* Typescript, Santa Barbara Historical Society, 1932.

Our Lady of Guadalupe Parish, Silver Jubilee, 1928–1953, Santa Barbara, California. Santa Barbara, 25 October 1953.

An Outline of Historical Research with Excerpts from the Minutes of the Common Council of the City of Santa Barbara, State of California, Dating from August 26, 1850, Robert R. Heatke, research editor. Compiled under the direction of Mayor Harvey T. Nielson. Office of the City Clerk, Santa Barbara City Hall.

Public Health Appraisal, Santa Barbara County, California, 1935. County Health Department and Chamber of Commerce Committee, R. C. Main Co., Santa Barbara, 1935.

Ritual del Club Mexicano Independencia. Legislative Commission, Santa Barbara, California, 1 January 1927.

Santa Barbara County Board of Supervisors' Minutes. Books C-H, 1878–1893, Santa Barbara County Clerk of the Board of Supervisors, County Administration Building.

Spaulding, Edward Selden. *Santa Barbara, 1898–1925, as seen by a boy.* Manuscript, Santa Barbara Historical Society, 1966(?).

Streeter, William A. *Recollections of Historical Events in California, 1843–1878.* Manuscript, Bancroft Library, University of California, Berkeley, 1878.

Whaley, Lillian. *Old Times in Old Town.* Typescript, San Diego Public Library, n.d.

III. Newspapers

La Gaceta de Santa Bárbara, 1879–1881.

San Bernardino Daily Sun, 1905–1930.

San Diego Labor Leader (also entitled the *Labor Leader*), San Diego County Federated Trade and Labor Council, 1919–1929.

San Diego Daily Union, 1871–1883, 1924–1931.

Santa Barbara Daily News, 1875–1876, 1913–1927.

Santa Barbara Gazette, 1855–1857.

Santa Barbara Independent, 1880–1918.

Santa Barbara Index, 1872–1877.

Santa Barbara Post, 1868–1869.
Santa Barbara Press, 1869–1930. (The various editions were known as the *Daily Press*, the *Morning Press*, and the *Weekly Press*.)
Santa Barbara Times, 1870–1873.

IV. Oral Interviews

All interviews were conducted in Santa Barbara, California. The following were the interviewees:

Acosta, Jesse. First interviewed on 20 September 1974; because of tape recorder malfunction reinterviewed on 29 January 1975.
Acosta, Luis. First interviewed on 20 September 1974; because of tape recorder malfunction reinterviewed on 29 January 1975.
Bonilla, Antonio ("Ike"). 21 August 1974.
Caballero, Albert. 24 August 1974.
Caballero, Lydia. 24 August 1974.
Castro, Anita. 25 September 1974.
Castro, Reyes. 25 September 1974.
Cordero, Angela. 21 September 1974.
Cordero, Herman. 21 September 1974.
Cordero, Ida. Interviewee and contact for prospective interviewees, 19 September 1974; intermittent consultant throughout August and September 1974.
Cordero, Leo. 20 September 1974.
Cordero, Walter. 19 September 1974.
Cota, Theodore. 11 September 1974.
Cuellar, Hortencia Castro de. 11 September 1974.
Domínguez, Alfred. 20 August 1974.
García, Miguel. 12 September 1974.
López, Federico. 7 October 1974.
Lugo, Luis. 15 September 1974.
Martínez, José. 25 September 1974.
Medina, Veronica. 16 August 1974.
Ortega, Mary. 14 September 1974.
Osuna, Yldefonso ("Poncho"). 23 August 1974.
Pérez, Nellie. 12 September 1974.
Ruiz, Alfred. 19 September 1974.
Ruiz, Russell A. 20 August 1974. Interviewee, consultant on local history, and contact for prospective interviewees.
Sánchez, Vereanda. 2 October 1974.
Vásquez, Daniel. 25 September 1974.
Vásquez, Dolores. 25 September 1974.
Villa, LeRoy. 20 August 1974.
Villa, Margarita. 20 August 1974.

Index